THE ENCYCLOPAEDIA
METALLICA

The Encyclopaedia Metallica
by Malcolm Dome and Jerry Ewing

A CHROME DREAMS PUBLICATION
First Edition 2007

Published by Chrome Dreams
PO BOX 230, New Malden, Surrey,
KT3 6YY, UK
books@chromedreams.co.uk
WWW.CHROMEDREAMS.CO.UK

ISBN 9781842404034
Copyright © 2007 by Chrome Dreams

Edited by   Cathy Johnstone
Cover Design   Sylwia Grzeszczuk
Layout Design   Marek Niedziewicz

A catalogue record for this book is available from the British Library.

Printed and bound in Great Britain by William Clowes Ltd, Beccles, Suffolk

THE ENCYCLOPAEDIA
METALLICA

Malcolm Dome and Jerry Ewing

THE AUTHORS WOULD LIKE TO THANK ...

...the following people for their support and assistance:

All at Chrome Dreams.

Adair & Roxy.

All at TotalRock: Tony Wilson, Thekkles, Tabitha, Emma 'SF' Bellamy, The Bat, Ickle Buh, The PMQ, Katie P.

Everyone at the Crobar/ Evensong: Sir Barrence, The Rector, The Crazy Bitch, The Lonely Doctor, Steve, Rick, Johanna, Bagel, Benjy, Maisie, Laura, Stuart, Steve Hammonds, John Richards, Dave Everley, Bob Slayer, David Kenny, The Unique One, Harjaholic, Al King, Jonty, Orange Chuffin' Goblin (Baby), Lady E., Smelly Jacques, Anna Maria, Speccy Rachel.

The Classic Rock crew: Scott Rowley, Sian Llewellyn, Geoff Barton, Ian Fortnam, Dave Ling is gay.

The Metal Hammer mob: Chris Ingham, Jamie Hibbard, Caren Gibson, Alex Milas, James Gill, Jamez Isaacs, Alex Burrows.

SOURCES FROM WHICH QUOTES HAVE BEEN TAKEN

Kerrang! magazine

Metal Hammer magazine

RAW magazine

Playboy magazine

Q magazine

Guitar World magazine

So What! official Metallica fanzine

www.encyclopedia-metallica.com

www.metallicaworld.co.uk

www.blabbermouth.net

www.metalhamer.co.uk

www.kerrang.com

en.wikipedia.org

INTRO

Metallica. Thrash pioneers. The most commercially successful metal band of all time. Mutliple Grammy Award winners. Over 100 million records sold…Yes, all that's true. But, for once, the facts don't even begin to encompass the magnitude of what this band have achieved just over a quarter-of-a-century since they began life, almost as a con trick perpetrated by drummer Lars Ulrich.

Con trick? Well, yes. Because this is the man who persuaded a record company owner to put a track from his 'band' on a compilation – even though, actually, the 'band' didn't exist. And this is the man who convinced guitarist/vocalist James Hetfield to join the mythical 'band', because they could do a song for the aforementioned compilation. Now, that is some piece of political trickery. And if you wanna know more, then you'd better get stuck into this book, right?

But that merely scratches the surface. Metallica's story encompasses death, insanity, bitterness, addiction, controversy, hirings, firings, therapists…it's more like a soap opera than any other band you'd care to mention. Moreover, this lot have never been afraid to show everything in public. Like the most brazen stripper, they conceal nothing.

And there's more. Without Metallica there might not have been a thrash movement at all. These guys have overcome accusations of 'selling out' across their career, to stand tall on their own principles. They might have made enormous musical and artistic mistakes, but they've done these on their own terms. They've literally used blood, semen and urine in pursuit of their artistic ambitions.

From the smallest clubs in California, Metallica have risen to headline the biggest stadia on the planet. From a demo recorded on a ghetto blaster they've gone on to give us the biggest selling metal album ever. It's the tale of a tennis protégé who swapped the racquet for drum sticks. And that of a man brought up in a Christian Science environment, who found fulfilment through a microphone and a guitar.

But beyond the facts there's the emotion, the passion, the music. A string of records that have inspired at least two generations of bands and fans. And a catalogue that will go on doing so for many years to come.

In the annals of the metal genre, only Iron Maiden and Black Sabbath can hope to compete with Metallica when it comes to influence – and neither come close to matching the Americans' remarkable commercial power and prowess. Any band who picks off a guitar and goes for a LOUD riff, is automatically plugging into the heritage, history and hirsute pursuits of Metallica. That's the law.

Metallica have also been responsible for expanding the parameters of metal. They have constantly evolved, and never shirked, from incorporating different musical ideals and ideologies. This is one act who refuse to accept that there are limitations, always searching and seeking to take their music further.

They've also been pioneers. They were the ones who made it cool to release albums solely consisting of cover versions. They made it credible for metalheads to work with an orchestra. And it's all been done on their terms. Even when they finally relented and did their first ever promo video, it was done to their own dictates, with no room for comfortable compromise.

Perhaps that's the greatest legacy Metallica have left us – the belief that it is possible to achieve astonishing success without ever having to relent and buckle, under business pressures. For this band, there is but one question to be asked: 'is it worthy of our own high standards?' How many others can say that so consistently.

What we have done with this book is present the story of Metallica as never before. Each detail, every fascinating facet has been unearthed. This isn't just a collection of bare facts, but a document that unravels the soul of the band, a documentary on the contributions made by disparate individuals and organisations to one of the truly legendary tales of rock history.

The only entry missing comes under 'F'. For 'Fans'. But now you're here, the story is complete. Enjoy.

Malcolm Dome and Jerry Ewing – London, August, 2007.

MALCOLM DOME

Malcolm Dome first heard Metallica in 1982 - and liked what he heard. A year later he reviewed their debut album, 'Kill 'Em All', for *Kerrang!* magazine – and, again, liked what he heard. Not that he ever expected Metallica to become megastars back then.

Dome started his carer in journalism with the now defunct weekly UK music paper *Record Mirror* in 1979. His first feature was on Samson (featuring vocalist Bruce Dickinson, now of Iron Maiden; back then he was merely Bruce Bruce). His first live review was Iron Maiden at The Marquee in London; his first album review was Samson's debut, and his first interview was with Hawkwind.

Since then he's written for any number of rock music magazines – *Kerrang!*, *Metal Mania, RAW*, *Metal Hammer*, *Classic Rock* and *Metal Forces*, to name but a small selection, and is regularly invited to contribute to television and DVD rock music documentaries.

Malcolm still writes for both *Metal Hammer* and *Classic Rock* and is heavily involved with the highly regarded radio station TotalRock (www.totalrock.com).

Dome's been involved with the rock/metal media in four separate decades, and is coming up to 30 years on the job. Phew! There seems to be no parole from rock 'n' roll – and he'd have it no other way.

JERRY EWING

By a bizarre twist of fate, being born in Exeter in the mid-60s never harmed Jerry Ewing and he somehow managed a typical Australian childhood growing up in North Sydney, lapping up the delights of sun, sea, surf and Skyhooks, mostly on his beloved Manly Beach. By the time he was old enough to drink a tinny of VB he was back in England and confronted by a multitude of Two Tone fans. Undaunted, his love of AC/DC kept him sane and he threw himself into the arms of the NWOBHM with aplomb.

Surviving an English higher education (via public school, but don't tell anyone, they won't believe you if you do) he found himself working on groundbreaking and respected UK metal mag *Metal Forces* in 1989, where only his hair was bigger than his ego. Since then he's edited, written for or generally bothered *Terror Magazine, Vox*, *Metal Hammer, Cutting Edge, Maxim, Stuff* and *Bizarre*.

Ewing devised and set-up *Classic Rock* magazine for Dennis Publishing in 1988, and continues to write for that journal to this day. He also works as a broadcaster on Total Rock Radio and is regularly featured on television and DVD with his views on metal and rock acts.

Jerry thinks 'Ride The Lightning' is the best Metallica album,

but accepts that 'Master Of
Puppets' is their finest. And he
still enjoys banging his head to
'Creeping Death' to this very
day. He has a beautiful daughter who he loves very much,
but still lists whingeing about
Chelsea football club and drinking with Malcolm Dome as his
hobbies. He once wrote a book
about Liverpool footballer
Steve McManaman, but
doesn't like to talk about it.

A YEAR AND A HALF IN THE LIFE OF METALLICA

'A Year And A Half In The Life Of Metallica', directed by Adam Dubin, was originally released as a double VHS back in 1992 (and currently to be found as a single, four hour DVD) and is a documentary centred around the making of 'The Black Album' and the early part of the ensuing three-year tour that followed in the album's wake.

The original VHS version featured, on its first tape, the making of the album segment and three music promo videos for 'Enter Sandman', 'The Unforgiven' and 'Nothing Else Matters'. The second tape concentrated on the 'Wherever We May Roam' tour, as well as Metallica's performance at Wembley Stadium at the Freddie Mercury Tribute Concert of 1992. That also featured two music promo videos, in this case 'Wherever I May Roam' and 'Sad But True'.

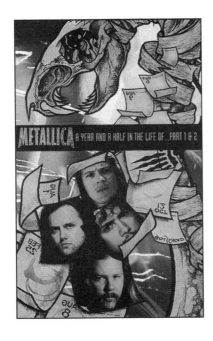

The film captures many of the disagreements between Metallica and producer Bob Rock through the recording process of 'The Black Album', owing to Rock's introduction of new and extreme working conditions, as costs spiralled to $1 million.

AIN'T MY BITCH

The opening song from Metallica's sixth studio album, 'Load', this goes a long way to disproving the theory supplied by disgruntled thrash fans that Metallica had either gone soft or had sold out. A furiously paced frenetic rocker, it sneers out at the listener in an act of supreme defiance, and in a manner the band who had recorded 'Kill 'Em All' would be proud.

The song began life in demo form simply titled 'Bitch', and was originally recorded in early April 1996. The 'Bitch' in the eventual title caused some controversy, but in truth only from a media looking for anything with which to have a dig at the band. In truth the message is simple: if there's a problem it's not mine and I don't care.

The song proved very popular while the band were performing material from both 'Load' and 'ReLoad', something they've proved increasingly reluctant to do of late. It was also the first Metallica track to feature Kirk Hammett playing slide guitar.

A&M STUDIOS

A&M Studios in Los Angeles was where Metallica recorded some of the material for 'The $5.98 EP: Garage Days Re-Revisited' in July 1987.

The studio, owned by the A&M Record Company, has been used by artists as wide ranging as Bruce Springsteen ('Lucky Town'), Leonard Cohen and Rage Against The Machine ('The Battle Of Los Angeles'), while Crowded House also recorded their 'Woodface' album there.

ALAGO, MICHAEL

Michael Alago was the Elektra Record Company executive who, if the mainstream press are to be believed, discovered Metallica. He was certainly the person responsible for signing the band from the Megaforce label in America, and acted as the group's A&R man.

In their 1992 book 'Metallica: A Visual Documentary' authors Xavier Russell and Mark Putterford allege that Alago used unusual tactics to sign the band, and allude to some sort of homosexual liaison between Alago and either Lars Ulrich or James Hetfield in order for Metallica to secure their desired deal.

Although Metallica have never openly commented on the allegations, in 1992 Jerry Ewing questioned Lars Ulrich on the subject when interviewing him for 'Metal Forces' magazine. Ulrich merely laughed it off before requesting the offending section of the book be faxed to him. Upon publication of 'Metallica: A Visual Documentary' the offending section was still intact.

Alago quit the music business in 2003, although he still manages the gay dance music star and ex-porn actor Colton Ford. He now works as a photographer and recently had a collection of homoerotic art published entitled 'Rough Gods'. In an interview with 'Gay And Lesbian Times' in July, 2007 Alago says that signing Metallica was one of the most memorable moments of his career, stating Metallica had "incredible energy" and were "great people". He goes on to add: "I love men. I love the look of them and the smell of them. And that inspires me to want to shoot their photographs". To the author's knowledge Alago

has never commented on the bizarre and unfounded allegations.

For the record both James Hetfield and Lars Ulrich are in happy, heterosexual relationships.

ALCOHOLICA

Nickname given to the band around 1985, because of their renowned partiality to beverages of an alcoholic nature. The band even did a jokey photo shoot around this time with 'Kerrang!' magazine's Peter Cronin , the legend 'Alcoholica' being used as a backdrop, in the style of the Metallica logo.

One fan even went so far as to adapt the 'Kill 'Em All' album cover, replacing the hammer and blood with an empty vodka bottle and split liquid of the same vintage, for a T-shirt. Needless to say the band's logo read 'Alcoholica' on this clothing item.

It is said that the band's management, Peter Mensch and Cliff Burnstein, were concerned at the

band's excessive love of bars and bottles. And they certainly were world-class libators.

ALL WITHIN MY HANDS

The final track from Metallica's eighth studio album, 'St. Anger', 'All Within My Hands' is a bare, open look at the psychosis suffered by mainman James Hetfield, who spent much of the album venting his spleen in an attempt to banish his demons.

At eight minutes and 49 seconds it is the longest track on the album as well as the most stark. 'I will only let you breath the air that I receive', Hetfield rages. 'Then we'll see if I'll let you love me'. It's shockingly open stuff from a man whose lyrics were once concerned only with religion, politics and social injustice. Yet, ever since some of the songs on 'The Black Album' Hetfield has become increasingly personal with his lyrics, as they became some kid of catharsis for the demons he was hiding. Now, having confronted those demons, the vitriol seems to pour out of him unabated, with the band putting in suitably stark, thrash metal performances.

AM I EVIL?

The most famous song from Metallica's favourite NWOBHM sons Diamond Head. 'Am I Evil?' originally appeared on Diamond Head's 1980 album 'Lightning To The Nations'.

It has appeared on no less than four Metallica demos and albums, including 'Ron McGovney's '82 Garage Demo', 'Metal Up Your Ass' (1982), the 1991 re-issue of 'Kill 'Em All' and 1998's 'Garage Inc.', as well as several B-sides including 'Creeping Death'.

Diamond Head

Diamond Head were one of Lars Ulrich's all-time favourite bands, and he even stayed with the group's Sean Harris and Brian Tatler (vocals and guitar, respectively) in 1981 while in England, catching as many NWOBHM bands as he could.

(ANESTHESIA) PULLING TEETH

Cliff Burton's bass showcase from Metallica's 'Kill 'Em All' debut album, and the only Metallica track on which James Hetfield doesn't have a writing credit. Lars doesn't have one either, but neither does he on 'Motorbreath'.

Allowed free reign, Burton displays the full range of his considerable musical expertise on '(Anesthesia) Pulling Teeth', which ranged from the classical influences he instilled into Metallica's songwriting, to jazz-fusion and straightforward heavy metal.

Perhaps not as accomplished as 'Orion' from 'Master Of Puppets', the piece is still remarkable for a young man starting out recording his first album with his first major band. And listened to through headphones with the lights off, it can induce a feeling that you are indeed having your teeth extracted.

...AND JUSTICE FOR ALL

Metallica's fourth album, and first following the tragic death of

Cliff Burton, '...And Justice For All', was always going to be a bittersweet affair. And so it proved. It's the album that gave them their first taste of mainstream acceptance and success and it contains some of their finest songs. Yet the production seems off-kilter and certainly at odds with the full-bodied sound of 'Ride The Lightning' and 'Master Of Puppets'. And you can barely hear that in Jason Newsted they have a new bass player.

Musically '...And Justice For All' is Metallica's most complex album, almost progressive thrash, with lengthy songs and thoughtful time signatures. At first listen it can sound unrelentingly inharmonious, but given time, songs like the excellent 'Harvester Of Sorrow', 'Blackened' and 'The Shortest Straw' are not without an inherent melody. Cliff Burton gets one writing credit, on 'To Live Is To Die', while Jason 'Newkid' Newsted also gets one on 'Blackened'.

However the one song that makes the album so pivotal, and equally debatable, in Metallica's canon of work is 'One'. An anti-war song, it opens slowly and melodically, misleading the listener that it might even be a ballad, before packing an almighty thrash punch as it builds to a brilliant climax. Based on Dalton Trumbow's novel and film 'Johnny Got His Gun', which tells the tale of a First World War soldier who has lost all his limbs and much of his face, yet retains his senses, it explores the idea of being aware but unable to communicate with the world around you.

Metallica chose to produce a promo video for the track, something they had never done before, and immediately faced further accusations of selling out from the narrow-minded element of their fanbase. And yet the full-length video, which included clips from the film 'Johnny Got His Gun' (for which the band purchased the rights to the film) intercut with footage of the band performing the song within the stark confines of a Los Angeles warehouse, remains one of Metallica's most impressive music promos, which of course became the norm for the band from then on in.

Production wise, however, '... And Justice For All' just doesn't seem to sit right. Indeed Metallica themselves have since claimed that they would love the chance to re-mix the album. In fact, rumour has it a re-mixed version with a more substantial bass sound has been doing the rounds for a while but has never been officially released. One suggestion concerning the almost total absence of a bass sound is that the band were still coming to terms with the tragic loss of Burton and that Newsted was too new to the fold to stamp his authority, and was not attendant at the mixing sessions. Newsted has also pointed out that the bass lines follow the rhythm guitar

parts very closely, which may go some way to explaining the lack of bass. Whatever, this was the final album handled by Flemming Rasmussen (who was brought in when things didn't work out with original choice, Mike Clink), and the band would look to Bob Rock for their next album.

Regardless, '...And Justice For All' was the album that broke Metallica into the arena league. It entered the US charts at number six and number four in the UK, while both 'Harvester Of Sorrow' and 'One' cracked the UK Top 20.

Initially the band found some of the song structures too complex to perform on stage, although 'One' quickly established itself as a live favourite, complete with pyrotechnical display. Lately more and more songs from the album have found their way back into Metallica's live set. 'Dyers Eve' got its very first airing on the 2003-2004 'Madly In Anger With The World' tour, while '...And Justice For All' itself was played for the first time since October 1989, at the beginning of the band's 2007 'Sick Of The Studio' tour.

In all, '...And Justice For All' is a triumph. But one still tainted by tragedy.

Tracklisting

'Blackened', '...And Justice For All', 'Eye Of The Beholder', 'One, 'The Shortest Straw', 'Harvester Of Sorrow', 'The Frayed Ends Of Sanity', 'To Live Is To Die', 'Dyers Eve'

ANTHRAX

Fellow members of what was termed The Big Four of thrash by the media, Anthrax and Metallica have always had a strong bond between them. Indeed, when Metallica were recording their debut album, 'Kill 'Em All', in New York, Anthrax allowed them to use their rehearsal room to stay in after they'd been thrown out of Johnny Zazula's house for breaking into his drinks cabinet. Devoid of any humanitarian facilities, Metallica were allowed to freshen up at the homes of various members of Anthrax.

John Bush, who would later replace singer Joey Belladonna in Anthrax, was, when fronting Armored Saint, asked to join Metallica prior to 'Ride The Lightning', with James Hetfield still not being entirely comfortable handling guitar and vocal duties.

Anthrax also sampled Metallica's 'Master Of Puppets' on their track 'I'm The Man!' and they covered 'Phantom Lord' for the album 'Tribute To The Four Horsemen'.

Anthrax were the band on tour with Metallica in 1986, when they suffered the fateful bus crash in Ljungby, Sweden, that claimed the life of Cliff Burton.

www.anthrax.com

ANTI NOWHERE LEAGUE

British punk rock band who are most famous for their cover of Ralph McTell's dusty old folk tune 'Streets Of London' and its B-side 'So What'. The latter track was covered by Metallica, originally as an extra track on the Japanese import of 'The Black Album', then later as the B-side to the single 'The Unforgiven'. The song also featured on 'Garage Inc.'.

The filth-laden 'So What' came about, allegedly, from the Anti Nowhere League overhearing a conversation between two men in a pub as they tried to outdo each other with more outrageous tales, and was written to rebuff those who embellish themselves with false tales. The Obscene Publications Squad didn't see things quite that way when the 'Streets Of London' single was released and promptly confiscated the lot, making it the Anti Nowhere League's most famous song. It can now be found on various Anti Nowhere League compilation CDs. The band called it a day in 1987.

However in 1992, when Metallica appeared at Wembley Arena, Anti Nowhere League singer Animal guested with the band as they played 'So What' as an encore. He said of the experience on his website at the time: "As I waited at the edge of the stage waiting to go on, it suddenly dawned on me I was just about to stand in front of 10,000 punters who didn't know me from Adam and sing a song I couldn't fucking remember. All

that kept running through my head was 'Run you silly old fucker!'."

The event acted as a catalyst for the Anti Nowhere League, and by 1993 the band were active again and have remained so to this day.

www.antinowhereleague.com

APOCALYPTICA

Arguably the most unusual Metallica tribute band of them all, the Finnish group Apocalyptica, started out in 1996, when four classically trained cellists (Eicca Toppinen, Paavo Lötjönen, Max Lilja, and Antero Manninen) got together to play Metallica covers.

Later that year they released the album 'Plays Metallica By Four Cellos', featuring only covers of the band, adapted for cello.

On 1998's 'Inquisition Symphony', they expanded their range with the album featuring just four Metallica covers, the rest of the tracks including songs by Pantera, Sepultura and Faith No More, as well as three original tunes.

By 2000's 'Cult', the new-look Apocalyptica (with a fresh line-up) were concentrating on their own songs, with just two Metalli-

ca covers making up the numbers, and 2003's 'Reflections' saw the covers dropped altogether.

Since then, they've brought in a number of major names to gust on their records - from Slayer drum maestro Dave Lombardo to HIM vocalist Ville Valo, Soulfly's Max Cavalera, Till Lindemann of Rammstein and Lacuna Coil singer Cristina Scabbia – but no-one from Metallica has yet appeared, even though they supported the band twice.

One for trivia fiends: Metallica used Apocalyptica's version of 'Master Of Puppets' in the documentary 'Some Kind Of Monster.'

www.apocalyptica.com

ASTRONOMY

A cover of a song by legendary US heavy metal band Blue Oyster Cult which appeared on Metallica's 'Garage Inc.'.

'Astronomy' first appeared on Blue Oyster Cult's 1974 album 'Secret Treaties'. It was taken from a poem written by the band's equally legendary producer Sandy Pearlman, titled 'The Soft Doctrines Of Immaginos', in which aliens guide a human, Immaginos, through history dabbling in events that would eventually leads to the outbreak World War I.

Blue Oyster Cult returned to the song on their 1988 album 'Imaginos', which was largely written over several years by the band's drummer, Albert Bouchard, with the intention of releasing a series of solo albums. Instead the record appeared under the Blue Oyster Cult moniker, but without the involvement of Bouchard himself.

It also appears on the Blue Oyster Cult live albums 'Some Enchanted Evening' and 'A Long Day's Night', and Swedish metal band Arch Enemy use the chorus of 'Astronomy' for the song 'Pilgrim' from their 'Burning Bridges'.

ATTITUDE

The 12th song from Metallica's seventh studio album, 'ReLoad', this reflects the rebellious nature that has always been inherent in the band, basically suggesting that there's nothing wrong with breaking the rules and being a rebel every now and then, a sentiment few Metallica fans would argue with.

The song was originally known in demo form as both 'Lenny' and 'Sweat'.

BAD SEED

One of the more forgettable tracks from 'ReLoad', and one that contributed to the album's generally less than great reputation. Lyrically, the song would seem to be about the dangers of tasting forbidden fruit, using allegorical references to the biblical tale of Adam and Eve.

Originally known as 'Bad Seed (Bastard)', the song has occasionally been played live, but only in jam form.

BATTERY

Arguably one of Metallica's greatest ever songs, and a fitting opener to their third album, 'Master Of Puppets'. Indeed, prior to the arrival of 'The Black Album'

Metallica would almost always open their sets with the rampaging 'Battery' which, despite its frenetic pace, saw the quartet direct its speedy metal prowess away from the confines of mere thrash metal.

The 'battery' in question is used as in 'assault and battery', hence the line 'Smashing through the boundaries, lunacy has found me, cannot stop the battery'. Said Hetfield of the song: "There's a good and a bad side of a battery. We were very good at the negative." Equally, the song's title is an indirect tribute to San Francisco's Old Waldorf venue, situated on Battery Street, where the band used to play.

The track has been covered both by Machine Head and Ensiferum, as well as a collective consisting of Flotsam & Jetsam's Eric AK, Dave Lombardo, Rob Trujillo and Mike Clark, on the album 'Metallic Assault: A Tribute To Metallica'. Ironically

Trujillo would join Metallica in 2003 while drummer Lombardo performed the song with the band at Download in 2004.

BAY AREA

The Bay Area refers to the scene that grew up around the San Francisco area from which thrash metal is widely believed to have developed, in much the same way as Florida is considered pivotal to the death metal scene.

Although Metallica actually formed in Los Angeles, they relocated to San Francisco's East Bay area in 1983, and it was the friendship between Kirk Hammett and Cliff Burton, and their link with bands such as Exodus (Hammett's original band) and Testament that helped forge a solid metal following in the area. Other names perceived to be part of the Bay Area scene at that time were Death Angel, Possessed, Vio-lence (featuring a young Robb Flynn, later of Machine Head) and Forbidden.

Notable venues included The Old Waldorf on Battery Street (honoured in Metallica's song 'Battery' – see above), The Fillmore, Ruthie's Inn, The Kabuki Theater, The Warfield and The Stone.

By the early 1990s the scene had pretty much died down, but a mini re-union of sorts occurred in 2001 with the 'Thrash Of The Titans' event to aid Testament singer Chuck Billy, who was suffering with cancer, and Death's Chuck Schuldiner, who had been diagnosed with a brain tumour (Death had recorded their 'Scream Bloody Gore' album in San Francisco). Among the performers were Vio-lence, Forbidden, Death Angel, Heathen, Anthrax, S.O.D. and Exodus.

BEATALLICA

For reasons best known to themselves this spoof band decided it would be a hoot to mix the music of The Beatles with Metallica.

The band's roots lay in Milwaukee's Spoof Fest at which, in 2001, original Beatallica guitarist Grg Hammetson (Michael Brandenburg) and singer Jaymz Lennfield (Michael Tierney) recorded the 'Garage Days Night' EP. A website grew up around the band who made their 'Grey Album', available online in 2004, with the additions of bassist Kliff McBurtney (Paul Terrien) and drummer Ringo Larz (Ryan Charles), the band began playing live and even supported Dream Theater at one point.

Unsurprisingly, Sony/ATV Music Publishing, who own the rights to The Beatles music, issued a Cease & Desist notice on the band. Ironically however, Lars Ulrich, who had spearheaded Metallica's legal battle with Napster (and possibly because of that), came to Beatallica's rescue, asking Metallica's attorney to help smooth things over with Sony. The move worked and Beatallica released 'Sgt. Hetfield's Motorbreath Pub Band' in 2007.

A typical Betallica track will combine a Metallica and a Beatles song, and be performed in a Metallica style. Such delights as 'Blackened In The U.S.S.R.', 'Leper Madonna' and 'A Garage Dayz Night' have thus far been offered up.

BEHIND THE MUSIC

Like most major rock acts of today, Metallica have been the subject of music station VH1's 'Behind The Music' which charted the band's rise from 'a garage band to the stadium rock act of today' – as VH1 put it on their website.

The Metallica show featured interviews with the band, as well as Ron McGovney, Anthrax's Scott Ian, Dave Mustaine, Primus' Les Claypool, Lemmy, Jerry Cantrell, producer Bob Rock and Torben Ulrich, Lars' dad.

Amongst various scenes, the band are captured joking about accusations they'd sold out, boasting that on 'The Black Album' tour they did indeed sell out – every night!

BETTER THAN YOU

The Grammy Award winning single from 'ReLoad'. Originally known as 'Better', the song deals with the arrogant view held by some, who believe they are, as the title says, 'Better than you'. Metallica of all bands, are well placed to know how it feels to have people looking down their noses at them.

The song won Metallica their fourth Grammy Award, at the 41st Grammy ceremony in 1998. It was released as a single in America, but clearly failed to impress the record buying public as much as the Grammy judges, since it failed to chart.

BIG FOUR, THE

As it became apparent that thrash metal was a serious sub-genre of heavy metal and not some flash-in-the-pan fad that would disappear overnight, so a hierarchy swiftly formed amongst the bands vying for contention. It didn't take long for the main front-runners to establish themselves and the press soon dubbed Metallica, Megadeth, Anthrax and Slayer: The Big Four.

Metallica were always head and shoulders above the rest of the pack, swiftly moving to distance themselves from thrash metal. Megadeth, led by ex-Metallica guitarist Dave Mustaine, spent much of their career sniffing at the coat tails of Metallica, yet were always unable to gain sufficient momentum to overtake them. New York's Anthrax made a decent fist of things with their 1987 album 'Among The Living', but their dalliance with rap music, while successful, always carried with it the whiff of gimmickry, and when singer Joey Belladonna was fired in 1992, the band never quite regained their momentum, despite creating some excellent music with new singer John Bush. And Slayer, who stuck doggedly to their task of delivering brutal and unrelenting thrash metal, were always at the more extreme end of the spectrum, and therefore unlikely to make an impact on the mainstream equal to Metallica's.

BLACK SABBATH

Seen by many as the originators of heavy metal, the Birmingham quartet's track 'Sabbra Cadabra' was covered by Metallica for 1998's 'Garage Inc.'. Taken from the band's fifth album 'Sabbath Bloody Sabbath' it might seem an unlikely choice, compared with the remaining new batch of covers selected for the album, but Ulrich has asserted that the band made a deliberate decision not to cover any of the more obvious Sabbath tracks such as 'Black Sabbath' or 'Paranoid'.

"Black Sabbath were not a direct influence on our music," Ulrich stated, "they had been going for too long. But they were a big influence on all four of us as we were growing up."

BLACKENED

The opener for Metallica's fourth album, '...And Justice For All' this is one of the album's faster tracks and is certainly as heavy as much of the rest of the album. It also features one of Kirk Hammett's most popular guitar solos. Indeed, when considering the guitar work on 'Blackened', it's interesting to note that the intro is made up of several different guitar parts which were recorded onto tape and then flipped, result-

ing in the entire opening actually being played backwards.

Lyrically it's bleak, discussing the dawning of a new ice age and nuclear destruction. It is the very first song written by Jason Newsted with Metallica and also his only writing credit on '...And Justice For All', although, as with much of the rest of the album, it features a spartan, almost non-existent bass sound.

The song was used as the set opener for the entire 'Damaged Justice' tour.

BLEEDING ME

This lengthy track from 'Load' was created in The Dungeon, Lars Ulrich's home studio on April 7, 1995. It deals with how someone reacts to being put through mental torture, taking the viewpoint of: don't put someone through what you wouldn't wish to be put through yourself.

"How did I know if the rest of the guys felt as much about the lyrics as I did?" Hetfield asked 'Kerrang! TV'. *"I could be singing 'Bleeding Me' with a tear in my eye and the rest of the guys might not have cared."*

The song was never released as a commercial single, but Elektra released it as a promo to radio in America.

BLITZER

One of three names shortlisted by Lars Ulrich and James Hetfield for their band, prior to choosing Metallica.

BLITZKRIEG

Blitzkrieg were a heavy metal band from Leicester who formed in 1980 and were signed to Neat Records. Their original line-up featured Brian Ross (vocals), Ken Johnson (guitar), Guy Laverick (guitar), Paul Brewis (bass) and Phil Brewis (drums). It was this line-up that recorded the 1981 single 'Buried Alive', the B-side to which featured the song 'Blitzkrieg' covered by Metallica, originally for the B-side of their 'Creeping Death' single in 1984.

Blitzkrieg split in 1981 with singer Ross going on to start a band called Satan. He re-formed Blitzkrieg in 1984 with a new line-up to release the album 'A

Time Of Changes' which again featured the track 'Blitzkrieg'.

On the back of Metallica's cover, Brian Ross has fronted various incarnations of Blitzkrieg over the years. Their most recent album was 2005's 'Sins And Greed'.

www.blitzed-alive.com

BLUE OYSTER CULT

Dubbed the thinking man's metal band, Blue Oyster Cult grew out of the ashes of Soft White Underbelly in the late '60s and were a seminal act in the development of American heavy metal. They are most famous for their 1976 hit 'Don't Fear (The Reaper)', featured in John Carpenter's legendary horror movie 'Halloween' as well as 'Godzilla' from 1977's 'Spectres' album.

Metallica covered the song 'Astronomy', taken from their 1974 album 'Secret Treaties' (although an updated version appeared on their 1988 album 'Imaginos') on 1998's 'Garage Inc' album. Ironically, bands like Blue Oyster Cult suffered a dip in popularity as thrash metal rose to prominence. However, the band doggedly stuck to their guns, and continue to record and tour to this day.

www.blueoystercult.com

BREADFAN

'Breadfan' is a track recorded by Welsh rockers Budgie, to be found on their 1973 album 'Never Turn Your Back On A Friend'.

Metallica covered the song in 1988 as a B-side to the single 'Harvester Of Sorrow'. It also features on the album 'Garage Inc.'.

BUDGIE

Welsh rockers Budgie received an unexpected shot in the arm when Metallica covered the song 'Breadfan' as a B-side to the single 'Harvester Of Sorrow' in 1988 (see above). The band also covered 'Crash Course In Brain Surgery' for 'The $5.98 EP: Garage Days Re-Revisited'. The original was on the 1974 album 'In For The Kill', but in America was a bonus track on the band's debut album, where it was credited as 'Crash Course'.

Although Budgie had been a going concern since 1967, they were mistakenly grouped in with the NWOBHM movement when they signed a new deal with RCA Records ,who pushed the band's 1980 album 'Power Supply' as part of the new metal movement. This is almost certainly where

Metallica's interest derives from, although the band are not without merit and well worth checking out.

Budgie regrouped sporadically throughout the '90s for the odd gig and re-issued their back catalogue on their own label in 2005. The band have now re-united and tour regularly.

www.budgie.uk.com

BURNSTEIN, CLIFF

Along with Peter Mensch, Burnstein is the brains behind the Q. Prime Management organisation who handle Metallica's affairs. Burnstein and Mensch worked with such acts as AC/DC, Scorpions, Aerosmith and Ted Nugent before setting up Q. Prime.

Initially, Burnstein ran the US side of operations from his flat in New York, while Mensch reciprocated

in London. The pair were signed on as consultants for the Rolling Stones' 'Steel Wheels' tour, and also by Madonna for her 'Ray Of Light' campaign. They also successfully guided UK pop metallers Def Leppard through the most acclaimed phase of their career.

Today their roster not only includes Metallica but also acts like Garbage, Lost Prophets, Snow Patrol and Gillian Welch.

BURTON, CLIFF

On September 27, 1986, Metallica suffered perhaps the biggest blow in their history, with the death of bassist Cliff Burton. To say that his loss was tragic is an understatement. To suggest that it was only after his passing that fans, media and the industry alike appreciated his crucial importance to the band is both fair and accurate. Born on February 10, 1962 (he spent the early part of his life in San Francisco), Burton was slightly older than the rest of the band. As a result, while drummer Lars Ulrich and

guitarist/vocalist James Hetfield were always seen as the leaders within the ranks, nonetheless both turned to Burton for guidance and advice on many occasions.

He had the insight, acumen and wit to see where Metallica's musical potential might lead. It's often suggested that the 'Black Album' might never have happened if he'd lived. On the contrary, it might have been recorded earlier, because Burton himself was a music fan, with a taste that went beyond metal and thrash. He enjoyed more mainstream and rootsy bands than the others in Metallica, and was a proud and

public supporter of southern rock, in particular Lynyrd Skynyrd. With his trademark flares, lashings of sweat-matted hair and the occasional cowboy hat, Burton stood apart from the rest of the thrash community.

A classically trained pianist who attended Chabot Junior College where he studied music, Burton started playing bass in 1976. One of his schoolmates back then also did well for himself – none other than 'Big' Jim Martin, who went on to find fame as guitarist with Faith No More. Burton's first band was EZ Street, named after a local strip joint. Musically they concentrated on covers and were never more than a stepping stone for him. Following this Burton got into local band, Trauma in 1982, and with them played at the famous Troubadour club on Sunset Strip in Los Angeles (although there are some who maintain it was actually the equally celebrated Whiskey A-Go-Go). Metallica, having just parted with Ron McGovney, were in the market for a new bassist. Both James Hetfield and Lars Ulrich were in the audience that night, when Burton played what was to become his trademark solo: '(Anesthesia) Pulling Teeth'. Impressed, the pair offered him the job on the spot. Ironically, given where Metallica would go, the bassist was keen to quit Trauma because they were becoming 'too commercial'.

Their first show with the new man was at The Stone in San Francisco on March 5, 1983. Two weeks later, on March 19, they play the same venue – their last concert with Dave Mustaine. This was actually filmed, and some of the footage was used in the 'Cliff 'Em All' video a few years later.

From the start, Cliff Burton showed he was his own man, unprepared to compromise without good reason. For instance, he was unwilling to relocate from San Francisco to LA, where Metallica were then based – he persuaded THEM to move.

Ironic that his first recording with the band coincided with the last of another member of the foursome, Dave Mustaine. It was a two-track demo featuring the tracks 'Whiplash' and 'No Remorse'. Variously known as the 'Megaforce' or the 'KUSF Demo' (KUSF being the local radio station that first played the tape on air), it helped to get the band their deal with Megaforce.

Now based in New Jersey, home to Megaforce, Metallica recorded and released the landmark 1983 debut album, 'Kill 'Em All', which included the aforementioned Burton solo trip. While there are many

standout tracks on that first record, a lot of attention was paid to '(Anesthesia)…', since the whole idea of a bass solo on an album was, to say the least, unusual. It also showcased Burton's unique ability to play conventionally in an unconventional way.

He really came into his own, however, on the second Metallica album, 'Ride The Lighting'. Listen to his intro to 'For Whom The Bell Tolls', which is so stunning most people believed it was a guitar moment, not a bass line. Likewise his solo on 'The Call Of Ktulu' is a highlight on the record, again proving that the rest of the band (with Dave Mustaine having been replaced by Kirk Hammett) had a lot of respect for his talents. Burton actually co-wrote all but two tracks on the album – more

than Hammett in fact. The songs 'Fight Fire With Fire', 'Ride The Lightning', 'For Whom The Bell Tolls', 'Fade To Black, 'Creeping Death' and 'The Call Of Ktulu' all bear his hallmark.

The band's 1986 breakthrough album, 'Master Of Puppets', again provided Burton with ample opportunity to shine. He performs heroically on the instrumental 'Orion', which he co-wrote and was one of his favourite Metallica songs. However, at the point when the band were poised to leave behind their thrash roots and fulfil their destiny as one of the great metal bands, tragedy struck.

On September 27, 1986, the tour bus carrying the band hit a patch of black ice on the road in the Ljungby Municipality in Sweden. It flipped onto the grass, rolled over and Burton was hurled out of his bunk, and through the window. The bus rolled on top of him… he didn't stand a chance. To make matters worse, when a crane was brought in to lift the bus in a vain effort to rescue the bassist, the chain snapped, and it fell back on him.

Various stories have done the rounds over the years, about the trick of fate which gave Burton the one bunk on the bus with a window unprotected by a wooden board. One theory is that, as this was the only comfortable bunk, each night the members of the band would draw cards to see who got it, and that night, Burton had won with an ace of spades. Another tale suggests that Hetfield was in the bunk, but couldn't get to sleep, so Burton agreed to swap with him.

There was also a rumour that the ice was a myth, and that the bus driver was drunk. Hetfield's even said to have walked down the road straight after the crash, vainly trying to find the patch of ice. However, a subsequent investigation exonerated the driver from any negligence. In reality, none of this matters. Burton was dead – fact.

The funeral was held on October 7, 1986 at the Chapel Of The Valley in his hometown of Castro Valley; Burton was cremated, with his ashes scattered over Maxwell Ranch, where he'd spent so much time. 'Orion' was played during the ceremony; subsequently, Metallica refused to play the song again in its entirety until June 3, 2006.

Burton has not been forgotten by band or fans. In 1987, Metallica released the 'Cliff 'Em All' documentary, a tribute to the man who's influence was so crucial. The album '…And Justice For All' features Burton's last songwriting credit, on 'To Live Is To Die', which includes a lot of his unused riffs. Mustaine also wrote his own personal message about Burton, through the song 'In My Darkest Hour' on 'So Far, So Good… So What!'. A memorial plaque has since been erected by fans at the fateful spot where Burton died.

Cliff Burton gave so much to Metallica – musically and image-wise. He's said to have been the one to introduce the Misfits as well as a love of southern rock to the band. Without question, his contribution to the band is immeasurably greater than the four years he was with them. His legacy will never be forgotten.

CALL OF KTULU, THE

The final track on Metallica's 'Ride The Lightning' album is the very first instrumental that all four band members played on. '(Anesthesia) Pulling Teeth' from debut album 'Kill 'Em All' had only featured Cliff Burton and Lars Ulrich. Equally, the bulk of the music for 'The Call Of Ktulu' had been written by Dave Mustaine during his tenure with the band (he also got a writing credit for the title track, 'Ride The Lightning') and this was originally known as 'When Hell Freezes Over'.

Cliff Burton had been a huge fan of H. P. Lovecraft and he had introduced the rest of the band to the legendary horror author's work. There's no doubt that 'The Call Of Ktulu' is inspired by Love-

craft's famous short story 'The Call Of Cthulhu': 'Ktulu' is an alternative spelling of the titular 'Cthulhu' used by Lovecraft later in his career.

The song won Metallica their sixth Grammy Award in 2001 for 'Best Rock Instrumental Performance'. Quite why it took the Grammy Awards panel 16 years to make the award only they know.

CAMP CHAOS

The people behind the Napster Bad cartoon series mocking Metallica for their role in the whole Napster controversy.

(see NAPSTER BAD!)

CANTRELL, JERRY

The guitar player with Alice In Chains, who were good friends with Metallica. Cantrell was among the group of musicians who played on 'Tuesday's Gone' at San Jose's KSJO radio station. Cantrell also performed the song with Metallica at the 1997 Bridge Benefit Concert.

He has also joined the band on 'The Four Horsemen', in an acoustic set in Boston during 1998.

CARPE DIEM BABY

The seventh song on 'ReLoad' is almost as simple as a direct translation of its title. Carpe diem means seize the day in Latin and this is a clarion call to live each day as if it is your last.

The song, known as 'Skimpy' in demo form, was originally recorded on March 2, 1995.

CAVE, NICK

Nick Cave is an Australian singer/songwriter who first shot to fame in goth band The Birthday Party, and gathered quite a cult following in the UK thanks to Cave's explosive stage performances and the band's hard driving music. When The Birthday Party split, as the drink and drug abuse became too much, the enigmatic frontman formed Nick Cave and the Bad Seeds, a more arty unit beloved of the indie press.

It was the Bad Seed's 1996 album 'Murder Ballads' (featuring duets with P.J. Harvey and, of all people, Kylie Minogue), that Metallica producer Bob Rock lent to James Hetfield, inspiring Hetfield to get Metallica to cover 'Loverman', a track taken from the Seeds' 1994 album 'Let Love In'.

"He's got the nice mellow stuff and goes straight into chaotic hell," Hetfield has said of Cave's work. "He builds these things into giant ugliness. That's the kind of stuff we were doing with 'Fade To Black'. Acoustic to heavy, one extreme to the other, and I saw a lot of that in Nick Cave."

Cave has recently formed the band Grinderman, a garage rock side project outside of The Bad Seeds, with whom he released a self-titled album in 2007. He has also pursued an interest in acting; Cave appeared in 'Johnny Handsome' alongside Brad Pitt in 1991, and recently wrote the screenplay for the Australian western 'The Proposition' starring Ray Winstone and Guy Pearce. He is currently working on a new album with the Bad Seeds.

www.nickcaveandthebadseeds.com

CLAYPOOL, LES

Leader and bass player with rock oddities Primus, Claypool was a childhood friend of Kirk Hammett's, and was auditioned for the role of bassist when Cliff Burton died. Although the band liked Claypool's style he was considered too "out there" for the band.

Kirk Hammett recorded with Primus on the tracks 'Tommy The Cat' from 1991's 'Sailing The Seas Of Cheese', as well as on a

Les Claypool

cover of Metallica's 'Master Of Puppets'. Hammett also appeared in the video for Primus' 'John The Fisherman' in 1990.

CLIFF 'EM ALL

Metallica's celluloid tribute to their late bass player Cliff Burton, originally released on VHS in 1987, and currently available on DVD.

The whole affair was shot in the form of a home video, using a mixture of fan clips, professionally shot footage of Burton during his time in Metallica and unseen TV footage. The whole thing is narrated by Lars Ulrich, James Hetfield and Kirk Hammett, who sit drinking beer throughout the programme. The footage goes as far back as 1983, with film of Cliff's second ever gig with the band at The Stone in San Francisco, and from Metallica's tour supporting Raven on the 'Kill 'Em All For One' tour. It also features footage from 1985's Day On The Green Festival in Oakland, 1986's Rosskilde Festival (Denmark) as well as the band's 1986 US tour with Ozzy Osbourne.

The informal nature and genuine warmth for Burton makes this a fan favourite as compared with the more recent 'Some Kind Of Monster'. It also provides a rare glimpse into the very early days of the band. The end credits and photos of Burton roll as an excerpt from 'Orion' (from 'Master Of Puppets') is played.

CLINK, MIKE

The original choice to produce '…And Justice For All'. Clink was replaced by Flemming Rasmussen, as James Hetfield revealed to 'Guitar World' magazine at the time.

"We started ('…And Justice For All') with Mike Clink as producer. He didn't work out so well, so we got Flemming to come over and save our asses," James Hetfield said at the time.

CONWAY STUDIOS

The studios in Los Angeles where Metallica recorded some of 'The $5.98: Garage Days Re-Re-visited', along with A&M Studios. Based on Melrose Avenue, the studios have played host to a wide range of artists, from blues legend Taj Mahal to Dave Matthews and UK rebel Billy Idol.

CORBIJN, ANTON

Anton Corbijn began life as a photographer for UK weekly music paper 'New Music Express' (NME) in the '70s. He later became better known as a director of music videos for the likes of David Sylvian and Echo & The Bunnymen, and creative director for bands as far ranging as Depeche Mode and U2.

It was Corbijn's photographs of Metallica, sporting their somewhat controversial new image, that appeared within the CD booklets for 'Load' and 'ReLoad'. These led to even more accusations that the band had abandoned their traditional roots and were actively seeking approval from different areas of the music business.

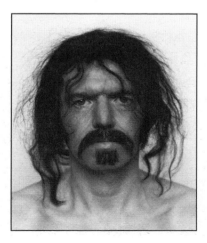

CORROSION OF CONFORMITY

Otherwise known as COC, Corrosion Of Conformity are a heavy metal band hailing from North Carolina and featuring guitarist Pepper Keenan, a friend of James Hetfield, who auditioned for the band as a prospective bassist following the departure of Jason Newsted in 2002.

The band formed in 1982, originally as a hardcore unit, featuring Woody Weatherman (guitar), Reed Mullin (drums), Mike Dean (bass) and Benji Shelton on vocals. By the time they released their debut album 'Eye For An Eye' they'd begun to dabble with heavy metal. Pepper Keenan joined on guitar and Karl Agell on vocals, in 1990, and 1991's 'Blind' was a much more straight forward heavy metal album which included the classic 'Vote With A Bullet'. Agell left to form Leadfoot, and Keenan took over on vocals for 1994's 'Deliverance', their first for major label Columbia, which showed a shift towards southern metal, a direction continued on 1996's 'Wiseblood', which in turn saw the band nominated for a Grammy. 2000's 'America's Volume Dealer' further developed the southern metal angle and in 2005 the band released the acclaimed 'The Arms Of God'.

Keenan appeared on Metallica's cover of Lynyrd Skynyrd's 'Tuesday's Gone' and James Hetfield sang backing vocals on the song 'Man Or Ash' from 'Wiseblood'.

www.coc.com

CRASH COURSE IN BRAIN SURGERY

A cover of a track by Welsh rockers Budgie taken from the band's debut album 'Budgie', released in 1971. Metallica recorded the song for 'The $5.98 EP: Garage Days Re-Revisited'.

Both 'The $5.98 EP: Garage Days Re-Revisited' and 1998's 'Garage Inc.' list 'Crash Course

In Brain Surgery' as having been recorded for 1974's 'In For The Kill'. In fact it was included on the US version of Budgie's debut album, released on the Kapp Records label, simply titled 'Crash Course'. The song was initially only released as a single in the UK, backed with the excellently titled 'Nude Disintegrating Parachutist Woman' in 1971.

CREEPING DEATH

Arguably one of Metallica's most enduringly popular songs, 'Creeping Death' was resurrected as set opener for the band's recent 'Sick Of The Studio 2007' summer tour and stands as a gem on 'Ride The Lightning'. No mean feat on an album packed with some of Metallica's best songs.

'Creeping Death' began life as a song called 'Die By The Sword' by Exodus, Kirk Hammett's original band. It never appeared on any Exodus album, but the band did record it in demo form. Inspired by watching the film 'The Ten Commandments', specifically the scenes dealing with the ten plagues of Egypt, which prompted Cliff Burton to comment that it was like watching "creeping death".

In the Bible, the creeping death was actually the tenth plague, the angel of death, whose arrival could not be seen but who had been sent by God to kill the first-born son of every family. Moses protected the Jews by getting them to paint their doors with lamb's blood, while the Egyptians' lack of knowledge of such a measure, resulted in their allowing in the angel of death.

James Hetfield ('Guitar World', 1991): "When we did the crunchy "die by my hand" breakdown in the middle, I sat in the control room after we did the gang vocals, and everyone was just going nuts! This was our first real big chanting gang vocal thing – there was almost some production value to it. The whole album was a big step for us."

'Creeping Death' was released as a single in the UK in 1984 by Music For Nations, who had issued 'Ride The Lightning', backed with covers of 'Am I Evil?' and 'Blitzkrieg'.

CURCIO, PAUL

Paul Curcio was the producer of Metallica's debut album 'Kill 'Em All'. Johnny Zazula was executive producer.

CURE

'Cure', taken from Metallica's 'Load' album is another example of James Hetfield venting his spleen against the religion that kept him shackled as a child.

Originally titled 'Believe' in demo form, the song refers to those who believe they will only find salvation in religion, thus leaving themselves with little hope in life.

Hetfield grew up in a Christian Science family. Christian Scientists believe God's love will cure all, even illness. Hetfield lost both his mother and father to cancer.

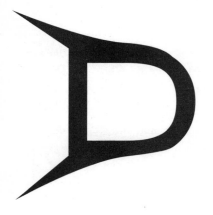

DAMAGE INC.

The closing track on 1986's 'Master Of Puppets' is, as its title implies, a tale of senseless violence and destruction. Equal in tone and pace to the vehement message carried in the lyrics, 'Damage Inc.' is one of the fastest tracks on 'Master Of Puppets', opening with a flurry of bass activity from Cliff Burton, before the rest of the band kick in, full steam ahead.

Dream Theatre

DAMAGE CASE

A Metallica's cover of Motorhead's 'Damage Case', originally from the latter band's 1979 album 'Overkill',was recorded at Motorheadache '95, a celebration for Lemmy's 50th birthday in December 1995. Metallica appeared onstage as The Lemmys, donning wigs and false facial hair to play a seven song set.

The song appeared on 'Garage Inc.', as the B-side to the 1996 UK single 'Hero Of The Day', on the Japanese version of 'Hero Of The Day' and on a strictly limited 'Hero Of The Day' – featuring the whole 'Motorheadache Mess' single.

The song has been covered by Dream Theater, who performed it with Napalm Death singer Barney Greenway and issued it on their '5 Years In A Lifetime' CD, as well as German thrash band Tankard, Funeral For A Friend, Razed In Black and hardcore band Shai Hulud.

DEVIL'S DANCE

One of the songs, along with '2 X 4', which was performed live during Metallica's performance at Donington in 1995 prior to the release of 'Load' and 'ReLoad' – and, inevitably, poor quality live versions were leaked onto the Internet.

'Devil's Dance' is another big rolling riff of a song dealing with the devil, and how he leads you on a merry dance as he dangles temptation in front of you.

DIAMOND HEAD

Easily one of the major influences on Metallica, especially Lars Ulrich, Diamond Head are the classic nearly men of British metal.

The band formed in Stourbridge in 1976, and became one of the leading lights of Lars Ulrich's beloved NWOBHM. The original, and indeed classic, line-up was Sean Harris (vocals), Brian Tatler (guitar), Colin Kimberley (bass) and Duncan Scott (drums).

Self-financed demos were enough to garner the band support slots with the likes of AC/DC and Iron Maiden but a major label deal was not forthcoming, despite interest – the fact that Sean Harris' mum, Linda, co-managed the band with her then boyfriend Reg Fellows (neither had any music business experience) has often been cited as a stumbling block, not least when Foreigner's manager Bud Prager came calling, offering to represent the band in America. This was turned down, much to the astonishment of many.

The band released the 'Sweet And Innocent'/'Streets Of Gold' single on Media Records, but forced to go it alone Diamond Head set up Happy Face Records and put out the 'Shoot Out The Lights'/'Helpless' single, before issuing their debut album, actually untitled but since referred to as 'Lightning To The Nations'. That was enough for MCA Records, who duly signed the band and for

whom Diamond Head released 'Living On... Borrowed Time', housed in a lavish, Rodney Matthews-designed sleeve, MCA's most expensive at the time. The album reached number 24 in the charts and it appeared that the faith of press and fans alike was to be paid back.

The more experimental 'Canterbury' followed in 1983, but the first batch of albums all jumped, which didn't help the group's progress. Neither did the fact that Diamond Head bowed to pressure from MCA and fired Kimberley and Scott. The band subsequently opened the 1983 Donington Monsters Of Rock, but soon after gave up the ghost.

In the interim period, Metallica arrived on the scene, professing

their admiration for the UK group and covering them aplenty. In 1991, Harris and Tatler put together a new line-up of the band, and Harris found himself working with Dave Mustaine, another longtime fan. Diamond Head released the good 'Death And Progress' in 1993, with contributions from Mustaine and Black Sabbath's Tony Iommi, and accepted the invitation to open for Metallica at the latter's performance at Milton Keynes Bowl, along with Megadeth and The Almighty. However, on the day Harris took it upon himself to skip onstage dressed as the Grim Reaper, befuddling an already confused set of fans who might have been aware of Diamond Head in a cursory manner, but weren't that interested in seeing them play live. Whatever imagery Harris believed he was projecting was lost. Diamond Head, it seemed,

had blown their big chance and split within the year.

Harris and Tatler gave it another shot in 2000, releasing an acoustic EP and finally got around to playing their first ever US show. But eventually the quirks and foibles of Harris proved too much and he left the band. Diamond Head continue to this day with singer Nick Tart and released 'All Will Be Revealed' in 2005.

One final point: at the time in the early 1980s when Metallica believed they needed a frontman, in order to allow an uncomfortable James Hetfield to concentrate on playing rhythm guitar, it's said the job was offered to Harris, who politely declined. But, whether there was ever any formal offer remains open to conjecture.

www.diamond-head.net

Die Krupps

DIE, DIE MY DARLING

A Misfits track appearing on their 1984 EP of the same name. This was the third Misfits cover undertaken by Metallica and was recorded especially for 1998's 'Garage Inc.'.

DIE KRUPPS

German band Die Krupps started life very much as an EBM/industrial act, featuring ex-members of pop band Propaganda. However in 1992 they began experimenting with more metallic sounds on 'Metal Machine Music'. They also released 'A Tribute To Metallica'. This album featured their own take on Metallica songs, including 'Enter Sandman', 'Nothing Else Matter's and 'Battery'. From there, they didn't look back, drafting in ex-Heathen guitarist Lee Altus for 1993's 'II: The Fi-nal Option' and getting progressively heavier over 1995's 'III: The Odyssey Of The Mind' and 1997's 'Paradise Now'. The band are still going today, but should be approached with some caution by those who think Metallica sold out after 'Kill 'Em All'.

www.die-krupps.de

DIJON, SAMMY

Singer with local band Ruthless, Dijon was brought in by Metallica in March 1982, at which point James Hetfield had decided he

wanted to concentrate solely on playing rhythm guitar. However, he never played a gig with Metallica and, after several rehearsals over a two-week period, he was told his services weren't needed.

DIRTY WINDOW

One of the few tracks from 'St. Anger' for which a guitar solo was added when performed live.

DISCHARGE

Metallica honoured their debt to Discharge by recording not one but two of the legendary UK punk band's songs, to appear on 'Garage Inc.', namely the excellent tracks 'Free Speech For The Dumb' and 'The More I See'.

Despite being viewed as little more than crusty punks in their home country, many metal bands have long cited Discharge as an influence, drawing inspiration from the band's metallic hardcore approach. Discharge songs have also been covered by the likes of Anthrax, At The Gates, Nasum, Monster Voodoo Machine, Sepultura, Soulfly, Napalm Death and Machine Head.

Formed in 1977 and featuring Terry 'Tez' Robberts (vocals), Tony 'Bones' Roberts (guitar), Roy 'Rainy' Wainright (guitar), Nigel Bamford (bass) and Akko (drums), the original line-up were very much a part of the punk scene instigated by the Sex Pistols. Two years later, now with Kelvin 'Cal'

Morris on vocals, the band had progressed to the grindingly metallic guitar and shouted vocals approach many deem to be classic Discharge.

The band have undergone many line-up changes over the years, and indeed their early proto speed metal came more to the fore in the '90s. The original line-up re-united in 2002, and although there have since been subsequent changes, the band continue to tour to this day.

http://myspace.com/discharge2k

DISPOSABLE HEROES

Offering up a very similar message to Dom Brautigam's striking cover painting for the album 'Master Of Puppets', 'Disposable Heroes' is a strident anti-war song delivered with steely intent and offering some of Metallica's most intricate guitar playing.

The song swings from the point of view of the foot soldiers in the front line to the generals who have sent them there, barking their orders, "Back to the front". The message is clear. War is futile, despite those who would glorify it.

The song was only ever performed once live with Cliff Burton, on September 14, 1985 at the Metal Hammer Festival in Germany (check it out at http://youtube.com/watch?v=hqNR33z-HhE), but has since re-appeared in Metallica's live set over the years, most recent-

ly making a welcome return during the band's Wembley Stadium appearance on July 8, 2007.

DOHERTY, STEVE

The man who gave the late Cliff Burtin bass lessons from September 1978 to January 1980. He is the person credited with introducing the young Burton to a range of styles, from classical to jazz. Says Doherty of Burton:

"He was a good student, very focused. He knew what he wanted and was a kind of student who always came in with the lesson prepared, which is not all that common.

"I can hear some of the odd metered rhythms we studied in his playings. I had many serious students, but Cliff had that rare inner drive to get out and do something about his music. I can't take credit for that; it was already there even when I taught him."

DONINGTON

Metallica appeared four times on the bill at Donington's Monsters Of Rock festival, headlining the event once in 1995.

They first appeared there in 1985 on a bill that ran (in reverse order): Ratt, Magnum. Metallica, Bon Jovi, Marillion and ZZ Top.

Set list: 'Creeping Death', 'Ride The Lightning', 'For Whom The Bell Tolls', 'The Four Horsemen', 'Fade To Black', 'Seek And Destroy', 'Whiplash', 'Am I Evil?', 'Motorbreath'.

Two years later they were back on a bill that also featured Anthrax but was headlined by Bon Jovi (full line-up: Cinderella, W.A.S.P., Anthrax, Metallica, Dio and Bon Jovi) which resulted in the letters pages of UK metal magazines being filled with claims that the event would constitute the ultimate pitched battle between hair metal fans and thrash heads. In the end the war between black and stonewashed denim never materialised.

Set list: 'Ecstasy Of Gold', 'Creeping Death', 'For Whom The Bell Tolls', 'Fade To Black', 'Leper Messiah', 'Phantom Lord', 'Welcome Home (Sanitarium)', 'Seek And Destroy', 'Master Of Puppets', 'Run To The Hills' (jam), 'Last Caress', 'Am I Evil?', 'Damage Inc.', 'Battery'.

Metallica returned in 1991, second on the bill to AC/DC (full line-up: The Black Crowes, Queensryche, Motley Crue, Metallica, AC/DC). On the day many expected Metallica to blow the headliners off the stage, but despite turning in a sterling performance, the sheer live spectacle that is AC/DC won the day – much as they had done

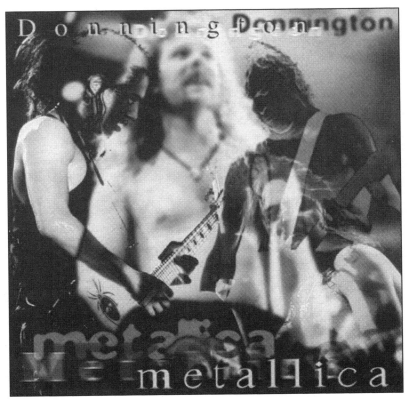

when they faced down the threat of Van Halen in 1984.

Set list: 'Ecstasy Of Gold', 'Enter Sandman', 'Creeping Death', 'Harvester Of Sorrow', 'Fade To Black', 'Sad But True', 'Master Of Puppets', 'Seek And Destroy', 'For Whom The Bell Tolls', 'One', 'Whiplash', 'Last Caress', 'Am I Evil?', 'Battery'.

No such problems for Metallica in 1995 when they headlined the entire event. With a massive main stage line-up that read: Corrosion Of Conformity, Warrior Soul, Machine Head, White Zombie, Slash's Snakepit, Slayer, Skid Row, Therapy? and Metallica, it remains one of the most remarkable Monsters Of Rock ever, with a heavy but varied bill over which Metallica rightly ruled supreme.

Set list: 'Ecstasy Of Gold', 'Breadfan', 'Master Of Puppets'/ 'Wherever I May Roam', 'The God That Failed', 'Fade To Black', '2 X 4', 'Kill/Ride Medley', 'For Whom The Bell Tolls', 'Devil's Dance', 'Holier Than Thou'/'Smoke On The Water'/ 'Slow And Easy'/'More Human Than Human'/'Welcome To The Jungle'/'Black Magic'/'Youth Gone Wild', 'Creeping Death', 'Welcome Home (Sanitarium)', 'Harvester Of Sorrow', 'Remember Tomorrow', 'The Unforgiven'/

'Nothing Else Matters', 'Sad But True', 'One', 'Last Caress', 'Seek And Destroy'/'London Dungeon'/ 'The Outlaw Torn', 'Enter Sandman', 'So What'.

DON'T TREAD ON ME

The title comes from the Gadsden Flag, which was hanging on the studio wall at the time of recording. The Gadsden Flag was flown by the US Navy during the American War Of Independence, as they attempted to hunt down British ships trying to carry war supplies through to British troops. All flags bore the legend 'Don't Tread On Me' and a coiled snake, which Metallica used on the cover of 'The Black Album'. It took the name from Colonel Christopher Gadsden who presented the flag to the Commander-In-Chief of the Navy, Commodore Esek Hopkins to use as his personal standard.

The defiance inherent in the lyrics of the track may have their roots in American patriotism, not least because the song was written as the first Gulf War had just begun. This may also account for why a snippet of 'In America' from 'West Side Story' is played at the beginning of the song.

'Don't Tread On Me' has never been played live, and in a 'Playboy' interview in 2001, James Hetfield suggested that songs like this one and 'Through The Never' simply weren't good enough.

DORIS

The nickname given the justice-style figure on the '...And Justice For All' album sleeve. Also a name given by Metallica to groupies in their early days.

DOWNLOAD

Metallica have appeared three times at the Download Festival, the modern alternative to Monsters Of Rock which is also held at Donington: in its inaugural year 2003, as an unbilled act, and as headliners in 2004 and 2007.

In 2003 Metallica had been contracted to headline the Reading Festival, but were also keen to put in an appearance at the very first Download. However, the promoters for Reading disagreed, so in one of the worst kept secrets in the music business, Metallica made an unscheduled appearance half-way down the bill on the Scuzz Stage on the Sunday afternoon (June 1). It was the first time UK audiences had either got to see the band with new bassist Rob Trujillo, or heard any material from 'St. Anger'.

Set list: 'Blackened', 'No Remorse', 'Harvester Of Sorrow', 'Welcome Home (Sanitarium)', 'Frantic', 'Sad But True', 'St. Anger', 'Masters Of Puppets', 'Creeping Death', 'Damage Inc.'.

In 2004, with Metallica headlining the event on the Sunday night (June 6), there was yet more controversy when Lars Ulrich failed to appear with the band, having been mysteriously taken ill on the flight over from Europe, and leaving the band frantically searching for a replacement backstage. In the end Slipknot drummer Joey Jordison and Slayer's Dave Lombardo, plus Ulrich's own roadie Flemming Larson, filled the drum stool, with Lombardo drumming on 'Battery' and 'The Four Horsemen' before Jordison took over for most of the main set.

Set list: 'Ecstasy Of Gold', 'Battery', 'The Four Horsemen', 'For Whom The Bell Tolls', 'Creeping Death', 'Seek And Destroy', 'Fade To Black', 'Wherever I May Roam', 'Last Caress', 'Sad But True', 'Nothing Else Matters', 'Enter Sandman'.

Metallica's last Download appearance thus far was in 2006, at the new look three-day festival, and thankfully went off without

a hitch. Metallica headlined the Saturday night (June 10) and were widely regarded as being the best of the three headline acts, Tool and Guns n' Roses supplying the competition. But when Metallica played the whole of 'Master Of Puppets, what do you expect?

Set list: Ecstasy Of Gold', 'Creeping Death', 'Fuel', 'Wherever I May Roam', 'The New Song', 'The Unforgiven', 'Battery', 'Master Of Puppets', 'The Thing That Should Not Be', 'Welcome Home (Sanitarium)', 'Disposable Heroes', 'Leper Messiah', 'Damage Inc.', 'Sad But True', 'Nothing Else Matters', 'One', 'Enter Sandman', 'Die, Die My Darling', 'Seek And Destroy'.

DUNGEON, THE

Lars Ulrich's home studio.

DYERS EVE

A young man feels anger towards his parents and how they behaved towards him when he was young. Hmmm, where do we think James drew inspiration for this one from? His Christian Science upbringing perchance?

Whatever, the closing track from '...And Justice For All' certainly gave Lars a stern test with some of the most complex drum sections ever in a Metallica song. Because of that, the song has rarely been performed live.

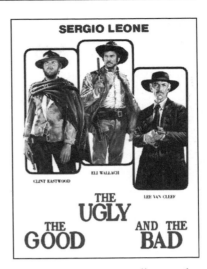

ECSTASY OF GOLD

'Ecstasy Of Gold' is part of composer Ennio Morricone's soundtrack score for Sergio Leone's 1966 spaghetti western 'The Good, The Bad And The Ugly'. This music accompanies the three-way Mexican stand-off between the stars Clint Eastwood, Lee Van Cleef and Eli Wallach at the film's climax. In the movie, Eastwood's character of 'Blondie' (a continuation of his enigmatic character 'The Man With No Name' from previous Leone westerns) shoots Cleef's 'Angel Eyes' as the three of them battle over hidden gold in a cemetery.

Wallach's character, 'Tuco', tries to fire his gun, only to discover Blondie has removed the bullets the night before. Blondie then forces Tuco to dig up the gold, before persuading him at gunpoint to balance on a rickety cross in the graveyard, placing his head in the noose that Blondie has tied to the branch of a tree. Meanwhile Blondie takes half the loot, with an irate Tuco screaming abuse, before turning and shooting to cut the rope, freeing Tuco and leaving him raging.

Metallica, long-time fans of Ennio Morricone, have used 'Ecstasy Of Gold, one of Morricone's most famous pieces, as their intro tape since 1983. It also features on the band's 1999 live album 'S & M', and has been covered by Metallica on the 2007 tribute album 'We All Love Ennio Morricone'.

ELEKTRA RECORDS

Elektra Records have been Metallica's US record label since 1984, when the band released 'Ride The Lightning'. Metallica were originally signed to independent label Megaforce, set up by the enterprising Johnny Zazula when no other label showed interest in signing the band. Megaforce issued Metallica's 1983 debut 'Kill 'Em All', but the swift rise of the band soon attracted the attention of the labels that had originally deemed them unworthy. Elektra, and in particular A&R man Michael Alago, subsequently won the band's signatures (after striking a deal with Megaforce for their release from the latter's contract), and have released every Metallica album in the US since.

Elektra Records was set up in 1950 by Jac Holzman and Paul Rickholt. By the 1960s the label was very much at the forefront of the folk boom, before signing both The Doors and Love in 1966 which led to them becoming the label most associated with the psychedelic movement by the late '60s. Since then, notable Elektra acts have included The Stooges, MC5l, Bad Company, The Cars, Dream

Theater, Dokken, Kyuss, Motley Crue, Tom Waits and Yes.

In the UK, Metallica remained signed to the independent Music For Nations label, before Phonogram stepped in for 1987's 'The $5.98 EP: Garage Days re-revisited' and 1988's '…And Justice For All', later also securing a deal to release the band's earlier albums.

ENTER SANDMAN

This is arguably Metallica's best-known, and undoubtedly most popular song, certainly for the more casual listener. 'Enter Sandman' is both the opening track and lead-off cut from 1991's 'Metallica' (or 'The Black Album') and it swiftly helped invest the band with an entirely new audience, ready to accept the combination of light and shade now added to their music. Thus it went a long way to establishing Metallica as the biggest metal band on the planet.

The song itself deals with the nightmares plaguing a young child as bedtime approaches, and producer Bob Rock's son joined Metallica frontman James Hetfield in reciting the popular children's prayer 'Now I Lay Me Down To Sleep' throughout the song. This helped to capitalise on the primal fears brought on by the presence of the 'Sandman' in sleep – fears that have haunted many people in the formative years of their life.

Originally the band had toyed with even darker themes for the song, exploring such tragedies as cot death, before settling for what was deemed a more palatable slant.

With its repetitive riff and ever expanding melody, the song proved a huge hit, reaching number five in the UK charts and number 16 in the USA. Ironically, the band had thought about releasing the harsher 'Holier Than Thou' as the first single from the album, but legend has it that Lars Ulrich pushed for 'Enter Sandman', believing it to be a more marketable commodity.

'Enter Sandman' has been a popular staple of the band's live set since the release of 'The Black Album', and has been performed at many major events including the 1991 MTV Music Awards, the 1992 Grammy Awards and at the 1992 Freddie Mercury Tribute gig at London's Wembley Stadium.

It is also by far and away the most covered Metallica song, with versions recorded by the likes of Anthrax, Judas Priest, Dream Theater, Pat Boone, The Mighty Mighty Bosstones, Apocalyptica, Motorhead, Beatallica, Vice Squad and Johnny Crass. The track has also been used in the sporting arena by a range of teams and individuals: professional wrestler Jim Fullerton for his character Sandman; The Cleveland Indians baseball team for player introductions and baseball players Mariano Rivera (New York Yankees) and by New York Mets' Billy Wagner as entrance music. Also the American football team The Virginia Tech Hockies use 'Enter Sandman' as the team enters the field of play for home games, as do hockey teams the Toronto Maple Leafs and Toronto Marlies.

ESCAPE

The sixth track on 1984's 'Ride The Lightning', 'Escape' is a shorter Metallica song, giving an indication of the style they would eventually develop with so much success on 1991's 'The Black Album'.

As the title implies, the song is all about a prisoner escaping from jail, although the interpretation can be taken to mean escaping anything you feel traps you. The use of police sirens towards the end of the song merely emphasises the chosen subject matter.

'Escape' has never been performed live by Metallica.

EXCITER

The Canadian thrash trio from Ottowa who were due to be part of the 'Hell On Earth UK tour' in 1984, which was also to feature headliners The Rods and Metallica. This event was intended to introduce all three bands to British audiences, but poor ticket sales led to the dates being scrapped. Exciter were actually the first of the three bands to play live in Britain, appearing at the Royal Standard in Walthamstow, North London, just days before Metallica marked their live debut in the UK at the Marquee Club in Wardour Street, Central London.

Still a going concern after three decades, Exciter's most celebrated album remains their debut, 1983's 'Heavy Metal Maniac'. The band were also briefly label-mates with Metallica, when they signed to Megaforce in America during 1984. They also featured on the Music For Nations roster in the UK/Europe at the same time as Metallica.

www.monsternation.se/exciter/

EXODUS

One of Metallica's contemporaries from The Bay Area thrash scene, it was from Exodus that Metallica would take Kirk Hammett to replace Dave Mustaine on guitar.

Exodus started in San Francisco during 1980, and originally featured singer/drummer Tom Hunting, guitarists Kirk Hammett and Tim Agnello plus bassist Carlton Melson. By the time the band recorded their three-track 1982 demo, vocalist Paul Baloff, guitarist Gary

Holt and bassist Geoff Andrews had joined the line-up, but by 1983 Hammett was gone, replaced by Rick Hunolt, and bassist Andrews was replaced by Rob McKillop.

This line-up recorded what is widely regarded as Exodus' finest hour, their debut album 'Bonded By Blood' (1985), which set the band up to make something of an impact in the wake of Metallica's success. However, Baloff left prior to 1987's 'Pleasures Of The Flesh', and was replaced by Steve 'Zetro' Souza. Exodus subsequently managed to retain a stable line-up, but despite albums like 'Fabulous Disaster' and 'Impact Is Imminent', never managed to emulate the success of Metallica, or even the likes of Megadeth, who swiftly usurped Exodus' position within the thrash movement.

Of late, both Souza and Baloff have fronted Exodus, although Baloff tragically died in 2002 from the effects of a stroke. Souza returned briefly for 2004's 'Exodus Of The Damned' but soon quit and has recently formed Dublin Death Patrol with Testament's Chuck Billy. Exodus have long been in the hands of guitarist Gary Holt, who has assembled a new line-up and continues to record and tour with Exodus, although in truth they remain something of a shadow of the band they were in the '80s.

www.exodusattack.com

EYE OF THE BEHOLDER

The third track from '...And Justice For All' was actually the first US single to be released from the album, although it failed to chart. It was backed with Metallica's cover of the classic Budgie song 'Breadfan'

The track deals with justice as you, the eye of the beholder, perceives it, railing against the limits on freedom of the individual by the law.

The song has often been played live, more frequently of late as part of a medley of material from the '...And Justice For All' album.

FADE TO BLACK

Track four on 1984's 'Ride The Lightning' album, this was a major step for Metallica, being the band's first ever move into ballad territory.

Unsurprisingly, it brought with it a raft of accusations of selling-out from disgruntled thrash fans, but it stands as a fine example of how the foursome's songwriting craft had developed tenfold within a year of their debut album. And, ironically, it swiftly became one of the band's most popular songs of all time.

While many people initially believed the track was about suicide, and in fact some fans felt compelled to write to the band saying that it had dissuaded them from a suicidal path, the song actually deals with James Hetfield's feelings, having just had a lot of his gear stolen at the Channel Club in Boston, MA in 1984. Included amongst the lost items was an amp given to him by his mother, just prior to her tragic death from cancer. The incident forced Metallica to borrow equipment from close friends, Anthrax. The song is imbued with a sense of losing the

will to go on due to the depression Hetfield felt at the time.

"The song was a pretty big step for us," Hetfield told 'Guitar World' magazine in 1991. "It was pretty much our first ballad so it was pretty challenging and we knew it would freak people out. Bands like Slayer and Exodus don't do ballads, but they've stuck themselves in that position. We never wanted to; limiting yourself to please your audience is bullshit."

Metallica were performing 'Fade To Black' when Hetfield suffered major burns to his hand and arm at a 1992 show in Montreal. The band's pyrotechnician had informed the group of new effects that were being used, but hadn't told them that the old ones were also still in use. Assuming the new effects cancelled out the old ones, Hetfield stood where a 12ft flame from the old pyro set up ignited, causing the damage.

'Fade To Black' has been covered by Disturbed, Apocalyptica, Dimmu Borgir and Sonata Arctica. Strangely, Flotsam & Jetsam, the band featuring Jason Newsted before he joined Metallica, also had a track in their repertoire entitled 'Fade To Black', although it was, in fact, a totally different song.

FAITHFULL, MARIANNE

Marianne Faithfull is the British singer and actress who acts as guest vocalist on the song 'The

Memory Remains', the first single taken from the 1997 album 'ReLoad'.

Best known in the '60s for her involvement with The Rolling Stones, Faithfull was actually discovered by that band's then manager Andrew Loog Oldham at a Rolling Stones party. Her early forays into music highlighted her sylph-like vocals on songs like 'As Tears Go By', but it was her relationship with Mick Jagger which scored her far more notoriety.

Faithfull was present at Keith Richards' house, Redlands, when the police raided it for drugs; she was found wearing only a rug. She was also responsible for lending Jagger the book 'The Master and Margarita' by Mikhail Bulgakov, which inspired Jagger to write 'Sympathy For The Devil', while Faithfull wrote the song 'Sister Morphine' and inspired the song 'Wild Horses'.

She battled various addictions during the '70s and '80s, but still scored in 1979 with the abrasive 'Broken English', by which time her voice, originally sweet and harmonious, had become ravaged by her lifestyle. She accepted Metallica's offer to join them on 'The Memory Remains' and her career has been reinvigorated of late.

As an actress Faithfull is best known for her role in the classic 1968 film 'Girl On A Motorcycle', and has also appeared in the TV sitcom 'Absolutely Fabulous' as God.

www.mariannefaithfull.org.uk

FANNING, SHAWN

Now a computer programmer, Shawn Fanning was the man responsible for creating the file-sharing software behind the Napster music website, with which Metallica would become embroiled.

Inspired by his college roommate's failure to access various MP3 files he was after while at Boston's Northeastern University, Fanning set about writing the code for a programme that would benefit the downloading of music. This became Napster, and Fanning even appeared on the cover of hi-tech magazine 'Wired'. But as Napster's popularity grew, the music business, which had thus far ignored the rise of digital media, realised they were losing revenue. The law suits began flying and were led by Metallica, who discovered a demo for the song 'I Disappear' from the 'Mission: Impossible 2' film online.

Fanning has since set up a new, legitimate digital media company. He also made a cameo appearance as himself in the 2003 film 'The

Italian Job', where he is accused by a character of stealing the Napster software from him, while he was taking a nap!

FIGHT FIRE WITH FIRE

The opening track from 1984's 'Ride The Lightning' album was the very first Metallica song to use an acoustic guitar intro, before it swiftly builds up a suitable head of steam. Written by James Hetfield, Lars Ulrich and Cliff Burton, the song deals with nuclear holocaust, and how atomic war would bring about Armageddon.

Written while the Cold War remained very real, nuclear obliteration was still perceived as a distinct possibility between the United States and the Soviet Union.

FIXXXER

Another personal lyric from James Hetfield on the closing track from 'ReLoad', this time discussing the pain a person, represented by a voodoo doll, has suffered at the hands of his father. Hetfield had a famously poor relationship with his own father, who walked out on the family when he was young.

A lengthy song, running at eight minutes and 50 seconds, it closes 'ReLoad' in much the same way that 'The Outlaw Torn' ended 'Load', a fact that didn't go unnoticed by Metallica fans.

$5.98 EP: GARAGE DAYS RE-REVISITED

The very first recording Metallica ever made with Jason Newsted, who had replaced the late Cliff Burton on bass. The EP features a selection of covers of tracks by NWOBHM acts as well as some punk and hardcore groups that had inspired the band.

The price tag was added to the EP's title in order to ensure fans were not overcharged for the record. This was later amended to $9.98 for the CD edition. The vinyl version has long been deleted and is now regarded as something of a collector's item.

In the UK the cover of Killing Joke's 'The Wait' had to be left off the record to remain within industry regulations concerning the length of an EP, but all five tracks were included on 1998's 'Garage Inc.' album. The EP reached number 28 in the UK charts in 1987 and number 29 in the US and has sold in the region of one million copies.

Tracklisting: 'Helpless' (Diamond Head), 'The Small Hours' (Holocaust), 'The Wait' (Killing Joke), 'Crash Course In Brain Surgery' (Budgie), 'Last Caress'/ 'Green Hell' (Misfits).

FLOTSAM & JETSAM

Flotsam & Jetsam were the Phoenix, Arizona thrash metal band, from which Metallica found bassist Jason Newsted to replace Cliff Burton, who had died in a tour bus accident in Sweden in September, 1986.

The band, formed in 1981, were originally known as Gangster, and later Dogz. Newsted joined in 1982, along with guitarist Mike Gilbert. Singer Erik A.K. was brought in a year later, with the band changing their name to Flotsam & Jetsam, inspired by a chapter title in J. R. R. Tolkien's 'The Two Towers' from 'The Lord Of The Rings' trilogy.

They recorded two demos, 'Iron Tears' and 'Metal Shock' in 1985, before appearing on the 'Metal Massacre IV' compilation, and subsequently signing a deal

with Metal Blade Records. Their debut album, 'Doomsday For The Deceiver', was produced by Metal Blade's Brian Slagel, and made serious inroads into the thrash scene upon its release in 1986. Newsted, who had been the band's main songwriter, left to join Metallica later that year, but Flotsam & Jetsam persevered and even secured a deal with Elektra Records – ironically also Metallica's US label.

'No Place For Disgrace' was released in 1988, but a fluctuating line-up and label change to MCA saw them lose momentum. 1992's 'Cuatro' flirted with grunge and in 1997 they returned to Metal Blade for 'High'. Flotsam then took a hiatus, and returned in the new Millennium with 2005's 'Dreams Of Death', a conceptual album based on returning singer Erik A. K.'s nightmares.

www.flotsam-and-jetsam.com

FOR WHOM THE BELL TOLS

Track three from 'Ride The Lightning' was yet further indication of how fast Metallica were developing as a band and, much like 'Creeping Death', remains one of their most popular tunes.

Inspired by the Ernest Hemingway novel of the same name (set in the Spanish Civil War), the lyrics centre around the section of the book in which five International Brigade soldiers try to escape the fascists with their stolen horses, but are killed by enemy fire from aircraft. It highlights James Hetfield's interest not just in contemporary literature but also in the injustices caused by war, religion and politics.

What was to become the intro to the song was written by Cliff Burton before he joined Metallica, and indeed played as a jam with his band Agents Of Misfortune. The actual intro to 'For Whom The Bell Tolls' is also played by Burton on his bass, through a wah-wah pedal. When performed live the song normally begins with a bass solo in honour of Burton's memory.

The song was released as a single, but failed to chart. It has been covered by Sunn O))) and was remixed by the DJ Spooky for the soundtrack to the horror film 'Spawn'.

The tolling bells that feature in the song were sampled and are played whenever the Chicago Bears American football team score a touchdown at their Soldier Field ground.

FOUR HORSEMEN, THE

The second track from Metallica's 1983 debut album 'Kill 'Em All' and was originally titled 'The Mechanix'. It was written by guitarist Dave Mustaine and originally appeared on the band's 'No Life 'Til Leather' demo.

Hetfield told 'Guitar World' magazine; "Dave brought that song over from one of his other bands. Back then it was called 'The Mechanix'. After he left Metallica we kind of fixed the song up. The lyrics he used were pretty silly."

Metallica's new lyrics were based very much on the Book Of Revelations from The Bible, in which chapter six is entitled 'The Four Horsemen Of The Apocalypse'. War, Pestilence, Famine and Death are sent forth to the four corners of the earth to announce Judgement Day. Figuratively, many people have drawn comparisons with Metallica as four metal musicians against the world.

Dave Mustaine kept the original, faster version of the song and re-titled it 'Mechanix' for Megadeth's debut album 'Killing Is My Business… And Business Is Good', where it still has many sonic similarities with Metallica's updated version.

The Four Horsemen is also one of the nicknames Metallica themselves are known by and was the name chosen for the band's secret appearance at the Download Festival in 2003.

FRANTIC

The opening track from 2003's 'St. Anger' album deals with the pain of addiction, something to the fore of Hetfield's mind at the time, having just endured his rehab session. There is also the addition of the Zen Buddhism concept of dukkha, that "Birth is pain, life is pain, death is pain", a theory also used in Samhain's song 'Macabre' (Metallica have long been fans of the work of Samhain mainman Glenn Danzig).

The spirit of the song is very much to seize the day, and when Hetfield introduced it at a live show in Orlando in 2003 he stated: "This song's about life. Like right fucking now." The accompanying video for the single features a man looking back at his life as he has a car crash. The song reached number 16 in the UK but failed to chart in America. The band also

performed 'Frantic' at the 2003 MTV Video Music Awards.

FRAYED ENDS OF SANITY, THE

One of only two songs from '…And Justice For All' never to have been performed live in its entirety (the other being 'To Live Is To Die'), 'Frayed Ends Of Sanity' deals with paranoia and the inability to deal with reality.

The opening chanting that can be heard in the songs is taken from the film 'The Wizard Of Oz', from the march of the Wicked Witch of the West's soldiers. The effect was later used by Prince.

FREE SPEECH FOR THE DUMB

A cover of a song by UK punk band Discharge that appeared on their 1982 album 'Hear Nothing See Nothing Say Nothing'. The lyrics feature just the one line, repeated over and over again, a tactic frequently used by Discharge to reinforce their message. "I think we've slowed it down a little bit and tuned it down to get more chug out of the riff," commented Hetfield on Metallica's version. "I like to think that they were the first crossover band, even before us, as in combining aggression and good riffs."

FUEL

The opening song from 'Re-Load' is, on the face of it, about driving your car as fast as you can for the sheer thrill of it. As James Hetfield says on 'Some Kind Of Monster', "We have to play 'Fuel' because it gets me so pumped up."

However scratch beneath the surface and you discover another song, one that also deals with the demons of addiction and what drives a person to become addicted.

The track proved immensely popular in America, where it was used in NASCAR broadcasts between 2001 and 2003, although for a while the opening scream was removed in the wake of the 9/11 attacks. It was also used by the Philadelphia Flyers ice hockey team before their home games for several seasons and has featured in various computer games, namely PlayStation's 'Hot Wheels Turbo Racing' and Xbox's 'Test Drive Off-Road Wide Open'.

Released as a single in both the US and the UK, it reached number 31 in the UK singles chart March 1998. 'Fuel' began life in demo form as a song called 'Fuel For Fire' and featured different lyrics. This version can be heard on the 'Cunning Stunts' DVD.

GARAGE INC.

Released in 1998, 'Garage Inc' collects together all of Metallica's cover versions to date. Split into two CDs, the first features new material recorded especially for the album, which ranges from classic rock tunes that surprised some Metallica fans, to hardcore punk covers. The second disc includes the band's covers from 'The $5.98 EP: Garage Days Re-Revisited' as well as various B-sides and extra tracks that have appeared on different versions of releases over the years.

The album reached number two in the US charts upon its release and number 29 in the UK and spawned three singles, including the Grammy Award winning 'Whiskey In The Jar', which reached number 29 in the UK Top 40 but didn't chart in the US. Neither did the band's versions of 'Turn The Page' despite being a huge radio hit in the US, or 'Die Die My Darling'.

To date, 'Garage Inc' has sold in the region of five million copies worldwide.

Tracklisting: CD One - 'Free Speech For The Dumb' (Discharge), 'It's Electric' (Diamond Head), 'Sabbra Cadabra' (Black Sabbath), 'Turn The Page' (Bob Seger), 'Die, Die My Darling' (Misfits), 'Loverman' (Nick Cave') 'Mercyful Fate' (Mercyful Fate – a medley), 'Astronomy'

(Blue Oyster Cult), 'Whiskey In The Jar' (Thin Lizzy), 'Tuesday's Gone' (Lynyrd Skynyrd), 'The More I See' (Discharge), 'Bridge Of Sighs' (Robin Trower).

CD Two - 'Helpless' (Diamond Head), 'The Small Hours' (Holocaust), 'The Wait' (Killing Joke), 'Crash Course In Brain Surgery' (Budgie), 'Last Caress'/'Green Hell' (Misfits), 'Am I Evil?' (Diamond Head), 'Blitzkrieg' (Blitzkrieg), 'Breadfan' (Budgie), 'The Prince' (Diamond Head), 'Stone Cold Crazy (Queen), 'So What' (Anti Nowhere League), 'Killing Time' (Sweet Savage), 'Overkill' (Motorhead), 'Damage Case' (Motorhead), 'Stone Dead Forever' (Motorhead), 'Too Late Too Late' (Motorhead).

GOD THAT FAILED, THE

One of James Hetfield's most intensely personal lyrics can be found on the tenth track from 'The Black Album', which primarily deals with the death of his mother through cancer while he was still young, but also with the wider issue of broken promises.

The fact that Hetfield grew up in the shadow of his parent's thrall to the Christian Science religion has often been quoted as the source for much of the alienation that he felt as youngster and which, to a great degree, helped to mould the personality of the young man who would go on to form Metallica.

He had to watch both his parents succumb to cancer; their religious beliefs decreed they would take no medicine, and that if it was God's will they would be saved by His love. 'The God That Failed' is a pointed attack on a subject Hetfield has also explored in songs like 'Dyers Eve' and also 'Mama Said'.

The number has been only sporadically performed live, first at a show in Buffalo, New York on May 30, 1994. Since then it has only been played during shows later that year and in 1995.

GRAMMY AWARDS

Although famously losing out to Jethro Tull in the 1989 edition with their very first nomination, Metallica have actually won seven Grammy Awards to date. The full list is as follows:

1990 Best Metal Performance ·'One'
1991 Best Metal Performance 'Stone Cold Crazy'

1992 Best Metal Performance
With Vocal
'The Black Album'
1999 Best Metal Performance
'Better Than You'
2000 Best Hard Rock
Performance
'Whiskey In The Jar'
2001 Best Rock Instrumental
Performance
'Call Of Ktulu' with Michael
Kamen and the San Francisco
Symphony Orchestra
2004 Best Metal Performance
'St. Anger'

GRANT, LLOYD

Metallica's original guitar player.
When Lars Ulrich managed to put

together the record 'Hit The Lights' for Brian Slagel's celebrated 'Metal Massacre' compilation album (the song that introduced the band to the world), Grant was there alongside Ulrich and James Hetfield (who played bass, rhythm guitar and also sang). This was during 1981, but by 1982 Grant had vanished from the Metallica line-up and has rarely been heard from since.

GREEN JELLY

Green Jelly were a joke heavy metal group, who began life intending to become the worst band in the world. They featured, at various times, future members of Tool. In 1991, having signed a deal with BMG Records subsidiary Zoo, they released their third album, 'Cereal Killer'. The track 'Three Little Pigs' became a freak hit from the album and features James Hetfield singing backing vocals.

The band were beset by lawsuits in the latter part of their career, including one from Metallica's management who objected to the partial use of 'Enter Sandman' in their song 'Electric Harley (House Of Love)'. Green Jelly 'ceased and desisted' making music in 1996, although they do still play the occasional live gig. They are currently listed as having an incredible 206 official members.

GRINDER

One of three names shortlisted by Lars Ulrich and James Hetfield for their band, prior to choosing Metallica.

HAMMETT, KIRK

Since joining Metallica in 1983, Kirk Hammett has grown in stature to become one of the most instantly recognisable guitarists in heavy metal. His incendiary solos have lit up many a Metallica album and many more Metallica shows, as he has moved from a prolific and talented thrash guitarist to becoming one of the finest of the heavy metal genre. Always happy to remain in the shadows of both Lars Ulrich and James Hetfield, Hammett has, for much of his career in Metallica, allowed his music to do his talking for him. So perhaps the less said about some suspect image changes around the time of 'Load' and 'ReLoad' the better!

Kirk was born in California on November 18, 1962. His mother was from the Philippines whilst his father was an Irish Merchant Marine. Their union did not last and Hammett's childhood was somewhat traumatic, as he revealed to 'Playboy' magazine in April 2001:

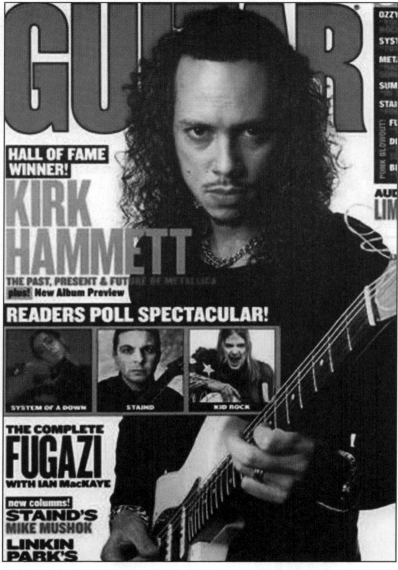

"James comes from a broken home and I come from a broken home, and when I joined the band we kind of bonded over that. I was abused as a child. My dad drank a lot. He beat the shit out of me and my mom quite a bit. I got a hold of a guitar and from the time I was 15. I rarely left my room. I remember having to pull my dad off my mom when he attacked her one time, during my 16th birthday – he turned on me and started slapping me around. Then my dad just left one day. My mom was

struggling to support me and my sister. I've definitely channelled a lot of anger into music. I was also abused by a neighbour when I was like nine or ten. The guy was a sick fuck. He had sex with my dog Tippy. I can laugh about it now – hell I was laughing about it then!"

Little wonder the young Hammett immersed himself in his older brother's record collection, citing Led Zeppelin, Black Sabbath, Status Quo, UFO and Jimi Hendrix amongst his earliest influences. He marvelled at his brother's guitars and by 15 was also marvelling at Jimi Hendrix, who he idolised and whose work he attempted to replicate.

Hammett's increased adeptness at guitar saw him moving swiftly from a Montgomery Ward catalogue guitar to his own customised Fender and eventually a 1974

Flying V. It also brought him into contact with other metal fans as the famous Bay Area Scene began to establish itself. Initially in a band called Mesh, in 1982 he formed Exodus with fellow guitarist Gary Holt and singer Paul Baloff. Hammett appeared on a 1982 demo by the band, but by April 1983 had accepted Metallica's offer to replace Dave Mustaine.

Hammett arrived in time to record Metallica's debut album, 'Kill 'Em All', in New York for Megaforce Records, with whom they'd already signed a deal. Despite the technical proficiency of his predecessor, Mustaine, there was no negative critic or fan reaction to the new guy – probably due to Hammett's own considerable abilities – in fact he was taking lessons from the soon-to-be legendary Joe Satriani at the time!

During his 24 years in Metallica, although largely seen as the band's lead guitarist, Hammett has contributed notable riffs, including 'Enter Sandman' and also 'Creeping Death' which was built around a riff he had originally come up with for an Exodus song named 'Die By The Sword'. Equally and understandably, the guitarist fought to have solos included on 'St, Anger' but was voted down. "We tried to put solos on there but they sounded like an afterthought," he said.

Outside of Metallica Hammett hasn't been too prolific. He's performed with the Spastik Children alongside James and Cliff Burton (later Jason Newsted was also involved), which was a side-project lasting from 1986 to 1990, and he has featured alongside Newsted in Voodoo Children. He has also recorded with Primus, Orbital, Pansy Division and Santana and lent his voice to an episode of The Simpson's called 'The Mook, The Chef, The Wife And Her Homer' as well as voicing various characters for the Cartoon Network show 'Adult Swim'.

Twice married (Hammett's first marriage ended in 1990, during recording sessions for 'The Black Album'), he currently resides with wife Lani in San Francisco with their young son Angel Ray Keala.

HAMMETT, LANI

Kirk Hammett's current, and second, wife. They were married in 1998. They have one son, Angel Ray Keala Hammett, born on September 29, 2006.

HAMMETT, REBECCA

Kirk Hammett's first wife. They were divorced in 1990, during the making of 'The Black Album'.

HARVESTER OF SORROW

The sixth track on Metallica's fourth album '...And Justice For All' featuring a splendid dual melody solo between James Hetfield and Kirk Hammett. It tells the story of a family torn asunder by a substance ravaged father and, as such, direct comparisons can

'Lightning To The Nations'. The song was co-written by Diamond Head vocalist Sean Harris and guitarist Brian Tatler. Metallica originally covered the song on 1987's 'The $5.98 EP – Garage Days Re-Revisited' and it later appeared on 1998's 'Garage Inc.' album.

be drawn between 'Harvester Of Sorrow' and Hetfield's early life when he had suffered at the hands of an alcoholic father.

"It was my mom's second marriage," he told 'Playboy' magazine in April 2001. "I have two older half brothers. I didn't really see any turmoil. They didn't argue in front of the kids. Then suddenly dad went on a 'business trip' – for more than a few years, you know? I was beginning Junior High. It was hidden that he was gone. Finally my mom said, 'Dad is not coming back'. It was pretty difficult."

'Harvester Of Sorrow' was the first single taken from '...And Justice For All' and only released in the UK on August 19, 1988. It was backed with covers of Budgie's 'Breadfan' and Diamond Head's 'The Prince' and reached number 20 in the charts.

HELPLESS

A cover of the Diamond Head song, which originally appeared on Diamond Head's 1980 album

HERO OF THE DAY

Featuring on 1996's 'Load', 'Hero Of The Day' has its roots in some of the album's earliest recording sessions. The original riff from which the song was built was titled 'Mouldy', so called because the demo on which it was recorded dates back to December 1994.

Lyrically, the song deals with the idea that people are always looking to the media to discover their heroes when, in fact, it is the people you meet in every day life who should be your role models. Musically it opens slowly before building into a heavier, more grounded song, not unlike 'Enter Sandman' but with a less emphatic build-up.

The accompanying video, directed by band photographer Anton Corbijn, shows a man channel flipping while watching television, with every shot featuring Metallica in some way; from a Western called 'Load' to a games show entitled 'Hero Of The Day'. A live video was recorded in Barcelona in September 1996, when

it took three takes to complete recording.

The song was also featured on the live album 'S & M', recorded with the San Francisco Symphony Orchestra, conducted by the late Michael Kamen.

'Hero Of The Day' was the second single taken from 'Load' and reached number 17 in the UK charts in September 1996. It currently stands as the band's tenth biggest hit.

HETFIELD, FRANCESCA

James Hetfield's Argentinian wife. They were married on August 17, 1997, and have three

children: Cali (born on June 13, 1998), Castor (born on May 18, 2000) and Marcella Francesca (born on January 17, 2002).

HETFIELD, JAMES

Seen by many as the figurehead of Metallica, James Hetfield has,

for many years, been regarded as both an icon and role model within the world of heavy metal. A commanding frontman on stage, Hetfield is a quiet and thoughtful, even intense person off it, and, although one who certainly knows how to enjoy himself when the mood takes him, it's easy to see why, when faced with competition like Axl Rose, it was Hetfield that the kids looked up to, as much for what he said, as for how he said it.

Born James Alan Hetfield on 3 August, 1963 in Downey, California, Hetfield's early life was as intense as he can sometimes appear himself, and it is clear that it has had a huge influence in shaping both the man and his music. Both his parents were strict followers of the Christian Science faith – not to be confused with Scientology – which rejects the use of medicines for curing ailments, while believing that the power of prayer can heal. This was of particular importance to the young Hetfield, whose mother Cynthia, a light opera singer, died of cancer when he was young. His father Virgil,

a truck driver, would also succumb to the disease. The effect on
Hetfield must have been immense
and has since surfaced in lyrics to
songs like 'The God That Failed'
and 'Until It Sleeps'.

Hetfield's first musical forays
were when he began piano lessons
aged nine. He later progressed to
playing on his brother's drum kit
before finally picking up a guitar aged 14. His first band were

called Obsession and his early musical influences ranged from Aerosmith, Black Sabbath and Led Zeppelin to Queen and The Beatles. Hetfield sang lead vocals for Obsession and it was during his time with them that he met Ron McGovney, who originally acted as roadie and later became a member of the band himself. Phantom Lord was Hetfield's next group, by which time he was singing and playing guitar before he once again hooked up with McGovney, living in a house owned by McGovney's parents. The pair formed Leather Charm, with Hetfield on vocals alone and McGovney on bass. As the band disintegrated and Hetfield was looking for a new drummer, ex-Leather Charm guitarist High

Tanner introduced him to Lars Ulrich.

Having formed Metallica, Hetfield was reluctant to take on the lead vocalist role and at one point John Bush, later of Armored Saint and Anthrax, was considered for the role. When Dave Mustaine was drafted in as guitarist the band even toyed around with the idea of Mustaine as sole guitar player. However Mustaine's time in Metallica was, as has been well documented, fraught with friction and Hetfield clashed with the guitarist several times. At one point he allegedly kicked Mustaine's dog, causing a fight between the pair, and eventually Mustaine's disruptive behaviour, blamed on substance abuse, led to his being kicked out of the band in favour of Kirk Hammett of Exodus.

Both Hetfield's character and talent as a musician developed tenfold as Metallica's career advanced, and the man singing on 'Ride The Lightning' bares little resemblance to the relative boy who performed on 'Kill 'Em All'. However his character took a huge body blow when, on September 27, 1986, much-loved bassist Cliff Burton was killed when Metallica's tour bus skidded off the road, turning over on a patch of black ice, near Ljungby in Sweden, and tossing a sleeping Burton out of the window. Rumour suggests that Burton was actually sleeping in Hetfield's bunk at the time, and the effect on Hetfield must have been immense. This horrific incident might go some way to explaining why Burton's replacement, Jason Newsted, never seemed completely welcomed into Metallica, and why Hetfield allegedly wears Burton's skull ring on his right hand.

A further incident occurred at a gig with Guns n' Roses at Montreal's Olympic Stadium in August, 1992, when Hetfield accidentally walked into the path of part of the band's immense pyrotechnic show. Although his guitar shielded much of his body from the blast, his left side suffered second and third degree burns. He made a swift recovery however, and was back on stage in a mere 17 days – although the band were forced to use John Marshall from Metal Church as a second guitarist until Hetfield's arm had recovered sufficiently for him to play guitar again.

Most recently Hetfield was forced to enter rehab during the recording of 'St. Anger' for alcoholism and obsessive-compulsive disorder. The band's excesses have been well-documented since the early days when they were nicknamed, much to the annoyance of then manager Peter Mensch, Alcoholica. Further decadence was made clear in an infamous feature in the UK lads mag 'Loaded' as well as a recent interview with 'Q' magazine.

In the end, Hetfield spent two months in rehab and a further seven with his family (he married wife Francesca in 1997, and the couple now have three children: Cali, Castor and Marcella) before returning to the band, where he was initially allowed to work for only four hours a day. The effect of Hetfield's absence could be seen in many areas, but was perhaps highlighted most strongly in Metallica's rather stark, and some might say unnecessary, 2004 film, 'Some Kind Of Monster'.

Hetfield has remained sober since his spell in rehab and has since undertaken a lengthy two-year tour in support of 'St. Anger' as well as two 'Escape From The Studio' tours in 2006 and 2007. At the most recent concert at London's Wembley Stadium, the band appeared completely re-invigorated, with a set that relied heavily on their classic earlier period, and Hetfield seeming totally in command.

An avid skateboarder – he has broken his arm on several occasions preventing him from playing guitar – Hetfield is also know to be a keen hunter, enjoys working on cars, is an avid fan of the Oakland Raiders American football team and also collects vintage guitars. He currently resides in Novato, California.

HIGH MAINTENANCE

A one-off alliance between Kirk Hammett and Lars Ulrich, with former Van Halen pair Sammy Hagar and Michael Anthony. They did a few numbers live at the Filmore in San Francisco on May 7, 2002.

High Maintenance

This was the last of three shows performed by Sammy Hagar & Waborites, with the Metalliduo coming on to play four songs from the self-titled, debut album by Montrose, another of Hagar's former bands. These were 'Rock The Nation', 'Space Station # 5', 'Rock Candy' and 'Bad Motor Scooter'.

High Maintenance were Sammy Hagar (vocals), Kirk Hammett (guitar), Michael Anthony (bass), Lars Ulrich (drums), plus Victor Johnson (rhythm guitar).

HIT THE LIGHTS

The first track on Metallica's 'Kill 'Em All' debut and one of the band's earliest songs, 'Hit The Lights' has its foundations in James Hetfield's early band Leather Charm. Hetfield and Ulrich worked out a new arrangement for the song and it initially appeared on Brian Slagel's original 'Metal Massacre' compilation album on the Metal Blade label. That version was recorded prior to Hammett and Burton joining the band and 'Hit The Lights' is one of the few songs from the Mustaine era still played live.

The song also appeared on Metallica's 1982 demo 'No Life 'Til Leather', a title taken from the opening lyric line of 'Hit The Lights', and on this version both Mustaine and bassist Ron McGovney also feature.

The band re-recorded the track for their debut album at Music America Studios in Rochester, New York, with producer Paul Curcio, this time with Kirk Hammett on guitar and Cliff Burton on bass.

Lyrically 'Hit The Lights' deals with Metallica and their relationship with their fans, of their being part of the heavy metal brotherhood and of life on the road. It was used as the opening song for many early Metallica shows to stir up a frenzied response from their already adoring fans.

HOLIER THAN THOU

Although there are those who believe that track three on 'The Black Album' is actually about the overly righteous approach of

it this bass heavy song was the choice of Hetfield, Newsted and Hammett to open the record, until Ulrich pushed for 'Enter Sandman'. But then he would say that, wouldn't he?

HOLOCAUST

Holocaust are a heavy metal band from Edinburgh in Scotland who were part of the NWOBHM, so beloved of Lars Ulrich, al-

Holocaust

us music critics, it is more likely to be concerned with hypocrisy, especially hypocrisy in religion, a particular bugbear of James Hetfield's who wrote this song with Lars Ulrich and Kirk Hammett. This is reinforced with the use of the lyric "Judge not lest ye be judged yourself", taken from Matthew 7:1 in the Bible.

Rarely played live following the band's 1991 tour, rumour has

though, to be honest, they were never widely regarded as leading lights within the movement. Their line-up featured Gary Lettice (vocals), John Mortimer (guitar), Ed Dudley (guitar), Robin Begg (bass) and Nicky Arkless (drums). They worked their way through the club scene during the late '70s and released 'The Nightcomers' in 1981. Featuring song titles like 'Heavy Metal Mania', 'Death Or

Glory' and 'Smokin' Values' it remains the band's seminal work.

They followed this with 1983's 'Live (Hot Curry And Wine)', from which Metallica famously covered 'The Small Hours' on 'The $5.98 EP: Garage Days Re-Revisited' and subsequently on 'Garage Inc.'. Holocaust disband-ed but re-grouped for 1984's 'No Man's Land' although only Mor-timer remained from the original line-up. They re-appeared in 1989 with 'The Sound Of Souls' and have been plugging away ever since but to little mainstream ac-claim. Their last studio effort was 2003's 'Primal' but their early albums, of most interest to Metal-lica fans, have recently been re-is-sued by the Sanctuary label. They have also had songs covered by Gamma Ray and Six Feet Under.

www.holocaustmetal.com

HORSEMEN OF THE APOCALYPSE

A 1983 self-released demo re-corded by the 'Kill 'Em All' line-up, it features the tracks 'Fight Fire With Fire', 'Ride The Light-ning' and 'The Prince' an early cover of the Diamond Head song. The demo appeared as a French vinyl bootleg in 1986, which as well as the original three tracks, added another seven from other early Metallica bootlegs: 'Killing Time' (a cover of the Sweet Sav-age song), 'Let It Loose' (a cover of the Savage song), 'The Four Horsemen' (originally a song penned by Dave Mustaine called 'The Mechanix'), 'Seek And De-stroy', 'Metal Militia', 'Phantom Lord' and 'Creeping Death'.

HOUSE THAT JACK BUILT, THE

Originally titled 'Jack' in demo form, the third track from 'Load', 'The House That Jack Built' deals with the effects of alcohol and drug abuse. The 'house' men-tioned in the title seems to refer to the user's mind. The song's lyrics focus on how drugs can take hold in the mind, offering their highs, but also their torrid come downs, followed by addiction.

The track features the use of a talkbox, popularised by Peter Frampton in the '70s. The guitar solo in this instance was played by James Hetfield, something he has tended to do with songs of particular significance to him, and possibly indicating that this one refers to his own experiences and feelings at the time, prior to entering rehab several years down the line.

Never performed live, 'The House That Jack Built' is rumoured to have been rehearsed backstage during the 'Poor Touring Me' tour of 1996.

HUGHES, BIG MICK

Renowned Metallica soundman, the affable Hughes became interested in sound engineering while at school, and got profes-

sional training when, as part of an apprenticeship at British Steel, he spent five years studying electronics at technical college.

In the early 1980s, the Birmingham-born engineer worked with bands like UB40 and The Armoury Show (featuring former members of Siouxsie & The Banshees and The Skids).

The latter band were managed at the time by Peter Mensch and Cliff Burnstein, who then asked Hughes to work with their latest signees, Metallica. This was in 1984, and he's been with them ever since, as their front-of-house sound engineer for over 1500 shows.

Hughes has also worked with the likes of Slipknot, Steve Vai, the Wildhearts and Def Leppard.

- HUMAN

Pronounced 'Minus Human', this song has only ever appeared on 1999's 'S & M' album, recorded with the San Francisco Symphony Orchestra, conducted by Michael Kamen. It was one of two new tracks recorded on the album, the other being 'No Leaf Clover'. The song has never been performed outside of the 'S & M' set up. Penned by Ulrich and Hetfield, it was originally known as 'Plod' in its demo form, and sonically is similar in tone to 'Sad But True' from 'The Black Album'.

I DISAPPEAR

The song Metallica wrote as the theme tune to the Tom Cruise film 'Mission: Impossible 2'. The track was recorded in Metallica's last studio sessions prior to bassist Jason Newsted leaving the band, and although Newsted appears in the video, producer Bob Rock actually plays bass on the track itself.

The video, produced by Wayne Isham, includes footage of Metallica members replicating various scenes from other classic films: James Hetfield is featured in a car chase ('Bullitt'), Kirk Hammett is seen being chased by a plane in the desert ('North By Northwest'), Lars Ulrich jumps off a building ('Die Hard') and, in perhaps the most interesting scene, Newsted, on the verge of leaving the band, is depicted struggling to walk past a tide of people inside a mansion.

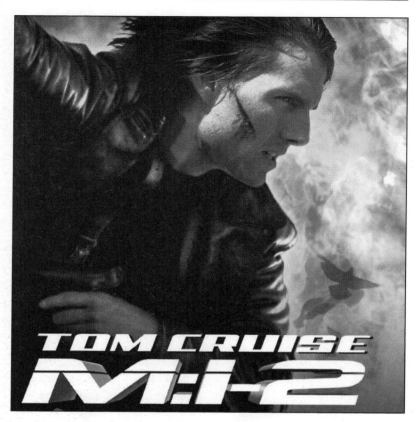

The single reached number 76 in the US charts and number 35 in the UK in 2000.

A demo version of 'I Disappear' was the track that was discovered on the Napster website, highlighting the whole file-sharing issue in which Metallica would become deeply embroiled and which would eventually bring down Napster.

INDIANA STATE UNIVERSITY (NAPSTER)

Legal action was brought against Indiana State University by Me-

tallica for not blocking the music file-sharing website Napster from their campus during Metallica's ongoing and very public battle with the latter organisation.

INEZ, MIKE

The bassist for Alice In Chains, good friends with Metallica, who responded to the band's new-look image at the time of the release of 'Load', by appearing on MTV's Unplugged with his band and uttering the words 'Friends don't let friends get Friends haircuts'. Initially Kirk Hammett was the only member of the band to re-grow his hair, although Lars Ulrich stated in interviews at the time of the band's 2007 appearance at Wembley Stadium that he too wanted to do likewise with what hair he had left.

INVISIBLE KID

Track five from Metallica's eighth studio album, this is one of the lengthier tracks on 'St. Anger' at eight-and-a-half minutes. Devoid of any guitar solo and bearing in mind the tinny production sound of the record in general, it remains, like many of the songs on the album, one of Metallica's less remarkable musical moments.

ISHAM, WAYNE

The director responsible for the videos for 'Enter Sandman', 'Wherever I May Roam' and 'Sad But True', all from 'The Black

Album'. He also directed the San Diego filming of 'Live Shit: Binge & Purge', and used live footage from this to accompany 'Wherever I May Roam' and 'Sad But True'.

He's also worked with bands such as Bon Jovi, Velvet Revolver, 3 Doors Down, Kid Rock and Def Leppard.

IT'S ELECTRIC

"That's where the shit came from, that's what spurred us on," says Hetfield of Diamond Head's 'It's Electric', which originally appeared on the Stourbridge band's 'Lightning To The Nations' album in 1980. This was one of Metallica's new cover versions recorded during 1997 and 1998 specifically for 'Garage Inc.' and is the second track on the first disc of the album.

Metallica have long been connected with UK metal band Diamond Head, and their cover of the band's legendary classic 'Am I Evil', originally recorded for 'The $5.98 EP: Garage Days Re-Revisited', can also be found on the second disc of 'Garage Inc.', as can their versions of 'Helpless' and 'The Prince'. Diamond Head also opened the show for Metallica at Milton Keynes Bowl in 1993.

JETHRO TULL

The British progressive folk rock band caused outrage amongst metal fans when, in 1989, they pipped Metallica to the Grammy for 'Best Hard Rock/Metal Performance Vocal or Instrumental'. Following the tragic death of bassist Cliff Burton in 1986 and their continuation in the face of adversity, not to mention the impact that the band were having on the world of heavy metal, most people thought Metallica were a shoe-in for the Grammy Award, for which 1987's '…And Justice For All' had been nominated.

At the ceremony itself, Metallica had just performed the track 'One', the most popular song

from '...And Justice For All', and were actually stood waiting in the wings ready to accept the award. However, amazingly the Grammy went to Jethro Tull for their 'Crest Of A Knave' album. Given that few people, least of all Tull themselves, even considered the band to be hard rock, let alone heavy metal, the result came as a shock, outraging fans and many metal magazines throughout the world. Tull didn't even show up at the Awards.

Metallica themselves responded with good grace, humorously stickering '...And Justice For All' with 'Grammy Award LOSERS'. In 1992, when accepting a Grammy for the single 'Enter Sandman', Ulrich referred to the incident by saying "We'd just like to thank Jethro Tull for not putting out an album this year."

JOHNNY GOT HIS GUN

'Johnny Got His Gun' is the 1971 film, written and directed by Dalton Trumbo, based on his own novel. The film, featuring Timothy Bottoms, Jason Robards and Donald Sutherland, centres around a young soldier, horrifically wounded in the First World War, left limbless and with much of his face blown away. He does, however, remain conscious and can reason, and much of the film focuses on this lead character trying to communicate to his doctors the feeling that he wishes to be placed on view in a circus sideshow to make people confront the horrors of war.

Metallica used clips from the film in one of three versions of the video for the track 'One', taken from '…And Justice For All'. The band had come in for criticism from fans for even filming a promo video for the track, having previously refused to pander to MTV by making promos for their songs. Of the three different versions, one features the band performing in a Los Angeles warehouse, one is a shortened version of this promo video and one shows the band performing, intercut with clips from the film.

James Hetfield was inspired by both the film and the novel, and used the idea of being cut off from the outside world, without any visible means of communication, as a theme for his own work. Metallica purchased the rights to the

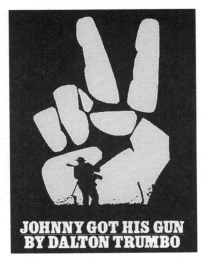

film so they could use clips in the video. The film is currently available on DVD.

JORDISON, JOEY

The diminutive Slipknot drummer stood in for Lars Ulrich at 2004's Download Festival when Ulrich was mysteriously taken ill on a flight from Europe. He has since blamed the incident on a panic attack, although far more colourful insinuations filled the

pages of the music press and the Internet in the wake of the incident. With Ulrich in hospital, Metallica were forced to hunt around for a replacement at short notice, with Jordison offering to fill the vacant drum stool. In the end he played on the bulk of the band's set, with Slayer drummer Dave Lombardo performing on two tracks and Lars' drum roadie, Fleming Larson, on 'Fade To Black'.

JUMP IN THE FIRE

The fourth track from Metallica's debut album 'Kill 'Em All' and written by Dave Mustaine, James Hetfield and Lars Ulrich. The original incarnation of 'Jump In The Fire', written by Mustaine alone, appeared on the 'No Life 'Til Leather' demo, and explored themes of a sexual nature.

By the time it appeared as a track on 'Kill 'Em All', Hetfield had reworded the lyrics to give a totally new perspective. The song is now written from the point of view of Satan, who is enjoying watching people murdering each other, happy in the knowledge that they will all 'Jump In The Fire' – or go to hell. There's no way they're getting away with their actions.

The song was released as Metallica's second single, but only outside the USA. It appeared in the UK on the Music For Nations label as a 12" single and 12" picture disc, the cover featuring a striking Satan figure surrounded by flames. The release included supposed live versions of 'Phantom Lord' and 'Seek And Destroy' on the B-side, but it later transpired that these were alternative versions of the songs with crowd noises overdubbed later.

Lars Ulrich has since claimed in interviews that the band were inspired by Iron Maiden's 'Run To The Hill's, which was popular at the time, and perhaps 'Jump In The Fire' was Metallica's attempt to emulate the British metal band.

M' album, as well as scoring the symphonic arrangements of the band's songs for the orchestra.

Educated at the New York High School Of Music and Art, and later at Juilliard, Kamen performed in the New York Rock & Roll Ensemble during the '60s, performing a mixture of classical and rock music similar to ELO. From there he became a successful and popular arranger of other people's music, and has worked with the likes of Pink Floyd, Kate Bush, Roger Waters, Queen, Aerosmith and Tom Petty amongst others. His work proved particularly successful when he linked up with Bryan Adams and producer 'Mutt' Lange, with whom he penned five songs, including the massively successful '(Everything I Do) I Do It For You' from the soundtrack of the film 'Robin Hood: Prince Of Thieves'.

KAMEN, MICHAEL

Michael Kamen is the composer who conducted the San Francisco Symphony Orchestra for the recording of Metallica's 'S &

In later years Kamen was equally successful as a composer of film scores and amongst his successes in this field were 'Highlander', 'X-Men', 'Licence To Kill' and the 'Lethal Weapon' and 'Die Hard' series.

Diagnosed with multiple sclerosis in 1997, Kamen died of a heart attack in 2003.

KEENAN, PEPPER

Best known as guitarist and vocalist with Corrosion Of Conformity, Keenan is a close friend of James Hetfield and sang the

second verse on Metallica's cover of Lynyrd Skynyrd's 'Tuesday's Gone' which features on 'Garage Inc.'. Other songs are known to have been recorded during these sessions but, as yet, nothing has seen the light of day. Hetfield can also be heard adding backing vocals to Corrosion Of Conformity's 'Man Or Ash' from 1996's 'Wiseblood' album.

Keenan auditioned for Metallica when Jason Newsted left the band, and this can be seen in Metallica's 'Some Kind Of Monster' film. Corrosion of Conformity released their latest album, 'In The Arms Of God', in 2005 and performed a rare London show in 2006. Keenan is currently working on a third Down album, the supergroup in which he performs with Phil Anselmo and Crowbar's Kirk Windstein.

KILL 'EM ALL

Metallica's debut album saw the light of day in 1983 and immediately spearheaded a new movement in metal: thrash. Despite the frequent denials that they were a thrash metal band, that would appear in the press after the release of 'Kill 'Em All', Metallica seemed more than happy to ride on the wave of this new genre, and were very much regarded as part of the Bay Area Scene, which also featured such acts as Exodus, Testament, Death Angel and Possessed. Or, as Lars Ulrich would

put it a year after the record's release, the band were on a path to world domination.

Metallica recorded 'Kill 'Em All' at Music America Studios in Rochester, New York with producer Paul Curcio, for Megaforce, a label originally set up by early band manager John Zazula to sign Metallica, as no other record company seemed interested at the time. Guitarist Dave Mustaine was fired immediately prior to the recording sessions for the album, owing to constant friction between himself and the rest of the band caused by his abrasive nature and heavy drinking. Indeed, Mustaine had been largely responsible for the departure of bassist Ron McGovney, due to an incident where Mustaine poured beer down the neck of the bass player's guitar so he got a nasty electric shock when he turned his amp on. However it should be noted that McGovney already felt

unappreciated in the band (he had to double for a time as manager) and the remaining members were actively seeking a replacement.

So it was that a line-up of James Hetfield (vocals/guitar), Lars Ulrich (drums), Kirk Hammett (guitar) and Cliff Burton (bass) recorded 'Kill 'Em All', helping to set in stone one of metal's most legendary groups. The sound of the album is one of youthful exuberance and a passion for their craft, and, even if by today's standards it sounds a bit undignified, it remains both an enthralling and thrilling listen. What is apparent from the off is that Metallica were already head and shoulders above their peers. One can't imag-

ine many of their Bay Area counterparts penning material with as much integrity and class as 'The Four Horsemen', 'Jump In The Fire' and 'Seek And Destroy', some of which remain staple parts of the band's live set to this day.

Equally, the ghost of the departed Mustaine looms large on the album with writing credits for '...Horsemen' (which would later feature on Megadeth's debut 'Killing Is My Business... And Business Is Good' but under its original title 'The Mechanix' as it had appeared on the demo 'No Life 'Til Leather'), 'Jump In The Fire', 'Phantom Lord' and 'Metal Militia'. Cliff Burton immediately begins to establish himself as a much-admired and loved bassist with his solo on the onomatopoeic '(Anesthesia) Pulling Teeth', and also on 'Whiplash', which must rate as Metallica's defining thrash metal moment.

After this the band would move on apace, constantly evolving their sound and refining their songwriting craft to a degree which few bands could ever hope to match. As such, viewed today, 'Kill 'Em All' sounds like a band 'in progress', which was indeed the case, but lest we forget, for many people this was the first time they had heard Metallica, and the impact of the album was immense on both a musical and social level. Fast, frantic, frenetic and fresh, 'Kill 'Em All' remains one of THE great debut albums.

Released on July 25, 1983, it did not chart initially in the UK. and only reached number 120 in the US when it was re-issued there on the Elektra label. That version featured covers of Diamond Head's 'Am I Evil?' and Blitzkrieg's 'Blitzkrieg', taken from the 'Creeping Death' EP, although both tracks were later dropped when 'Garage Inc.' was released. To date 'Kill 'Em All' has sold approximately three million copies.

Tracklisting: 'Hit The Lights', 'The Four Horsemen', 'Motorbreath', 'Jump In The Fire', '(Anaesthesia) Pulling Teeth', 'Whiplash', 'Phantom Lord', 'No Remorse', 'Seek & Destroy', 'Metal Militia'.

KILLING JOKE

One of the most important bands to have emerged from the post-punk movement of the late 1970s and early '80s, Killing Joke have, throughout their chequered but impressive career, interwoven such diverse styles as dub, indus-

trial, heavy metal, punk, dance and synth-led music and have been a major influence on the likes of Nine Inch Nails, Nirvana, Prong, Soundgarden, Big Black and Faith No More throughout their 28 years on the planet.

Metallica chose to cover 'The Wait' from Killing Joke's 1980 debut album 'Killing Joke' for 'The $5.98 EP: Garage Days Re-Revisited'. The Metallica version is much harsher than Killing Joke's original, although this is almost certainly down to advancements in production techniques rather than anything else – as anyone who has ever caught Killing Joke live will tell you, they remain one of the most intense bands anywhere. Typically, Metallica chose to include a guitar solo in their version, whereas Killing Joke guitarist Geordie Walker is well known for never playing solos. The track also appears on 'Garage Inc.'.

KILLING TIME

Although they once shared management companies and record labels in the UK, most people would assume there is little to link pop metallers Def Leppard with Metallica. But there is one connection – Irish metal band Sweet Savage, who, in their original incarnation, featured current Def Leppard guitarist Vivian Campbell. One of the more obscure NWOBHM bands, they only ever recorded an EP with Campbell, which included the song 'Killing Time'.

Metallica first featured a cover version of the track on 'Ron McGovney's '82 Garage Demo' and would later re-record the song as the B-side to the single 'The Unforgiven'. That version appeared on 'Garage Inc.'.

Vivian Campbell left Sweet Savage to join Dio, followed by Whitesnake, River Dogs, Shadow King and Def Leppard. Sweet Savage reunited in the '90s, probably on the back of interest generated by Metallica's cover, and released 'Killing Time' in 1996 and 'Runes' in 1998.

KING NOTHING

The fifth track on Metallica's sixth studio album 'Load', 'King Nothing', in keeping with much of the record, is one of Metallica's more melodic tracks, even veering towards a slightly alt-

Vivian Campbell

metal stance. The song is all about those who covet everything – be it money, possessions, power – for their own and then find, when it all comes crashing down, that it counts for nothing. At the end of the song the words 'Off to Neverland' can be made out, a line taken from Metallica's 'Enter Sandman' – not wholly dissimilar to 'King Nothing'.

The song was released as a single in America only, where it reached number 90 in January 1997. The promo video for the single was directed by Matt Mahurin who also handled the video for 'The Unforgiven'. The single was backed with a live version of 'Ain't My Bitch'.

'King Nothing' has featured in Metallica's live set, and at a show in Seattle on June 23, 2000 the band segued the song into a snippet of Nirvana's 'Come As You Are'. The track was covered by the band Castle Of Pain for the album 'Overload: A Tribute To Metallica'.

KINNEY, SEAN

Sean Kinney, the drummer from Alice In Chains, was one of the musicians who played in the 1997 session during which 'Tuesday's Gone' was recorded for 'Garage Inc.'. He appeared alongside Alice In Chains guitarist Jerry Cantrell.

drum kit at concerts. In 2004, when Ulrich missed the band's performance at the Download Festival (due a last minute illness), Larson filled in for part of the set.

LAST CARESS/GREEN HELL

A combination of two songs by US punk band The Misfits that Metallica first included on 'The $5.98 EP: Garage Days Re-Revisited'. The song also features on 'Garage Inc.'.

'Last Caress' originally appeared on an EP titled 'Beware' released by the Misfits in 1980 whilst 'Green Hell' is taken from the 1983 album 'Earth A.D.'.

An out-of-tune snippet of Iron Maiden's 'Run To The Hills' can be heard towards the end of the track. This Maiden song is an enduring favourite with Metallica, and Lars Ulrich has stated that it inspired the band to write 'Jump In The Fire'.

LARSON, FLEMING

Fleming Larson is Lars Ulrich's drum roadie. Also from Denmark, the long-serving Larson is one of the main reasons the Danish flag is always seen flying from Ulrich's

Fleming Larson

LEMMY

Not surprisingly there has long been a connection between Motorhead, *the* metal band of the '70s and early '80s, and Metallica, who took on the mantle for the late '80s, '90s and beyond. In 1995, the then line-up of Metallica appeared as The Lemmys at Motorheadache '95, a 50th birthday party bash for the perennial Motorhead mainstay, at the legendary Whiskey-A-Go-Go (ironically, probably the very same venue at which Hetfield and Ulrich had originally met Cliff Burton). Donning wigs and fake facial hair, the band performed a selection of songs for Lemmy, who was obviously in attendance. The seven song set consisted of: 'Overkill', 'Damage Case', 'Stone Dead Forever', 'Too Late Too Late', 'The Chase Is Better Than The Catch', 'We Are The Road Crew' and a reprise of 'Overkill'. Four of the songs made it onto 'Garage Inc.' having previously appeared as B-sides to Metallica singles, the four being: 'Overkill', 'Damage Case', 'Too Late Too Late', and 'Stone Dead Forever'.

Lemmy appeared with Metallica at Lollapalooza, in Irvine, California in 1996 to perform a cover of Motorhead's 'Overkill'. James Hetfield returned the favour, appearing with Motorhead at the Maritime Hall in San Francisco on May 28, 2000, again performing 'Overkill'. He allegedly appeared for the final song of the band's set and announced to the audience, "These are the Godfather's of heavy metal!"

LEPER MESSIAH

The sixth song from Metallica's third album, 'Master Of Puppets', sees Hetfield tackling one of his favourite subjects, religion, head on. In this case it is the TV evangelists, so popular in America but who, at the same time, extract millions of dollars from their television flocks in the name of faith. Despite the fact that many of the most famous of these people, including Jimmy Swaggart, Jim and Tammy Faye Bakker, Pat Robinson and Jerry Falwell, have been embroiled in scandals and notoriety, often forcing appallingly crass, tearful and, most likely, fake confessions from them, the practice remains popular in America. Hetfield, who grew up in a strict Christian Science family, has often railed against religion, and in 'Leper Messiah' points out the exploitation and lack of real care and faith of such people, and even of organised religion itself. Indeed, Hetfield once sarcastically dedicated the song in concert to the Bakkers, who were found guilty of embezzling millions of dollars of charity money.

The song was first performed at London's legendary 100 Club when the band appeared there at a secret gig as Damage Inc. on August 20, 1987. It has also been performed live as a pre-encore jam, as seen on the 'Cunning Stunts' DVD, filmed at Fort Worth in Texas in September 1997.

Early Metallica guitarist Dave Mustaine laid claim to writing the main riff for the track. This was refuted by Kirk Hammett in an interview in the February 2006 issue of 'Guitar World' magazine.

The song has been covered by UK indie rock act Fightstar for a 'Kerrang!' magazine CD, 'Master Of Puppets: Remastered', as well as the novelty act Beatallica, who mixed it with The Beatles 'Lady Madonna' for the song 'Leper Madonna'. Funny guys!

LIVEMETALLICA.COM

"This is the next logical step," says Lars Ulrich in his introduction on LiveMetallica.com, *"in a process that began back in 1991 when we first introduced the 'Taper Section' at our shows, where our fans were encouraged to bring in their own gear to record the show, and then take home their very own "bootleg" of the show they'd just seen. This technology will enable our fans to get the best possible recording of the show, without having to hold a microphone in the air for the entire night."*

As Ulrich says, LiveMetallica.com is the place to download entire Metallica shows. Of course, you have to pay for them (at the time of writing the pricing seems to be $9.95 for MP3 and $12.95 for FLAC). Artwork is also supplied with each show. There are plenty of free downloads available on the site as well, ranging from a 1982 gig at the Old Waldorf in San Francisco, to a 2003 gig at Orlando's Citrus Bowl. However, you will at least need to have opened an account with LiveMetallica.com before you can get your hands on even the free material.

In the wake of Metallica's dispute with Napster, some might see LiveMetallica.com as a hypocritical venture, not least because Metallica were perceived as having benefited enormously from the tape-trading scene which grew up around thrash metal. However, offering good quality recordings of live shows to

fans via the Internet is becoming an increasingly popular practice by bands such as Queen.

LIVE, SHIT: BINGE & PURGE

Metallica's biggest release undertaking at the time, 1993's 'Live Shit: Binge & Purge' is a hefty box set containing no less than nine hours of Metalli-music on three CDs and two DVDs (originally it was released with VHS videos). On top of that, fans were given an extra incentive to part with their hard-earned cash by the addition of a backstage pass (obviously out of date), a stencil and a booklet full of photos and relevant information, all housed in a special box.

The CDs feature songs recorded at a show in Mexico City, whilst the DVD's carry material from shows in Seattle in 1989 and San Diego in 1992. The set was criticised upon release for its high price and the perceived tackiness of the gimmicks inside, but the tracklisting remains, to this day, a Metallica fan's dream. It reached number 26 in the US charts and number 54 in the UK.

Tracklisting

CD One: 'Enter Sandman', 'Creeping Death', 'Harvester Of Sorrow', 'Welcome Home (Sanitarium)', 'Sad But True', 'Of Wolf And Man', 'The Unforgiven', 'Justice Medley: Eye Of The Beholder/Blackened/The Frayed Ends Of Sanity/...And Justice For All/Blackened', Solos (Bass/Guitar).

CD Two: 'Through The Never', 'For Whom The Bell Tolls', 'Fade To Black', 'Master Of Puppets', 'Seek And Destroy', 'Whiplash'.

CD Three: 'Nothing Else Matters', 'Wherever I May Roam', 'Am I Evil?', 'Last Caress', 'One', 'So What', 'The Four Horsemen', 'Motorbreath', 'Stone Cold Crazy'.

DVD One: San Diego, '92: 'The Ecstasy Of Gold', 'Enter Sandman', 'Creeping Death', 'Harvester Of Sorrow', 'Welcome Home (Sanitarium)', 'Sad But True', 'Wherever I May Roam', 'Through The Never', 'The Unforgiven', 'Justice Medley: Eye Of The Beholder/Blackened/The Frayed Ends Of Sanity/...And Justice For All', 'The Four Horsemen', 'For Whom The Bell Tolls', 'Fade To Black', 'Whiplash', 'Master Of Puppets', 'Seek And Destroy', 'One', 'Last Caress', 'Am I Evil?', 'Battery', 'Stone Cold Crazy'.

DVD Two: Seattle, '89: 'The Ecstasy Of Gold/Blackened', 'For Whom The Bell Tolls', 'Welcome Home (Sanitarium)', 'Harvester Of Sorrow', 'The Four Horsemen', 'The Thing That Should Never Be', Bass Solo, 'Master Of Puppets', 'Fade To Black', 'Seek And Destroy', '...And Justice For All', 'One', 'Creeping Death', Guitar Solo, 'Battery/Frayed Ends Of Sanity', 'Last Caress', 'Am I Evil?', 'Whiplash', 'Breadfan'.

LJUNGBY

For most people, the tiny municipality of Ljungby in Southern Sweden will barely register on the radar. Surrounded by forests, lakes and plains, like much of the local area it is a popular destination with German holidaymakers. However, it is here that Metallica bassist Cliff Burton lost his life on September 27, 1986, when Metallica's tour bus reportedly skidded on a patch of black ice, throwing Burton, allegedly sleeping in James Hetfield's bunk, through a smashed window, killing him when the bus fell back on top of him, while the authorities were trying to winch it clear.

LOAD

Metallica's sixth album, 'Load', remains an enjoyable collection of songs delivered in a mature and engaging fashion and which, for many bands, would have been hailed a triumph. But some 13-years after their debut, some of the effects of thrash metal continued to hang around their collective necks like an albatross. Given thrash metal fans' notorious distrust of change in any shape or form, often resulting in a collective accusation of selling out, 'The Black Album' had been considered, by some, as something of a disappointment, while in the opinion of others, Metallica were evolving into the excellent, classy and very heavy metal band they'd long promised to be. Five years

down the line 'Load' was deemed a step too far by purists.

Not only did the Metallica of 'Load' sound markedly different – akin to the more melodic moments from the previous record – but they looked different too! They'd cut their hair, they'd changed their image – some said Kirk Hammett now looked like a pimp. They'd even changed their logo! A section of their fanbase rose as one, mirroring the character Garth in the film 'Wayne's World', and announced "We fear change!" Or they might as well have done.

Yes, Metallica looked different – prompting long-time friend Mike Inez, bassist with Alice In Chains to pronounce, "Friends don't let friends get Friends haircuts" – but did they sound drastically different from the band that had released 'The Black Album' in 1991? Not if the likes of opener 'Ain't My Bitch' and the rolling riff that is '2 X 4' are anything to go by. 'Hero Of The Day' and 'King Nothing' would sit happily alongside some of the last album's more melodic moments and even the first single from the album, 'Until It Sleeps', in which

Hetfield addresses the death of his father from cancer, seems to mirror 'Enter Sandman' in tone if not style.

Perhaps if anything, where 'Load' does fall down is in the fact that at 78 minutes and 59 seconds, it is just too long – certainly the lengthiest Metallica studio album that has been recorded. In fact, had it been any longer the CD would probably have jumped when played! But it's a sad fact that advancements in technology meant that, whereas in the '70s a band merely had two sides of vinyl to contend with (or four if they were called Yes or Emerson, Lake And Palmer), the advent of the CD allowed more room for songs and more pressure from record companies to fill up as much space as possible, in order to make a more marketable commodity. As such, perhaps Metallica fell foul of modern day market forces.

But, of course, it really should be all about the music, and few people will argue that 'Load' is regarded as the point where it seemed, with the band's authority being questioned, things began to go awry – a state of affairs from which the foursome only now seem to be extricating themselves. Certainly the change of logo is the kind of thing that is likely to bother hardcore thrash fans. More so, perhaps, the accompanying booklet that for once didn't feature the lyrics to the songs, but merely snippets, accompanied by 'artistic' shots of the band members, courtesy of renowned photographer and film maker Anton Corbijn, until now best known for his work with U2 and Depeche Mode. The fact that the front cover was based on a work entitled 'Semen And Blood III' by the artist Andres Serrano, in which he mixed bovine blood with his own semen between sheets of plexiglass, was probably met with a derisive snort in bedrooms all over the world.

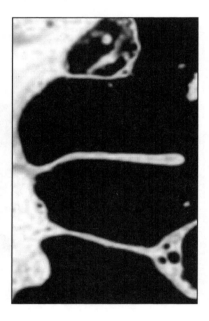

'Load' was created with long-time producer Bob Rock in a similar fashion to previous Metallica albums. James Hetfield and Lars Ulrich would generate the demos for the material that would eventually make up the record in Ulrich's basement studio, known as The Dungeon. By the time the band entered The Plant Studios in Sausalito, California they had 30 potential tracks to work on, along with Rock, Hammett and Jason

Newsted. Interestingly, however, Newsted gets no writing credit on 'Load' – the very first time this had been the case for any bass player on a Metallica album. In fact, Newsted would only get one more credit – on 'ReLoad' – before his tenure with the band came to an end.

'Load' may have come in for some unnecessarily harsh criticism, but it has still sold in the region of five million copies worldwide. The album also hit the top spot in the charts on both sides of the Atlantic, upon its release on June 4, 1996. Not bad for a supposedly weak album.

Tracklisting

'Ain't My Bitch', '2 X 4', 'The House That Jack Built', 'Until It Sleeps', 'King Nothing', 'Hero Of The Day', 'Bleeding Me', 'Cure', 'Poor Twisted Me', 'Wasting My Hate', 'Mama Said', 'Thorn Within', 'Ronnie', 'The Outlaw Torn'.

LOLLAPALOOZA

Lollapalooza is the once-travelling American arts festival that had been the brain child of Jane's Addiction and Porno For Pyros frontman Perry Farrell, one that mixed music from indie, hip-hop, punk and alternative rock acts as well as featuring dance and comedy. It is widely seen as mirroring the influence of, as well as interest in, the alternative music and lifestyles that swept through youth culture in the '90s, thanks largely to the grunge explosion that emanated from Seattle. The original festival ran from 1991 to 1997 before poor ticket sales spelt its end. It was revived in 2003, but again poor ticket sales forced the cancellation of the 2004 event. It reappeared in 2005, not as a travelling festival but as a three-day event at Grant Park in Chicago.

Metallica have only once played at Lollapalooza, headlining the event in 1996. The band's appearance that year was deemed by some in the alternative world to be symptomatic of the festival having become too mainstream.

LOMBARDO, DAVE

Best-known as the impressive drummer of fellow Big Four members Slayer (he also featured in Grip Inc. during his time out of Slayer), Dave Lombardo stood in for Lars Ulrich at Download Festival in 2004, when the drummer

was mysteriously taken ill prior to the festival. Although Slipknot's Joey Jordison drummed for the majority of Metallica's set, Lombardo appeared for the songs 'Battery' and 'The Four Horsemen'.

LOVECRAFT. H.P.

Howard Philips Lovecraft is widely regarded as one of the forefathers of modern horror literature. The impact of the Rhode Island-born author has been felt far and wide, from authors like Clive Barker and Stephen King to film directors such as John Carpenter and artist H. R. Giger, as well as countless poor, straight-to-video horror films. Amongst his most famous works is 'Call Of Cthulhu', a short story which introduces the mythical creature Cthulhu, from which the Cthulhu Mythos arose, concerning repeated themes and creatures in Lovecraft's work.

Cliff Burton was the first member of Metallica to become intrigued with Lovecraft's work, introducing the rest of the band to 'The Shadow Over Innsmouth',

a collection of his short stories. Interest rapidly spread throughout the whole band who particularly admired the tale 'Call Of Cthulhu'. It was on this that Metallica based the track 'Call Of Ktulu' – the first recorded instrumental to feature all four members of the band performing together and which appears on 'Ride The Lightning'. The re-spelling 'Ktulu' reflects the way Lovecraft occasionally referred to 'Cthulu' in later works. The writer's influence can also be found in other Metallica songs, 'The Thing That Should Not Be' being one example.

LOVERMAN

'Loverman' is a song by Australian goth rockers Nick Cave And The Bad Seeds. It was covered by Metallica for 'Garage Inc.' and is one of the new tracks recorded especially for that release. The recording of the song was instigated by James Hetfield, who got into Cave's work when producer Bob Rock lent him Cave's album 'Murder Ballads'.

"I thought, 'Woah, these are cool songs, they're all about murders'," Hetfield has since said. *"That made me investigate his other material and I was turned on by it completely. The moods it creates. He's got the nice mellow stuff and goes straight into chaotic hell. He builds these things into giant ugliness. That's the kind of stuff we were doing with 'Fade To Black', acoustic to heavy, one extreme to the other, and I saw a lot of that in Nick Cave. And that's what 'Loverman' was about."*

LOW MAN'S LYRIC

The 11th song on 'ReLoad', 'Low Man's Lyric' sees Metallica again using the hurdy gurdy, so prevalent on the single from 'ReLoad', 'The Memory Remains'. In both instances the instrument was played by David Miles. Lyrically the song explores the thoughts of a hopeless and homeless drug addict.

The track was originally known as 'Mine Eyes' in demo form and, despite its laidback feel, was actually used to open a San Francisco Metallica show in October 1997.

LYNYRD SKYNYRD

Along with The Allman Brothers Band, Lynyrd Skynyrd are the forefathers of Southern Rock, a genre of music much loved of James Hetfield, who, for much of the time around the release of 'The Black Album', took to wearing a Stetson and cowboy boots, and speaking openly of his fondness for country rock music (Hetfield was close friends with the late outlaw country rocker Waylon Jennings).

Metallica covered Skynyrd's 'Tuesday's Gone', originally taken from their debut album 'Pronounced Leh-nerd Skin-nerd', on 'Garage Inc.' and, in a change for them, the recording sessions featured an array of guests. Pepper Keenan of Corrosion Of Conformity appeared alongside Sean Kinney and Jerry Cantrell from Alice In Chains, Primus' Les Claypool, 'Big' Jim Martin, formerly with Faith No More and original Lynyrd Skynyrd guitarist Gary Rossington.

"This is the only one with guests," Hetfield has since said. *"It was live from the radio show we did last year so there's all these people singing out of key. We gave Randy (Staub, producer/engineer) the tapes of it and said, 'Here, mix these' and he was like, 'Holy shit, there's 20 guys on it', and it had a great vibe. I always loved that one. It's a movin' on song. You're splitting, you're leaving your woman at home. You're off doing your own thing. It really fits the road."*

MCGOVNEY, RON

Not all members of some of Metallica's earliest incarnations are easy to track down. Anyone know where Lloyd Grant is, for example? Ron McGovney, the band's bass player for the first two years of their existence, is a little easier. Although Cliff Burton might be the best loved and most missed bassist ever to perform with Metallica, McGovney's role should not be underestimated.

Born on November 2, 1962, McGovney met James Hetfield at high school and the pair became friends through their love of heavy metal. It was Hetfield who persuaded McGovney to take up the bass, and it was also he who taught McGovney to play during the time the two shared a house owned by McGovney's parents, one that had been slated for demolition to make way for a new highway. The two formed a band, Leather Charm, that also featured a succession of other musicians, but it was guitarist Hugh Tanner, who had previously quit Leather Charm to go into man-

Hetfield, McGovney, Ulrich, Mustaine

Lloyd Grant and Ron McGovney

agement, who introduced the pair to a young Danish drummer by the name of Lars Ulrich.

McGovney was not impressed with the new drummer, deciding to take his leave of Leather Charm and return to photography. Yet with Ulrich and Hetfield continuing to play at the house McGovney and Hetfield shared, he could not escape so easily. One day a young guitar player named Lloyd Grant and a bassist known only as Glen turned up for a jam, but the latter proved to be so bad

McGovney found himself drawn back into the band. At that point Leather Charm found themselves morphing into Metallica.

Dave Mustaine eventually replaced the short-lived Lloyd Grant and it was this line-up that recorded what is known as 'Ron McGovney's Garage Demo' on March 14, 1982. McGovney would appear on a further four Metallica demos; 'Power Metal', the legendary 'No Life 'Til Leather' and 'Metal Up Your Ass' from 1982 and 'The Horsemen Of The

Apocalypse' from early 1983. It was on these demos that soon-to-be Metallica classics were initially forged. Songs like 'Jump In The Fire', 'The Mechanix' (later 'The Four Horsemen'), 'Seek And Destroy', 'Whiplash' and 'Ride The Lightning' as well as the band's predilection for covering tracks by those who had inspired them, like Diamond Head's 'The Prince' and 'Am I Evil?', Sweet Savage's 'Killing Time' and Savage's 'Let It Loose'.

McGovney was in the band when, for a very short period, they flirted with someone other than James Hetfield taking the microphone. Feeling he wasn't a good enough singer, Hetfield wanted to solely play rhythm guitar and a new singer, one Sammy Dijon from a local band named Ruthless was enlisted. Dijon never played a live show with Metallica, but rehearsed with them for three weeks. After which time, however, Hetfield was back behind the mic.

McGovney's tenure with Metallica was sometimes fraught. He was also chosen to act as the group's manager and was responsible for the early 'Power Metal' slogan used by the band on business cards. Additionally he had to drive the band to gigs and eventually tired of the drunken antics

of the other three members. Yet no-one clashed with him more than the abrasive Dave Mustaine. When Mustaine poured beer down the neck of McGovney's bass, giving him an electric shock when he turned his amp on, he decided enough was enough.

The actual reasons for McGovney's departure have become clouded in the mists of time, with rumours suggesting they were actively pursuing Cliff Burton while he was still in the band. In a 1997 interview with 'Shockwaves', McGovney said; "After I heard them talk about Cliff I had some idea. I remember after that show it was raining like a mothafucker and I saw Cliff, all in denim, just standing there in the rain. I said to him, 'Hey dude, do you want a ride home?'. I kinda felt sorry for the guy. I kinda saw the writing on the wall. We played at Mabuhay Gardens the next day, it was a little hole in the wall. That was the last gig I did with Metallica. I never ever heard them tell me, 'You're out the band'. What happened was, after Dave fucked my bass up I confronted the band when they came over for practice and said, 'Get the fuck out of my house'. And I said to James, 'You have to go, too'. And they were

Ron McGovney and Dave Mustaine

gone within the next couple of days. They packed all their gear and moved to San Francisco."

Disillusioned, McGovney sold a lot of his musical equipment but was, for a brief while, enticed back into the spotlight in a band called Phantasm with Hirax man Katon W. DePena, but it was short-lived. In a 2004 interview with the All-metallica website, McGovney referred to himself as a blue-collar worker with three children living in North Carolina. He still has his basses and amps and jams with his kids at weekends.

MAHURIN, MATT

Director of the clips for 'The Unforgiven' and 'King Nothing', he turned down the chance to do 'One' because he didn't want to use extracts from the film 'Johnny Got His Gun'.

Mahurin has also worked with Motley Crue, Queesnryche and Bonnie Rait.

MAMA SAID

On an album of which it is said James Hetfield wrote some of his most personal lyrics, looking inwards rather than at the political and social injustice around him, the gentle, acoustic-led 'Mama Said' must rate as one of his most personal songs ever. In the past though, tracks like 'The God That Failed' had also echoed Hetfield's distaste for religion, particularly with reference to his own childhood, growing up in a Christian Science household and seeing both his mother and father succumb to cancer when, because of their faith, they believed that God's love would overcome all without the need for medical intervention.

With lines like 'I took your love for granted' the song tackles the painful issue of Hetfield's relationship with his mother and her death, although he does so through a central character in the song who expresses the writer's own loss and remorse.

The track was criticised by hardcore fans, who also poured plenty of scorn on the album itself because they felt it represented a shift away from Metallica's metal roots. Certainly, with its steel guitar, 'Mama Said' represents the softer side of the band's output and also reflects Hetfield's own love of country music. He performed the song with Jessi Colter, the widow of Waylon Jennings, at Country Music Television's 'Outlaw Concert' and the pair also performed a cover of Waylon's 'Don't You Think This Outlaw Bit Done Gone Got Out Of Hand'. Hetfield has been known to play this rarely heard song live on his own.

'Mama Said' was released as a single outside the US, and reached number 19 in the UK charts in December 1996. Ironically, given the laidback nature of the song, the B-sides on the two-CD set were live versions of 'King Nothing', 'Whiplash', 'So What' and 'Creeping Death'.

MARQUEE CLUB

Although Metallica may not have played London's legendary Marquee as many times as other notable metal acts, their shows at the club have always been memorable, not least for those who were in attendance. The band were due to support The Rods and Exciter on their 'Hell On Earth' UK tour in 1984, but when the dates were pulled due to poor ticket sales, Metallica took the opportunity and bowled on up to the Marquee Club, at its Wardour Street home, to play their first ever UK shows.

Such was Metallica's rapid rise through the metal ranks that they never returned to the Wardour Street venue again, and by December 1984 they were headlining The Lyceum down the road in the Strand. They would, however, make one more appearance at the Marquee Club, but at its new Charing Cross Road home, where they played support to Metal Church under the name Vertigo in 1990. Fans entering the venue might have guessed what was going on when they clapped eyes on a huge white double bass drum kit dwarfing that of Metal Church and resplendent with Danish flags. Metal Church singer Mike Howe introduced the 'support' act, asking the crowd to give "this new young band a chance".

MARSHALL, JOHN

The Metal Church guitarist was actually Kirk Hammett's guitar tech and long-time friend when he was originally called in to replace James Hetfield after the frontman broke his arm skateboarding while the band toured with Ozzy Osbourne in 1986. Being already familiar with Metallica's guitar parts he was the natural choice to replace Hetfield. Marshall began his stint playing off stage, only appearing when Hetfield would introduce him. However, at the insistence of Cliff Burton, Marshall took to the stage for the whole show after the fourth gig.

Marshall joined Metal Church in 1989 and remained with them until 1993, rejoining for a second stint between 1998 and 2001. He appears on the band's classic albums

'Blessing In Disguise' (1989) and 'The Human Factor' (1991).

When Hetfield was severely burned by pyrotechnics during Metallica's 1992 co-headlining American tour with Guns n'Roses, the band once more turned to Marshall as stand in. And despite the fact he was now a member of Metal Church, he once more duly obliged. Metallica returned the favour by playing as secret support act under the name Vertigo when Metal Church played London's Marquee Club in 1990.

MARTIN, 'BIG' JIM

The ex-Faith No More guitar player went to school with Cliff Burton, with whom he was a close friend. In fact, in the promo video for Faith No More's 'Epic', Martin can be seen wearing a T-shirt bearing the legend 'A Tribute To Cliff Burton'. He is also friends with both James Hetfield and Jason Newsted. Hetfield played on

Martin's own 'Milk And Blood' solo album and he was also one of the musicians in Metallica's legendary session during which their cover of Lynyrd Skynyrd's 'Tuesday's Gone' was recorded. The pair are also keen hunters.

As for Newsted, Martin was one of the very first collaborators with Echobrain, the band Newsted joined upon first leaving Metallica and the two are known to jam together frequently.

MASTER OF PUPPETS (ALBUM)

Metallica's third album has quite rightly gone down in history as one of the all time greatest of its genre. In the space of three short years since their impressive debut, and having already taken immense strides with 1984's 'Ride The Lightning', they now found themselves staring in the face of true greatness with a stunning third album. If both 'Kill 'Em All' and 'Ride The Lightning' had suggested Metallica's peers would have difficulty keeping apace with them, then 'Master Of Puppets' must have sent many shivers down the spines of the likes of Slayer, Megadeth and Anthrax – fellow members of what the music press tagged The Big Four – who watched on with not a little trepidation. It did, however, put an equal number of smiles on the faces of metalheads the world over.

By 1985, when James Hetfield, Lars Ulrich, Cliff Burton and Kirk Hammett entered Sweet Silence Studios in Copenhagen with engineer Flemming Rasmussen, they were already a well-oiled machine, even if a relatively new one. With two genre-defining albums under their belts they certainly knew their way around a song and a recording studio. They were also already a great live act and easy in each other's company. In fact, three short years into their career, the tribulations that they would find themselves facing throughout the start of the new millennium were so very far away. It was all still fun for Metallica.

Which probably explains why 'Master Of Puppets' sounds the way it does. It's still powerful, bordering on dangerous and full of aggression, yet carries with it a spirit of youthful exuberance and a continued love of the music. It's not thrash metal by a long shot, but in the likes of 'Disposable Heroes' and 'Leper Messiah' you can hear the spirit of the genre that Metallica grew up with in the Bay Area. But what really sets 'Master Of Puppets' up as such a great album is the growth in songwriting that's on show. 'Creeping Death' and 'For Whom The Bell Tolls' on 'Ride The Lightning' hinted at the progressively inclined epics Metallica could write. 'Master

Of Puppets' is almost overflowing with them. From the awesome opener 'Battery', through the defiant title track to 'The Thing That Should Not Be' and the stunning 'Welcome Home (Sanitarium)' Metallica are simply jaw-dropping.

In 'Orion' Cliff Burton got what would be his final chance to display his stunning bass technique on a solo that far outstrips '(Anesthesia) Pulling Teeth' from 'Kill 'Em All'. Although the song had been performed live in part following Burton's tragic death, it was only on the 20th Anniversary of the release of 'Master Of Puppets' that the piece was played in its entirety as Metallica tore through the whole of 'Master of Puppets' at shows on their 2006 'Escape From The Studio' tour, including their set at the Download Festival that year.

At the time of its release, with hair metal riding high in the charts and with little promotion and no promo videos, 'Master of Puppets' sold in the region of half-a-million copies, reaching number 29 in the US charts and number 41 in the UK, making it Metallica's first ever certified gold record. Although not a thrash album, it changed the face of both thrash metal and heavy metal at once, and proved that bands playing extreme music that received little airplay could still make a major impact on the music world. 'Master Of Puppets' is a true classic album.

Tracklisting

'Battery', 'Master Of Puppets', 'The Thing That Should Not Be', 'Welcome Home (Sanitarium)', 'Disposable Heroes', 'Leper Messiah', 'Orion', 'Damage Inc.'.

MASTER OF PUPPETS (SONG)

The title track of the band's third album is rumoured to have been Cliff Burton's favourite ever Metallica song. It deals with the subject of addiction and, as one of the band's all-time classics, it has long been a staple of Metallica's live set. 'Guitar World' magazine ranked Kirk Hammett's solo number 51 in their '100 Best Solos' in 1998.

"I think we wanted to write another song like 'Creeping Death'," James Hetfield said of 'Master Of Puppets' in an issue of 'Guitar World'. *"With open chords carried by the vocals and a real catchy chorus. On 'Master of Puppets' we started getting into the longer, more orchestrated songs. It was more of a challenge to write a long song that didn't seem long."*

'Master Of Puppets' has been covered by Primus, Trivium and Apocalyptica, has been performed live by Limp Bizkit and Dream Theater and also features in an episode of 'The Simpsons' called 'The Mook, The Chef, The Wife And Her Homer'.

MEGADETH

After his dismissal from Metallica, Dave Mustaine wasted little time in setting himself up in his own band. Megadeth was the chosen name, and unsurprisingly the band's output bore a close resemblance to the music that he'd been making with Metallica, although it had, perhaps, a more aggressive edge.

"After getting fired by Metallica all I remember is I wanted blood," says Mustaine in the liner notes for the remastered edition of their first album 'Killing Is My Business... And Business Is Good'.

"Theirs. I wanted to be faster and heavier than them." And by the time Megadeth had settled on a stable line-up (anyone remember their original drummer Dijon Carruthers? Thought not), signed a deal with New York label Combat and released their debut in 1985, this was more than apparent. With albums like 'Peace Sells... But Who's Buying' (1987) and 'So Far, So Good, So What' (1988) that followed, it was evident that Megadeth were pursuing a similar path to Metallica, redefining their sound and constantly evolving, although they perhaps remained slightly more faithful to their thrash roots.

A newly sober Mustaine with a new-look Megadeth released 'Rust In Peace' in 1990 and the band moved into what was easily

their most creative and successful period. Still edgy enough to please thrash fans, the band displayed real progression on material like 'Holy Wars... The Punishment Due' and 'Hangar 18' and the album sold over a million copes in the States and was nominated for a Grammy for 'Best Metal Performance'.

1992's 'Countdown To Extinction' fared even better, debuting on the US chart at number two and at number five in the UK. It brought the band a second Grammy and swiftly went double platinum in the States. A year later Mustaine and his band supported Metallica at the Milton Keynes Bowl. It was the first time that the former bandmates had played on the same stage in ten years. Megadeth's stock continued to rise – in 1993 they were nominated for another Grammy, this time for their contribution to 'The Beavis & Butt-Head Experience'

with the song '99 Ways To Die', and in 1994 they released the excellent 'Youthanasia', their most commercial recording to date and which sold quicker than any Megadeth album up to that time.

1997's 'Cryptic Writings' continued the upward trend, giving the band their first real taste of mainstream radio success in the US with the song 'Trust', and they chose to work with producer Dann Huff once more (Huff had been a member of AOR band Giant) for 1999's 'Risk'. This time, however, things did not fare so well. Easily the band's least metal album, long-time fans deserted in droves and in 2000 Megadeth split with their long-time record label Capitol after 2000's 'Capitol Punishment: The Megadeth Years'.

Since 2000 the band have undergone even more changes than during their early 'revolving door' period – something which, in the long term, must have hindered their progress to some extent. In 2001, signed to Sanctuary, they released the metallic 'The World Needs A Hero', but in 2002 a freak injury to Mustaine caused nerve damage to his left hand, leaving him fearing he would never play again. He recovered enough for 2004's 'The System Has Failed', intended as a solo album but ending up, due to contractual obligations, being released under the name Megadeth. Mustaine tried to re-form the 'Rust In Peace' line-up but failed, and despite reasonable success – the album hit number 18 in the US charts – and following the tour to promote it, he announced that Megadeth was finished and he would now concentrate on a solo career.

In 2005 Mustaine announced the formation of Gigantour, an annual heavy metal festival tour and, while playing in Argentina in October of that year, confirmed from the stage that Megadeth would, in fact, continue. The band signed a deal with Roadrunner Records and in 2007 released 'United Abominations' which entered the US charts at number 8, their highest charting album since 1994's 'Youthanasia'. Megadeth's stock is, it appears, as high as ever after all!

Despite Mustaine's sometimes abrasive nature, and a band that regularly seemed to fall into substance abuse and an ever-changing line-up, Megadeth have survived. That Mustaine is talented has never been in doubt – seven consecutive Grammy nominations and

a string of successful and mostly excellent albums pay testament to that. We await Mustaine's next move with much interest.

MEGAFORCE

Megaforce is the record label set up by Johnny Zazula specifically for Metallica to record and release 'Kill 'Em All' when no other company showed any interest in signing the band. Originally based in Old Bridge, New Jersey, Zazula acted as the executive producer, alongside producer Paul Curcio, for the band's debut. Metallica would sign to Elektra Records in America for 1984's 'Ride The Lightning' (although Megaforce retained an interest), while in the UK they would remain with independent label Music For Nations up to and including 'Master of Puppets', before Phonogram stepped in to sign the band for '...And Justice For All', and also pick up their back catalogue.

Post Metallica, Megaforce became the home to many metal acts and their roster boasted the likes of Anthrax, Testament, Stormtroopers Of Death, Kings X, Ace Frehley and Manowar. Eventually it was bought out by major label Atlantic and is now distributed by Sony / BMG Music Entertainment. Recent signings include hardcore legends Bad Brains, Ministry, Rose Hill Drive and Mushroomhead.

MEMORY REMAINS, THE

Track two from 'ReLoad', 'The Memory Remains' was the first single taken from Metallica's seventh studio album. It was also the very first song from 'ReLoad' to be performed live prior to the album's release, in a jam at Deer Creek Field, Nobelsville, Indiana on July 2, 1996.

The song deals with someone lost in their own glory days. So much so that they have become detached from reality and driven mad facing up to their own obscurity. It has been suggested the 1950 Billy Wilder film 'Sunset Boulevard', which features a similar theme, was the inspiration behind the song.

Metallica were joined by legendary '60s chanteuse Marianne Faithful as guest vocalist. She also appears in the promo video for the song and was the inspiration behind adding some of Marilyn Monroe's lines from the film 'The Misfits'. When performed live, Metallica urge the audience to sing the vocal parts handled by Faithful.

The single reached number 28 on the US charts upon its release in 1997, and number 13 in the UK.

MENSCH, PETER

Along with Cliff Burnstein, Mensch heads Q. Prime, the management company that has handled Metallica's affairs since 1984, taking over from Johnny Z of Megaforce Records. Legend has it that then 'Kerrang!' writer Xavier Russell suggested to Lars Ulrich that he get in touch with Mensch concerning management of the band and Ulrich called Mensch, who was living in London's Earl's Court at the time, from a London telephone box.

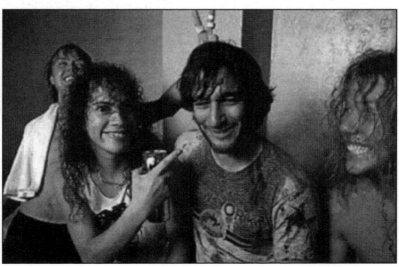

The first gig Metallica played under Q. Prime was their 1984 headline show at The Lyceum in London.

Mensch formed Q. Prime in 1982 with Burnstein, having already worked with such rock heavyweights as AC/DC, Aerosmith, Ted Nugent and the Scorpions. Alongside Metallica they have also handled Def Leppard, the Rolling Stones and Madonna and currently look after the likes of Shania Twain, Garbage, Muse, Lost Prophets, Snow Patrol and Fountains Of Wayne.

MERCYFUL FATE

A Danish heavy metal band, much loved by Lars Ulrich, and who Metallica covered on 'Garage Inc.' recording a medley of Mercyful Fate material, featuring the tracks 'Evil', 'Curse Of The Pharaohs', 'Satan's Fall', 'Corpse Without A Soul' and 'Into The Coven'. At 11 minutes 11 seconds it remains the longest studio recording ever laid down by Metallica.

Mercyful Fate formed in Copenhagen in 1980 and were instrumental in developing various metal genres, including power metal, black metal and progressive metal. Led by the fanciful King Diamond, resplendent in face paint that would eventually get him sued by the fiscally minded Kiss man Gene Simmons for breach of his copyright, Mercyful Fate first released 'Nuns Have No Fun' on the Dutch label Rave On, before signing with Roadrunner Records and releasing the classic albums 'Melissa' (1983) and 'Don't Break The Oath' (1984). King Diamond left to go solo in

1985 whilst the remainder formed AOR act, Fate.

They re-united in 1992 and recorded 'In The Shadows' for Metal Blade, which features Lars Ulrich on drums on a re-recording of an early Mercyful Fate track, 'Return Of The Vampire'. Though with diminishing returns, the band continued to record throughout the '90s, but have been inactive since 1999's '9', with King Diamond returning to his more lucrative solo career.

www.covenworldwide.org

METAL BLADE

Metal Blade Records is the American record company that gave Metallica their first break by including the band on the very first of their 'Metal Massacre' compilations. The label was set up by metal fan and Woodland Hills, California resident Brian Slagel on the back of 'The New Heavy Metal Revue Presents Metal Massacre' album, which featured, alongside Metallica, the likes of Cirith Ungol, Steeler, Malice, Avatar, Bitch and, er, Ratt! Having sold out of all 5000 copies he pressed, Slagel signed a deal with Enigma Records and formed Metal Blade in 1983.

The label released Slayer's 'Show No Mercy' album, as well as those by the likes of Warlord and Armored Saint, and would go on to sign such bands as Flot-sam And Jetsam (featuring future Metallica bassist Jason Newsted), Sacred Reich and Corrosion Of Conformity. Involved with WEA Records in the past, Metal Blade remains one of the leading independent metal labels in the world and currently features Six Feet Under, Job For A Cowboy and Hate Eternal amongst others.

METAL CHURCH

A heavy metal band from Aberdeen, Washington (Kurt Cobain's home town) formed in 1981 out of the ashes of Shrapnel. Always one of the more melodic of the thrash metal bands, Metal Church released their self-titled debut album in 1984 and by the time of 1986's 'The Dark' were already supporting Metallica. Mike Howe replaced vocalist David Wayne for 1989's 'Blessing In Disguise' album and also featured on 1991's excellent 'The Human Factor', but the band split after releasing 'Hanging In The Balance' in 1993.

Metal Church guitarist John Marshall was once Kirk Hammett's guitar tech, and stood in for James Hetfield on guitar when

Hetfield broke his arm skate-boarding whilst Metallica were touring with Ozzy Osbourne in 1986. He once more stood in for Hetfield when he suffered horrific burns following an accident with pyrotechnics when the band were on tour in North America with Guns n' Roses in 1992. In 1990 Metallica supported Metal Church at London's Marquee Club, billed as Vertigo.

Some of the band's original members reunited in 1998, and in 2006 released 'A Light In The Dark'.

www.metalchurch.com

METAL MANIA

'Metal Mania' is the title of a fanzine run by local San Francisco metal promoter Ron Quintana, the man credited with coming up with the Metallica name. Quintana had asked Lars Ulrich to help think of a name for his new fanzine promoting UK and US metal. Quintana drew up a list that included Metallica while Ulrich's list included both Metal Mania and Hesse. Quintana was forced to run with Metal Mania when Ulrich decided to use the name Metallica for his own band.

METAL MASSACRE

'Metal Massacre' is a series of heavy metal compilations released on Brian Slagel's Metal Blade label, which famously gave Metallica their first break by featuring the song 'Hit The Lights' on the very first volume in 1982. Recorded by the Hetfield, Ulrich, McGovney, Mustaine line-up, the version on that album is slightly rougher than the one that would appear on 'Kill 'Em All'.

A 'Metal Massacre' album came out every year between 1982 and 1989, since which time they have only been released sporadically. The final compilation in the series was released in 2006 and differed from previous ones by mainly featuring unsigned bands, instead of acts on the Metal Blade roster.

The full tracklisting of the 'Metal Massacre' compilation featuring Metallica is:

'Chains Around Heaven' – Black 'N' Blue; 'Live For The Whip' – Bitch; 'Captive Of Light' – Malice; 'Octave' – Avatar; 'Death Of The Sun' – Cirith Ungol; 'Dead Of The Night' – Demon Flight; 'Fighting Backwards' – Pandemonium; 'Kick You Down' – Malice; 'Hit The Lights' – Metallica.

METAL UP YOUR ASS

Metallica's legendary live demo from 1982 recorded at San Francisco's Old Waldorf. The band performed all the original material they had to that point, which was everything from the 'No Life 'Til Leather' demo and two new songs that would eventually appear on the 'Megaforce' demo, as well as covers of Diamond Head's 'Am I Evil?' and 'The Prince', although the latter does not feature on the demo as the tape ran out.

Ironically Metallica were supported on the night by Exodus, featuring future Metallica guitarist Kirk Hammett. The album sleeve depicts a fist clenching a knife reaching up from a toilet bowl and this, as well as the 'Metal Up Your Ass' title, were intended to be used for Metallica's debut album, before they changed their minds at the suggestion of the record company.

Tracklisting

'Hit The Lights', 'The Mechanix', 'Phantom Lord', 'Jump In The Fire', 'Motorbreath', 'No Remorse', 'Seek And Destroy', 'Whiplash', 'Am I Evil?', 'Metal Militia'.

METALLICA

Otherwise known as 'The Black Album', 1991's 'Metallica' must rank not just as Metallica's most famous record, but one of heavy metal's most famous as well. Housed in an almost entirely black sleeve (shades of Spinal Tap's 'Smell The Glove' perchance?) only the band's logo and a coiled snake are just about visible – the snake being lifted from a Gadsden flag that was hanging on the wall of One On One Studios in Los Angeles where the band recorded the album and which also bore the legend 'Don't Tread On Me'. And yet the music contained therein would have a profound affect on both Metallica and metal.

'The Black Album' features a different sounding Metallica to that which had gone before, yet there are still traces of the thrash band that started out life in the early '80s on show too. Much of the change in sound is down to the presence of producer Bob Rock, a man whose CV prior to working with Metallica bore such names as Motley Crue, The Cult, David Lee Roth and Blue Murder. Rock built upon the bedrock of sound that Metallica had captured on 'Master Of Puppets' but seemed to lose on '…And Justice For All', creating a rich, bass heavy, metallic sound that suited both the heavier songs and the new departures into way more melodic territory. The latter tracks, of course, brought forth scorn from diehard Metallica fans who accused the band of selling out. But then, as the group pointed out in interviews at the time, they'd been accused of selling out ever since they released 'Ride The Lightning' in 1985.

The opening track on 'Metallica' sets the tone for the rest of the album and remains one of the band's most easily identifiable tunes. With the immediately recognisable, building riff, nightmarish tales and morbid visions of 'Enter Sandman' the album explodes into life. From there, the record is split between the heavy

The reaction of fans was split. A hugely successful record – to date 'The Black Album' has sold almost 15 million copies and entered the charts at number one on both sides of the Atlantic – it nevertheless infuriated some thrash metal fans, always some of the most resistant to change of any kind, because of the ad-

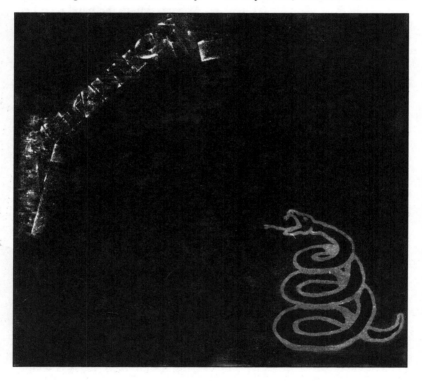

('Sad But True', 'Holier Than Thou', 'The God That Failed') and mellower moments that horrified diehard fans ('Nothing Else Matters', 'The Unforgiven') and, although there are one or two less emphatic moments ('Don't Tread On Me', 'Through The Never'), the album remains a hugely impressive body of work.

vancements in sound that Metallica had clearly made. And as for the inclusion of what they saw as ballads in 'The Unforgiven' and 'Nothing Else Matters', well that was tantamount to treason.

Things didn't run entirely smoothly during the recording of the album however. Initially Metallica had just wanted Bob Rock to mix it, having been impressed with the sound of Motley Crue's 'Dr. Feelgood'. In the end though, they felt Rock could bring out the best in them and went with him as producer. However, as can be seen on the DVD 'A Year And A Half In The Life Of Metallica', Rock introduced a whole new work ethic to a band who had been used to working with Flemming Rasmussen for their last three albums, and there were plenty of personality clashes. But the ends most certainly justified the means, and Bob Rock went on to produce every Metallica album up to and including 'St. Anger'.

The band were awarded a Grammy for the album, their third, and hit the road for three years to promote the release. Their position as the world's finest heavy metal band was now well established.

Tracklisting

'Enter Sandman', 'Sad But True', 'Holier Than Thou', 'The Unforgiven', 'Wherever I May Roam', 'Don't Tread On Me', 'Through The Never', 'Nothing Else Matters', 'Of Wolf And Man', 'The God That Failed', 'My Friend Of Misery', 'The Struggle Within'.

METALLICA.COM

Metallica.com is the band's official website, not to be confused with LiveMetallica.com, where fans can purchase live shows in their entirety, and MetClub.com, the band's official fan club online.

METCLUB.COM

(See Above)

MILTON KEYNES BOWL

One of the most regularly used of all open air venues for festivals in the UK. Metallica have headlined here twice. The first time was on June 5, 1993, topping a bill that also featured Megadeth, The Almighty and Diamond Head. Their set that day was: 'Ecstasy Of Gold', 'Creeping Death', 'Harvester Of Sorrow', 'Welcome Home (Sanitarium)', 'Of Wolf And Man', 'Wherever I May Roam', 'The Thing That Should Not Be', 'The Unforgiven', 'Disposable Heroes', Jason Newsted solo, 'Orion', 'To Live Is To Die'/'The Call Of Ktulu', Kirk Hammett guitar solo, 'The Four Horsemen', 'For Whom The Bell Tolls', 'Fade To Black', 'Master Of Puppets', 'Seek And Destroy', 'Battery', 'Sad But True', 'Nothing Else Matters', 'Last Caress', 'One', 'Enter Sandman', 'So What'.

The band returned on July 10, 1999 and this time the bill was a lot larger – in fact, there were two stages. The list of acts performing is as follows:

Main Stage: Metallica, Marilyn Manson, Ben Harper, Ministry, Sepultura, Creed.

Kerrang! Stage: Terrorvision, Monster Magnet, Pitchshifter,

Symposium, Queens Of The Stone Age, Mercyful Fate.

Metallica's set that day was: 'Ecstasy Of Gold', 'Breadfan', 'Master Of Puppets', 'Of Wolf And Man', 'The Thing That Should Not Be', 'Fuel', 'The Memory Remains', 'Bleeding Me', 'Seek & Destroy', 'For Whom The Bell Tolls', 'King Nothing' (with a brief extract from 'The Outlaw Torn'), 'Wherever I May Roam', 'One', 'Fight Fire With Fire', 'Nothing Else Matters', 'Sad But True', 'Creeping Death', 'Fixxxer', 'Die, Die My Darling', 'Enter Sandman', 'Battery'.

MISFITS, THE

The Misfits are an American punk band who gloried in their '50s B-movie schlock horror image and are perhaps most famous for being fronted by Glenn

Danzig, who now leads his own band, Danzig. Named after the final Marilyn Monroe film (from which Marianne Faithful takes some lines in the song 'The Memory Remains') the band formed in 1977, although their unique take on horror punk wouldn't be developed for a good year. They soon came to be viewed as America's answer to The Damned and released such albums as 'Walk Among Us' and 'Earth AD'. By 1983 the band had split with Danzig going on to form Samhain and later Danzig in 1987.

Metallica have covered three Misfits songs, 'Last Caress', 'Green Hell' and 'Die, Die My Darling', all of which appear on 'Garage Inc.'. Both 'Last Caress' and 'Green Hell' (taken from 1980's 'Beware' EP and 1983's 'Earth AD' respectively) were segued together, originally for the '$5.98 EP: Garage Days Re-Revisited', whilst 'Die, Die My Darling' was recorded especially for 'Garage Inc.'. Says James Hetfield; "Awesome ugly shit. I always liked their poppy modulations combined with singing about death."

A version of The Misfits still tours and records today, as do Danzig.

www.misfits.com

MISSION: IMPOSSIBLE II

Metallica recorded the theme tune, 'I Disappear', for this, the second film in the franchise starring Tom Cruise.

MORE I SEE, THE

A song by UK punk band Discharge, covered by Metallica and which appears as one of the new tracks recorded especially for 'Garage Inc.'. The song was released as a single by Discharge in 1984. The group have long been hailed by thrash and hardcore outfits as a major influence on their sound.

"I love singing Discharge stuff," commented James Hetfield. "You've only got three lines sung 50 times over. But the riffs, that guitarist Bones was pulling off some serious metal riffs."

MORRICONE, ENNIO

Morricone is the legendary Italian composer noted for his film scores, particularly the Spaghetti Westerns like 'Fistful Of Dollars', 'For A Few Dollars More' and 'The Good, The Bad, And The Ugly'.

Born in 1928, Morricone has composed the score for over 400 films and TV productions, making him the most prolific com-

posers of all time in this field. Amazingly, despite being known for his spaghetti western themes, these account for just 30 of his works. He was also responsible for the music accompanying 'Cinema Paradiso', 'Lolita', 'The Untouchables' and 'The Mission'. He is one of just two composers to be awarded an honorary Oscar for lifetime achievements. In all, he's been nominated four times for Oscars, including for 'Bugsy' in 1992.

Metallica have used 'Ecstacy Of Gold' from 'The Good, The Bad And The Ugly' as an intro tape since 1983 and even lent their own version to 2007's tribute album 'We All Love Ennio Morricone'.

MOTORBREATH

This is a track from the 'Kill 'Em All' album and is also featured on the 'No Life 'Til Leather' demo, the latter being the template for the debut record anyway. It's notable for being the only song in the history of the band to be credited solely to James Hetfield, and one of only two not to have a Lars Ulrich writing credit – the other being the bass solo '(Anesthesia) Pulling Teeth'.

The song seems to have an obvious meaning of living life to the full because this isn't a dress rehearsal. Try everything and be your own person. However, there are some who believe it might be about either cocaine or amphetamines. The title itself is certainly similar to that of the song 'Motorhead' by the band of the same name and which is about a speed freak. So, is it just possible that Metallica are referring to the smell on the breath of someone addicted to speed? That would certainly make sense of lines like: 'Getting your kicks as you are shooting the line/Sending the shivers up and down your spine'.

The track is featured in the background during a locker room scene in the movie 'Any Given Sunday' and also on the soundtrack for the game 'MTX: Motortrax'. It's also been covered by Canadian punks D.O.A.

MOTORHEAD

One of the seminal bands in the history of heavy metal, Motorhead actually transcend any attempts to pigeon hole them. They appeal as much to punks as to metalheads, while mainman Lemmy has more than once described the band thus: "We're rock 'n' roll, that's all. Nothing more. Nothing less."

Lars Ulrich in particular, seems to hold Lemmy in high esteem: "In 1981 I ran some of the Motorhead appreciation stuff and also following them around on tour. A few years later, when they were in LA, I went down to the hotel room to see Lemmy. I started drinking and ended up passed out in his room having thrown up over myself. He took a picture of that and put it on one of Motorhead's records."

That isn't the only time that Ulrich's made the mistake of trying to emulate the Motorman's legendary capacity for drink. On another occasion, at an after-hours drinking establishment in Central London called the St. Moritz, he

decided to go head-to-head with Lemmy on the drinks front.

"I'll have exactly what you're drinking," he foolishly challenged. It wasn't long before the hapless drummer was staggering out of the club and ordering a taxi to take him to Denmark – at the time he was living at the house of manager Peter Mensch in West London. Lemmy? He was still rather sober!

But seriously, while these incidents might have slightly embarrassed the Metallica man, there is much mutual respect between the bands. And Motorhead's influence on their sound has never been questioned.

Lemmy started up the band in 1975, having been thrown out of Hawkwind for being excessively into drugs – and given that lot's legendary capacity for partaking of substances, that was a remarkable feat.

When he began Motorhead – American slang for someone into taking speed – the bassist/vocalist famously said: "If we move in next door, your lawn would die!" And that was the philosophy of the band throughout: play hard, play fast, play dirty – and turn it up. Constantly.

Amazingly, they became enormously successful in the early 1980s as albums such as 'Ace Of Spades' and the live 'No Sleep 'Til Hammersmith' made them not just heroes for the rock community, but also turned them in a mainstream phenomenon. It was often said that they were the one metal-style band that the commercial world could accept.

There was something inviting, warm, friendly, yet still edgy about the trio at the time. Lemmy, guitarist 'Fast' Eddie Clarke and drummer Phil 'Philthy Animal' Taylor were the real deal, but

there was a charisma and charm that endeared them to those who would normally hide behind their New Romantics albums – Lemmy even got to record with The Nolan Sisters in that era!

The mustachio'd bassist himself has become an articulate, well-rounded spokesman for the metal generation. He takes no prisoners and brooks no fools. When asked in recent times if he felt he was betraying his roots by moving out of England to live in Los Angeles, he snapped back: "Does that mean that if I were born in a plane, then I'd have to live my whole life in one?"

Given their love of high speed, gnarly riffage, it's no wonder that Motorhead became an inspiration for the whole thrash movement. They were unruly and unfettered. They went onstage the way they'd walk into a pub – no fancy haircuts, no preening, no stage clothes.

What you might see in the street is what you'd get in a performance.

Thrash itself had no pretensions, it was born on the streets and raised in the gutter. So a band like Motorhead would certainly appeal.

Like most bands, Motorhead have had their triumphs and failures over the years. It's always been a source of irritation to Lemmy that people talk about the band's 'golden era', when the above trio were in their pomp. Now, it cannot be denied that the most important albums of their career are the holy trinity of 'Overkill', 'Bomber' and 'Ace Of Spades', but they've consistently released strong albums and while many of these might have been overlooked, time has proven they've an abiding resonance.

Lemmy himself has become something of a cultural icon. He's been in movies, notably 'Eat The

Rich', 'Tromeo & Juliet' and 'Hardware'. He's even appeared in a TV advert for Kit-Kat – playing the violin. And he was one of the few to come out of the infamous 1980s metal documentary 'Decline Of Western Civilization Part II: The Metal Years' with any credit.

Motorhead finally got some form of industry recognition in 2005, when they received a Grammy for 'Best Metal Performance'. How ironic it was that this was for their cover of 'Whiplash' by... Metallica (this appeared on the 'Metal Attack. Metallica: The Ultimate Tribute Album').

Ironic? Yes, because Metallica themselves have recorded a few Motorhead covers. In fact, on December 14, 1995, the band appeared at the Whiskey A-Go-Go Club in West Hollywood as The Lemmys in tribute a to the Motorhead frontman on his 50th birthday. They dressed up in black wigs, drew on moustaches, and each member used a maker pen to draw a tattoo on one arm in honour of Lemmy – except that all of them chose the wrong arm!

That night The Lemmys did seven Motorhead covers. They had also recorded four songs by the band as a further tribute to the great man – 'Damage Case', 'Overkill', 'Stone Dead Forever' and 'Too Late Too Late'.

All four of these were used a year later on the 'Hero Of The Day' single. 'Overkill' and 'Damage Case' were part of the first CD, with 'Stone Dead Forever' and 'Too Late Too Late' used on the second. And they all subsequently turned up on the double CD 'Garage Inc.', which collects together all the covers Metallica have recorded over the years.

And, just to cement the relationship between the bands, Lemmy got onstage with them on August 3, 1996 – James Hetfield's birthday – to perform 'Overkill'.

Yep, the ties between Motorhead and Metallica are stronger than the bond between Metallica and almost any other band.

www.imotorhead.com

MR. FISSE

One of a number of rude Danish language pseudonyms used by Lars Ulrich to check into hotels over the years. This one literally means 'Mr. C**t'. It became infamous when the drummer used it to check into a hotel in Omaha, Nebraska one night – only to find that the female receptionist spoke perfect Danish. Embarrassed by the incident, Ulrich dropped the idea of using his native tongue as a resource for rude names.

MUSIC AMERICA STUDIOS

Located in Rochester, New York, this is where, with producer Paul Curcio, Metallica recorded that all important debut album in 1983.

Ulrich recalled those times as follows: "We spent six weeks up in Rochester, New York, recording the album at the Music America Studio. The actual studio is in the basement of this huge old colonial-type of club house. Up on the second floor there's this huge ballroom which is perfect for getting a good drum sound. The only problem is the place is fucking haunted, so I had to have someone else up there the whole time I was recording. My cymbals would start spinning, you know shit like that. It was scary, but I would love to record there again."

MUSIC COMPANY, THE

Lars Ulrich attempted to move into the realms of record company executive in 1998 when he founded The Music Company, in association with a former Metallica tour accountant, Tim Duffy. It's worth stressing the term 'attempted', because, like so many other major names over the years, Ulrich found the process to be a little beyond his talents. Try as he might – and the drummer seemed genuinely determined to make it happen for the bands he signed – in the end the project failed.

But he did sign and release the following:

DDT
The first act to be snapped up by The Music Company, DDT were from Canada and mixed up rap,

ska and punk – not the usual food for the Ulrich soul. Their only album for the label, 'Urban Observer', was released in August, 1999.

Goudie

From Austin, Texas, this band combined an element of Radiohead with certain Placebo influences, which sounds a lot more like the kind of music Ulrich would have been attracted to at the end of the 1990s. The Music Company released their album, 'Peep Show', in July 2000.

Systematic

A hard rocking band from San Jose, California, they released their debut album for the label in 2001. Called 'Somewhere In Between', it actually charted in America, making number 143 on the 'Billboard' charts. No doubt its success was helped by a stint on the US Ozzfest tour. Former Slayer drummer Paul Bostaph joined in time for their second album, 'Pleasure To Burn', which

came out in 2003. But a year later the band split up.

Brand New Immortals

From Atlanta, Georgia, the band featured one-time Black Crowes bassist Johnny Colt. They were recommended to the label by producer Brendan O'Brien, a man with a pedigree that includes Pearl Jam, the Black Crowes, Rage Against The Machine and Korn. He had produced their demos, and was impressed enough to bring in Ulrich. Their debut album, 'Tragic Show', was released in June, 2001.

Despite the promise of all of these signings, eventually The Music Company had to close its doors, through a combination of little commercial success, and Ulrich's commitments with Metallica.

This is one of a number of projects outside of Metallica which have occupied Ulrich's time over the years. When Diamond Head re-formed in 1993, he acted as an advisor on their reunion album 'Death & Progress'.

He also played drums for Mercyful Fate on their re-make of 'Return Of The Vampire' which appeared on their 1993 album 'In The Shadows'.

In 1990, he teamed up with then Kerrang! editor Geoff Barton to put together a compilation called 'NWOBHM – '79 Re-Visited'. This was a celebration of the New Wave Of British Heavy Metal, a double album that featured the following artists: Diamond Head, Sweet Savage, Saxon, White Spirit, Raven, Paralex, Def Leppard, Weapon, Hollow Ground, Samson, Girlschool, Witchfynde, Iron Maiden, Jaguar, Tygers Of Pan Tang, Gaskin, Sledgehammer, Venom, Angel Witch, Trespass, Holocaust, Vardis, Blitzkrieg, Dragster, AIIZ, Witchfinder General, Black Axe, Fist and Praying Mantis.

It was very much a labour of love for the drummer as it paid homage and tribute to the era in music that had inspired him in the first place.

MUSIC FOR NATIONS

The British label to whom Metallica were signed for their first three albums. One of the first independent record companies in the UK to deal with metal, Music For Nations established a reputation for being meticulous, pioneering and enthusiastic.

Unlike many of the majors around at the time, MFN was run by people who understood what bands wanted from a deal and what fans demanded from the bands and the records.

The company was launched in 1983 by Martin Hooker, a former EMI executive who'd previously run the Secret label. Although that was predominantly a punk outlet, it had made a huge impact by signing Twisted Sister in 1982 for their debut album, 'Under The Blade'. At a time when no-one else would take a risk with the oddball Yanks, Secret – Martin Hooker and his longtime lieutenant Gem Howard – dived in, and got the plaudits.

Thus, when the pair decamped to start Music For Nations – not the most metal-oriented company name, it must be said – they already had a good reputation. Their first signing was a New York band called Virgin Steele. They released their self-titled debut album in 1983 in the UK and Europe – thereby giving this band the distinction of being the first to release a record through MFN.

W.A.S.P.

Over the next several years, it was principally through shrewd American signings that the label made its name. Among those they picked up were:

Ratt

The cover of their self-titled debut EP which the label released features the lower half of a woman with rats climbing up her stockinged legs. That woman was Tawny Kitaen, who'd go on to find fame through her roles in the Whitesnake videos for the '1987' album.

W.A.S.P.

Although signed to Capitol Records, there were certain obvious problems when the Los Angeles band announced that their first single was to be called 'Animal (F*** Like A Beast)'. The major label decided they didn't want to be associated with such a terrifying title and licensed it out to Music For Nations, who didn't have the difficulty of dealing with blue-rinse shareholders who might not understand the subtleties of such a song. It was a huge hit for MFN and remains, arguably, the band's most famous – or infamous – song.

Manowar

The proto-battle metallers were ignored by everyone apart from the UK when they signed up to release 'Into Glory Ride'. And such was the commitment shown by Music For Nations in the way they marketed and supported the band that their next album was titled 'Hail To England'. And then they were gone to bigger things.

Slayer

The first three Slayer releases ('Show No Mercy', 'Haunting The Chapel' and 'Hell Awaits') were all on the label, before they departed for Rick Rubin and Def American.

But the jewel in the MFN crown was obviously Metallica. They released their first three albums on the label and they are the three that many regard as the band's purple period – 'Kill 'Em All', 'Ride The Lightning' and 'Master Of Puppets'. They slowly built the band's profile, and there was a genuine rapport. Gem Howard even acted as their European tour manager.

Yet when the time came for the contract to be renewed, Metallica didn't want to know. Or rather, co-managers Peter Mensch and Cliff Bunstein took them to Phonogram (now Mercury). Music For Nations insisted their offer had been better, but the decision was probably taken long before offers were even put on the table. What's more, Phonogram acquired the rights to those first three albums as well.

While MFN put on a brave face and looked forward, it's fair to say the shock of losing Metallica was one they never truly got over. Working with a band like that had given them the chance to take a step up themselves, and the people involved at the label genuinely thought they'd done the best job anyone could have done, and yet they ended up feeling used. They'd built up Metallica's profile, only to have someone else benefit.

Music For Nations was never quite the same again. True, they continued to support and promote a raft of fine acts – even Frank Zappa got involved, while others of note included Opeth, Anathema, Cradle Of Filth, Godflesh, Venom and Paradise Lost. The relationship with Metallica had been a special one, but in the end hard-nosed business considerations overrode all else.

Music For Nations was eventually bought out by the Zomba Group, a major music business company taking in studios, publishing, record companies and management. But the halcyon days had gone and in 2004 MFN was unceremoniously closed down, its vast back catalogue put in mothballs, waiting to be re-discovered.

MUSTAINE, DAVE

Is there anyone else in the entire history of Metallica who's proven to be more controversial, more bitter, more contentious... and yet

more talented? Dave Mustaine is a troubled soul, a man who, in his time, has railed and raged against the band with whom he spent such a short period of time. In fact he joined the group in early 1982 and was fired in April the next year, about 14 months in all, during which time he recorded three demos – 'Ron McGovney's Garage Demo', 'Power Metal' and 'No Life 'Til Leather'. That's it. There have been people who've spent considerably longer in bands that subsequently went on to find success but who have a lot less animosity about what happened to them than Mustaine. Guitarist Dennis Stratton, fired about the debut, self-titled Iron Maiden album. Guitarist Pete Willis, fired after two albums with Def Leppard, the band he founded. And yet, has there ever been anyone who's carried the hate and resentment in his heart for as long as Mustaine has towards Metallica?

Why? Perhaps because he knows the enormous contribution he actually made to the band in the first place. When Mustaine answered an advert in the local paper, little did he know that he was about to replace Lloyd Grant as the new guitarist in this young band called Metallica – and what it would all go on to mean.

David Scott Mustaine was born in La Mesa, California, on September 13, 1961. His first proper band were called Panic, a local act for whom tragedy would strike in

a road accident when their drummer and driver were killed – Mustaine was fortunately not in the car at the time. Even though the band soldiered on, the guitarist knew it was destined to go nowhere, and that wasn't a town on his road map. So he jumped ship, rode hard to the sound of the Metallica sirens, and played a huge role in focusing their style.

Listen to those early demos, and what you get is a sense of Mustaine being the musical leader. James Hetfield had a developing voice, but it was the young lead guitarist who really stood head and shoulders above everyone else. And he could write a mean tune as well. Witness 'The Mechanix', from 'No Life 'Til Leather' – the man had startling talent. And while the others were slowly coming to grips with the demands and responsibilities of being in a band with ambition, Mustaine was well down the track already.

Those lucky enough to see Metallica at this time agree that the man was a special talent. While Hetfield struggled with his role upfront, Mustaine was a natural, a leader born. But he had a dark side as well.

Mustaine was dabbling in heavy drugs at the time as well as drinking far too much. He was an uncontrollable force to be reckoned with – unpredictable, unreliable, moody and dangerous. If the late Syd Barrett became an acid casualty and slipped away from Pink Floyd at the end of the 1960s, then Dave Mustaine was an altogether more actively psychotic creature.

He attacked Hetfield for allegedly kicking his dog – a dog that was usually employed in guarding Mustaine's stash of drugs. He deliberately poured a can of beer over Ron McGovney's bass, causing him to be thrown across the room by an electric shock when he plugged it in. In general he did enough to unnerve everyone associated with the band and by the time they'd travelled across America to New Jersey in search of their dream, Mustaine was a nightmare that had to be exorcised.

Metal Blade owner Brian Slagel said of Mustaine at the time:

"Dave was an incredibly talented guy, but he also had an incredibly large problem with alcohol and drugs. He'd get wasted and become a real crazy person, a raging maniac, and the other guys just couldn't deal with that after a while. They all drank of course, but Dave drank more... much more. I could see they were beginning to get fed up of seeing Dave drunk out of his mind all the time."

On April 1, 1983, Metallica contacted Exodus guitarist Kirk Hammett and asked if he'd be interested in flying to New York for an audition. This was all done without Mustaine's prior knowledge, and eight days later, on April 9, when the band played at L'Amours Club in Brooklyn, it was to be their last ever gig with him. He was told that he'd been fired – and that this time it was for good. He had been ousted once before, after kicking Hetfield's dog on the same night that he also attacked McGovney, but was let back in. This time though, it was for real. The band helped Mustaine pack up his stuff, drove him to the station and put him on a Greyhound bus back home.

The end... or so they must have thought.

Talking about the sacking, Lars Ulrich says:

"We went in where he was sleeping and woke him up. I was the one who was definitely closest to him at the time and I didn't want to say anything, and as Cliff was the newest member he didn't want to say anything, so we both pointed to James to do the dirty deed. We told him and he looked at us, and didn't really know what to do. He was sitting on the bus home before I think it hit him. In retrospect, it may have been a dirty way to do it, but he was so unpredictable it was certainly the safest!"

Mustaine picked himself up, dusted down his bruised ego, and set about putting together his own band, Megadeth. It's a name that resonates as one of the 'Big Four' of thrash. Constant line-up changes and more problems with drugs and alcohol haven't prevented Megadeth from accruing a portfolio of successful and acclaimed albums. But still the bitterness over Metallica hurts Mustaine. In the early days of Megadeth he'd attack them as having relied on his music and ideas, slam Hetfield for copying him and generally make it known that they were inferior to him when it came to talent.

Slowly he seemed to come to terms with things. But the problem was to rear its head again. His appearance in the 'Some Kind Of Monster' documentary rekindled the animosity and he confronted Ulrich on his feelings about being fired by Metallica.

"I asked them to let me see what they were gonna use before the film came out," insists Mustaine. *"I didn't trust them. And then... nothing. The film came out, my part was cut down almost to a soundbite. I was angry at this latest betrayal. It made me look stupid. They went back on their word."*

Since then? Well, more confusion. Mustaine hinted that he'd love to work with Ulrich and Hetfield again, but quickly retracted this when it became obvious that the pair weren't remotely interested. Subsequently he seems to

be back on an even keel with the band – for now, at least.

Is this the longest running and most pointless feud in metal? Probably. It's all one-sided, but the thing is, would Dave Mustaine be the same talent without this dark side, this aspect of his character that leads to these ongoing feuds with people? Probably not.

For the record, apart from the members of Metallica, Mustaine also has ongoing battles with Phil Anselmo of Pantera, Mike Muir of Suicidal Tendencies, Kerry King of Slayer, and former Megadeth bandmates Dave Ellefson and Chris Poland. He does like a good scrap.

MY FRIEND OF MISERY

Song from 'The Black Album', and the only one on this record to have a co-writing credit for Jason Newsted (alongside the usual pairing of James Hetfield and Lars Ulrich).

Apparently the song is based on a bass riff that Newsted had written before joining Metallica. In fact, when he heard they were looking to carry on after Cliff Burton's death, he had sent them a tape of it in the hope it would impress them enough to get him an audition – it did.

Originally, Newsted was hoping this could be the instrumental track on the album, following a tradition that stretched back to '(Anesthesia) Pulling Teeth' on

'Kill 'Em All' and had been continued by 'The Call Of Ktulu' on 'Ride The Lightning', then 'Orion' on 'Master Of Puppets' and, finally, 'To Live Is To Die' from '...And Justice For All'.

Despite Newsted's hopes, the track wasn't to continue the trend. Some have speculated that this was another in a long list of slights against the bassist. Although he was in the band for '...And Justice For All', 'To Live Is To Die' was actually written by Hetfield, Ulrich and Burton. Since Burton was no longer alive it's just possible that Hetfield and Ulrich felt it inappropriate for the band to carry on the tradition and that in some way Newsted didn't rank quite as highly as his predecessor in their minds.

Lyrically, it tries to understand those wallowing in misery and seeming to have the weight of the world on their shoulders. The narrator is telling the unknown person that things are not black all the time, they should be positive and look at life in a new way or else they'll miss out on so much. There's also a strong element of care and affection as the narrator displays more pity than frustration or anger at his friend's inability to see past the hell they've created for themselves.

The song itself has never been played live by the band, although Newsted did use part of the bass riff in his own solo spot.

Sweden's Dark Tranquillity covered this on the album 'Tribute To The Four Horsemen: A Tribute To Metallica'.

MY WORLD

A track from the 'St. Anger' album, 'My World' opens with the emotive line: 'The muthaf**kers got in my head/Trying to make me someone else instead'. And this has led to a lot of speculation regarding what exactly the band are referring to. Or, more specifically, what is James Hetfield on about, since he wrote the lyrics?

One interpretation is that this is a plea for Metallica fans to understand that the band had been under intense pressure to conform and be what others wanted them to be – presumably this is a reference to music industry people – but that, despite this, they were determined to battle through and stand up for themselves.

Now, it's also possible that they're referring not to the industry, with whom Metallica have had little truck over the years, but

the fans themselves. 'Load' and 'ReLoad' got lukewarm responses from some that saw the band as not being 'theirs' anymore. They were the ones demanding that the band change back, reverting to type. So, when Hetfield snarls that, 'It's my world, you can't have it', might he be telling those who want old school Metallica that this band doesn't belong to them, that they don't have any say in the direction it takes.

It's also possible that Hetfield's alluding to the ludicrous situation in which Metallica found themselves during this period – surrounded by extraneous people and in a world of turmoil. Is this the moment when Hetfield in particular, and Metallica in general, hit back, looking to take control again?

The song is biting and angry although, like much on the album, lacks the focus and vision that has made Metallica such a force over the years. It's as if they were so bound up with what had been going on in their lives, as was seen in the 'Some Kind Of Monster' documentary, that they had to let the rage out in a torrent. The record might have suffered, but as both people and musicians Metallica re-discovered themselves.

There may also be hints here that, for Hetfield at least, 'St. Anger' was a doomed project. But he was prepared to pay the price to get his band back. As he says towards the end of the song: 'Look out muthaf**kers here I come/ Gonna make my head my home'.

NAPSTER

The filesharing service that so angered Metallica, in particular Lars Ulrich, that the band took decisive and divisive action against them and played a significant role in forcing them off the proverbial board. So, what annoyed Metallica? Simple. This was a free service, therefore thousands of people were able to get their music for absolutely nothing, robbing them of a fortune.

It was, however, very much a moot point, a moral, legal and economic issue that turned a lot of people against Metallica, believing that they were showing an unacceptable greed, one that went against everything they had claimed to stand for. But before looking at the arguments on both sides, let's explain just what Napster was at the time.

The service was started by Shawn Fanning and Sean Parker in 1999, while the former was still attending Northeastern University in Boston. The name comes from Fanning – it was his nickname.

Based in San Mateo, California, Napster went live on September 1, 1999 and was the first service to offer peer-to-peer file sharing systems. Although it was not strictly peer-to-peer, as it used central servers to maintain lists of connected systems and the files they provided, all actual transac-

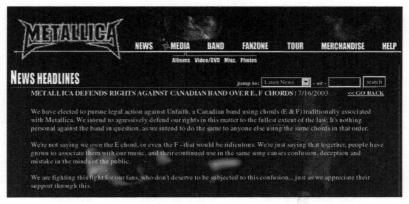

tions were done directly between relevant machines. Napster specialized exclusively in music in the form of MP3 files, and had a user-friendly interface. What all this meant was that it was relatively easy for users to upload tracks for others to find, while people in search of specific songs found it equally simple to locate and download them. A cyber musical utopia, one might say.

Of course, one of the problems was that people would download music, and then burn their own CDs – thereby circumventing the requirement of paying any royalties to the artists concerned. And this is where the problems started. Metallica discovered that a demo of the song 'I Disappear', which was to be used for the soundtrack of the 'Mission: Impossible 2' movie, had found its way onto the napster system. As a result,

a number of radio stations across America had started to give it airplay – something the band most certainly did not want.

To make matters worse, further investigations discovered that everything the band had recorded was readily available via Napster – a situation they were not prepared to tolerate. So, in 2000 Metallica launched their law suit, designed to prevent this pirating of their music. Shortly afterwards, rap artist Dr. Dre, who used the same legal representatives as Metallica, issued his own suit following Napster's refusal to remove all of his material from their system.

At the same time, Metallica prepared and submitted a list of thousands of names they claimed to be those of people who were pirating their songs. They demanded that these 'activists' be barred from the service, something which Napster agreed to do – only to find that, through internet cunning, the ban could easily be reversed.

Come 2001, Napster was set against the full weight of the music business as several major labels, and even the powerful Recording Industry Association of America took significant legal steps to shut the service down. By July the same year they'd seemingly succeeded. But two months later Napster agreed to pay $26 million as reparation for lost royalties, and $10 million as an advance against future payments. It seemed Napster was going legit. However, the ony way they could afford to make these payments was to become a subscription service, and the problem there was that they couldn't obtain the necessary licenses to operate. An attempted sale to the giant Bertelsmann entertainment company failed when Napster was refused permission to file for Chapter 11 protection under US bankruptcy law, which would have allowed them to reorganise. Forced to sell off their assets, Napster closed, with the website offering the farewell message: 'Napster was here'.

Since then, as broadband speeds have dramatically increased, file-sharing has actually become ever more prevalent. So the action of shutting down Napster hardly

Shawn Fanning

served as a warning to others. If anything, it's been an irrelevance.

Metallica's part in all of this has seen them lambasted in many quarters as poachers turned game-keepers. Why? Because the band encouraged tape-trading in their early days and also went so far as to establish particular areas at shows for people to record the gig – as long as the tapes were for private use. At a time when bootleg-ging was seen as a blight on the music business landscape, Metal-lica were very much supporting the practice.

But what's the difference be-tween Napster filesharing and the other activities of which the band were so supportive? Simple and obvious. Tape-trading was a fast track demo system, a way of spreading the word about a band who couldn't get any media expo-sure. So, release a demo into the wild and watch the word mush-room and grow. There was no ar-tistic copyright to protect, because nobody was gonna buy a tape by an unknown band – it was used only as a promotional tool.

Bootlegging, in its strictest sense, is about going to a show and tap-ing it. In other words, recording a gig that the band themselves had no interest in releasing officially. And, by its very definition, this was restricted to diehard fans, the sort who'd go out and buy everything from a band, whatever the quality. Bootlegging would never harm official sales, so Metallica felt comfortable in backing it.

But filesharing... that was akin to home taping, wherein one person would buy an album and several others would borrow it, tape it, and save their money. Except that this was on a massive scale. Clearly Metallica believed that those using Napster were actually affecting the financial status of the band, and that the altruistic nature of the service – free music for everyone – was naïve as well as illegal.

Whatever the pros and cons of the argument, the fact remains that Metallica scored a massive own goal in the way they went about tackling the problem. From being a band of the people, some now saw them as the enemy, a corporate rubber duck bobbing happily on the gentle waves generated by millions of sales, and now flying into action to tackle what they saw as turbulence.

They were vilified, ridiculed and parodied, and to this day have yet to fully recover. It's hard to estimate how many actual sales were lost by Metallica. And, who knows, they might also have found a few new ones along the way. The one thing free music does is encourage you to listen to tracks and bands you've never heard of before. And in one case, Radiohead's 'Kid A' album, Napster was deemed to have played a significant role in its huge sales, as the interest generated by track leaks sent the album soaring.

Was Napster evil and pernicious? Were Metallica maligned artists? The truth probably lies somewhere in between. Perhaps Judge Marilyn Hall Patel summed it best, when ruling on the case in February 2002 thus: "Despite Napster's unclean hands, any balancing of equities must account for the fact that the Napster

Shawn Fanning

service is no longer functioning and thereby not infringing. When it became apparent to Napster that it could not comply with this court's injunction, it disabled the ability of its users to share music files. In contrast, (the record labels') allegedly inequitable conduct is currently ongoing and the extent of the prospective harm is massive. If Napster is correct, plaintiffs are attempting the near monopolization of the digital distribution market. The resulting injury affects both Napster and the public interest."

NAPSTER BAD! (BY CAMP CHAOS)

'Napster Bad!' was a series of flash cartoons created by one Bob Cesca during the period 2000-3, under the 'Camp Chaos' banner. It spoofed the controversy sur-

rounding Napster and especially lampooned Lars Ulrich and James Hetfield for their stand against them.

Ulrich is portrayed here as a greedy and rather crude, grubby little man, wearing incredibly small shorts, a tight tanktop and no shoes. He talks far too much and is often seen running around like a headless chicken. James Hetfield is very much a Neanderthal, Frankenstein-type, a beer monster with only says two words: 'Bad' and 'Good'. He also hates fire, which might have been a reference to his pyro accident onstage in 1992. Other characters in the series include Nutty McShithead, the official spokesman for R.A.P.E. (Recording Association for Popsong Economics) – a giant pile of shit fashioned into human shape and wearing a tuxedo and a blond wig. He rapes those who dare download free MP3s.

There are eight episodes in all, which are as follows:

'Napster Bad!'
Ulrich and Hetfield discuss their lawsuit against Napster, which is being brought due to the fact that Napster downloads are free, and as a result, Metallica get no profits. The pair are in a room filled with bags of money.

'Metalli Cops'

The Metallica duo are seen as cops trying to stop people using Napster to download songs. Their target here is one Pip McDuddy, who was spotted downloading 'Welcome Home (Sanitarium)'. Ulrich verbally assaults him, while Hetfield slams his head into the computer's monitor.

'Metallica Millionaire'

Here Hetfield is a contestant in the TV series 'Who Wants To Be A Millionaire?', during the show's 'Rock Star Week'. Ulrich is the friend he chooses to phone to help with the answers. Naturally, Hetfield gets nothing right.

'MP3 Music – Good Or Goblin?'

This cartoon features Recording Association for Popsong Economics spokesman Nutty McShithead with Sheryl Crow, discussing the problems of free MP3 downloading, specifically the dangers to the artists themselves. During the episode, Nutty sodomizes a confessed Napster user.

'Camp Chaos – Sue All The World'

This is a song featuring various artists who are against free music downloading. A parody of the Live Aid song 'We Are The World', among those joining in the fun are Hetfield, Ulrich and Jason Newsted, together with Michael Kamen, Elton John and Madonna. Kirk Hammett is seen as the closing credits role, realising that he'd missed the recording session.

'Bizarro Napster Bad'

Here, Larz Chipwich and Jaymez Hatfielder from Metallicock have their own anti-Napster tirade. They claim that, thanks to the new law forcing Napster to block files of certain bands (including Metallica), rip-off and tribute bands were now getting their songs downloaded for free more frequently than before. This prompts Metallicock to sue Napster, Metallica, the illegal downloaders, and their mothers.

'Fire Bad!'

This is a game where you have to put out the fires which spontaneously appear on Hetfield's body. If you get a bad score, he'll burn up and disappear as ashes.

'Napster Dead?'

Ulrich, Hetfield and Nutty Mc-Shithead have a party in a bath filled with beer as they celebrate the end of Napster. But when they hear that a court has ruled that Napster can stay online, their excitement quickly goes. They decide the party should remain their secret.

Inevitably, the series didn't go down at all well with Metallica fans – even now, hate mail is received by the 'Camp Chaos' organisation – and it's mentioned by Hetfield and Ulrich when they defend their stance on Napster in the 'Some Kind Of Monster' documentary.

In a twist, there's a 'Camp Chaos' cartoon featuring Motley Crue, during which they slam Metallica (referred to as 'Metalligreed') for their attitude to Napster, claiming it was only done to get publicity for an upcoming tour. It seems the Crue had chosen this medium as the best way to get that message across – and they did the voices themselves.

All of these cartoons may still be accessed for free at http://www.campchaos.com/

NEWSTED, JASON

The man who took over from the late Cliff Burton and the bassist who's been with the band for the longest period. And yet, did Jason Newsted ever get beyond being called Jason Newboy by all and sundry? Was he ever truly accepted as a fully-fledged Metallica man by the fans, or even the band?

The fact is, like Brian Johnson in AC/DC, Jake E. Lee in Ozzy Osbourne's band and Paul Rodgers with Queen, he was replacing a dead icon, a folk hero. Johnson found it impossible to fill Bon Scott's shoes. Lee had the same trouble with Randy Rhoads, and, although Rodgers wasn't strictly speaking taking over from Freddie Mercury (the band have re-titled themselves Queen + Paul Rodgers), nonetheless most people saw it that way.

And when you are the next in line after someone like Cliff Burton, then the best you can hope to achieve is that people will just begrudgingly go along with the choice. It wasn't Newsted's fault. He never made the decision that the band should carry on – James Hetfield, Lars Ulrich and Kirk Hammett did that. And, once those three had elected to continue, can anyone blame the young hopeful Jason for going after the job?

Says Newsted:

"My friend woke me up at six in the morning and said, 'Cliff's gone'. I said, 'No f**king way. Why are you doing this to me this early in the morning?' And he said, 'No, it's real. Go look in the paper'. So I looked in the paper and I had this epiphany, watching and just thinking, and I was like, 'I'm going to be the dude. I'm going to do it. If they're going to go on then I'm the man. I'm going to do it'. And from that minute on I wasn't going to let anybody else get it."

Newsted wasn't the first choice at the time. In an effort to 'keep it in the family' as it were, Metallica offered the position to Joey Vera from Armored Saint, a band with whom Metallica had toured and one that also had the same management team (Peter Mensch and Cliff Burnstein). But he turned it down.

"I really felt at the time that Armored Saint were going somewhere," says Vera now. *"So I didn't want to split up the band – one that I believed to be 'my band' – in order to join Metallica."*

So they turned elsewhere, and this is the point at which Jason Newsted enters the picture. Born in 1963, in Battle Creek, Michigan, he joined Arizona thrashers Flotsam And Jetsam in 1982, a name taken from the Tolkien book 'The Two Towers'. In 1985 they released two demo tapes, 'Iron Tears' and 'Metal Shock'. Newsted sent copies to 'Kerrang!' magazine, who were very enthusiastic about the group's brand of thrash, full of energy and enthusiasm.

A deal with Metal Blade led to the release of their 1986 debut album 'Doomsday For The Deceiver', which was produced by

Brian Slagel – the man who had given Metallica their big break a few years earlier by putting the song 'Hit The Lights' on his first 'Metal Massacre' compilation. At this time Newsted was the main songwriter in the band. But he was soon to depart.

Metallica decided to hold auditions to find the right man to take over from Burton. In all, some 60 bassists passed through the door, including such notables as Les Claypool of Primus, Willie Lange of Laaz Rockit and Troy Gregory of Prong fame – who knew Hammett from algebra classes! It was Slagel who reluctantly recommended Newsted to Ulrich. On the one hand, he felt that the young bassist had all the attributes to step into those giant shoes, while on the other, he didn't want to unsettle a band on his own label, one that had started to make their mark.

Legend has it that, after auditioning him, the three Metallica members took Newsted out for a drinking session at a place called Tommy's Joynt in San Francisco. At a certain point in the evening, Hetfield, Hammett and Ulrich went to the toilets together – to talk over their views on the Flotsam man. They came to an agreement there and then, went back to Newsted, and Ulrich is said to have casually asked: "Want a job?"

Ulrich recalls:

"We did about 60 people in one week and we decided that we wanted to ask four of them back. Jason was second of the four. We played all day and then went out for a meal. And then we went for the big test, which was obviously the drink test. Somehow, and I swear it wasn't planned, me and Kirk and James ended up in the toilet together, pissing. So we're standing there at three in the morning, out of our faces, all of us

in a line and not saying anything, and I just said without looking at anybody, 'That's him, right?' And the other guys said, 'Yeah, that's him'. And that was it!"

Metallica had a new man in place. Newsted made his live debut with them on November 8, 1986 at the Country Club in Reseda, California – barely six weeks after Burton's death. The next night they played at Jezabel's in Anaheim. Three numbers in, during 'Master Of Puppets', the power cut, leaving only the bass amp working. An impromptu jam between Ulrich and Newsted followed – it got a great reaction.

On record, Newsted was first heard on 'The $5.98 EP: Garage Days Re-Revisited' collection of covers released in 1987. Interestingly, the sleeve shows the band in what might well be a toilet – a tribute to Tommy's Joynt and that fateful urinals decision? Recalls Newsted:

"It was a f**king blast, man. You walked into the room, set up your amp the way you would live, put a microphone in front of it and play the song. We recorded it there and then, mistakes and all."

In 1988, Newsted appeared on his first fully fledged album, '...And Justice For All'. Not only does he get just one songwriting credit – on 'Blackened', and remember, this man was used to penning all the songs for Flotsam And Jetsam – but his bass lines are often buried so far into the mix it's almost impossible to hear them. However, Ulrich insists that this isn't the case, and that Newsted was doubling up on the rhythm guitar parts, which is why his sound is somewhat lost.

Newsted was the butt of all the band's practical jokes during the ensuing tour, especially during a five-date trip to Japan. Some of the more mentionable ones include having his stuff thrown out of the hotel window and having drinks charged to his room. In addition, he'd taken to signing autographs as 'Bassface' and on more than one occasion another member of the band would rub out the 'B'! They also told fans that their new bassist was gay, which led to more than one tricky moment for him.

Newsted has always claimed that, far from being some sort of initiation into the band, the jokes never stopped. He was always the victim. Perhaps this is the root cause of why he felt alienated from the other three?

But the success kept coming. 'The Black Album' proved to be the biggest selling true heavy metal album of all time, and Newsted played a full part, although again he was restricted to one co-writing credit, on 'My Friend Of Misery'.

But the writing was on the wall when the 'Load' and 'ReLoad' albums appeared in 1996 and 1997, respectively. The records marked even more of a departure from the strict metal regime than had been the case with even 'The Black Album'. Determined not to stand still, Ulrich – with enthusiastic

support from Hammett – wanted to make Metallica a more modern band. He even wanted photoshoots in… ulp, make-up! Hetfield and Newsted found themselves allies in adversity, baulking at the suggestion. But to a large extent, the Ulrich-Hammett axis won out.

And in January 2001, Newsted quit Metallica, after just over 14 years in the band. He gave his last performance with them at the VH1 Awards, finishing with 'Fade To Black'. But he felt bitter about a lot of things. He claimed that Hetfield had wanted to block his side project Echobrain, and accused the frontman of being too controlling. He also believed that

he'd never been fully accepted by the rest of the band.

Since then, Newsted has worked with Ozzy, Voivod, Rock Star Supernova (alongside Motley Crue's Tommy Lee) and Government Mule. As for Metallica, it seems that his relationship with the rest of the band has eased somewhat. But for a time comments like this one did him no favours. When talking about what he expected from 'St. Anger', Newsted railed:

"I don't think they have any idea. I am a fan of Metallica again, I did my thing with them and I'm proud of that shit. What they are doing now is such an

obvious cash thing and has nothing to do with the music that we're supposed to be fighting for. Kirk got quoted about their new record sounding like (Swedish band) Entombed. Who is playing bass to make it sound like Entombed? James is a good bass player, but c'mon! Lars? He hasn't practiced enough drums over the years – he let his art fall away from him, he doesn't have the same finesse as he used to have."

One final point: Newsted was the band's fourth bassist, following on from Hetfield (who filled the role very briefly in the early days), Ron McGovney and Cliff Burton. He's also the longest serving one. More recently, he's concentrating on his commitments with Voivod, working on the Canadian band's next album.

NIELSEN, CONNIE

Danish actress and Lars Ulrich's current girlfriend. They have a son together, Bryce Thadeus Ulrich-Nielsen, born on May 21, 2007.

Nielsen, who also has a son named Sebastian from a previous relationship, was born on July 3, 1965 in Frederikshavn. After training in France she made her acting debut in the French film 'Par Où T'es Rentré? On T'a Pas Vu Sortir' in 1984. Her major breakthrough, however, didn't come till 1997 when she played the role of Christabella Andreoli in the movie 'The Devil's Advocate', alongside Al Pacino and Keanu Reves. This led to roles in 'Permanent Midnight', 'Rushmore' and 'Soldier'.

Since then, she's appeared in 'Gladiator' (playing Lucilla) and 'Mission To Mars', as well as TV series including 'Law & Order: Special Victims Unit'.

METALLICA
WITH **MICHAEL KAMEN** CONDUCTING
THE SAN FRANCISCO SYMPHONY ORCHESTRA

In 2004 she picked up an award for 'Best Actress' in Denmark for her performance in 'Bodre', her first Danish language movie. The role later won her the same accolade at the San Sebastian International Film Festival.

NO LEAF CLOVER

One of two tracks specifically composed for the orchestral album 'S&M', the other being '- Human'. This features a number of riffs that James Hetfield had stored over the years, but for which he'd never previously found a decent use. The song is based on the idea of a four leaf clover bringing you luck. A notion Hetfield adapted to talk about situations in which you get so close to reaching your goal, but in the end something prevents it happening. He talks about a light at the end of a tunnel being no more than, 'Just a freight train coming your way'.

There's also a feeling of inevitability here. That whatever you do to change your circumstances and luck, nothing can prevent the onset of your fate. And, in the end, death is a certainty. Be it real or imagined.

There may also be a hint here that Hetfield was talking about the demands put on him as some sort of celebrity, and that while this may have its positive side, nonetheless, ultimately it will destroy him.

One or two people have claimed that the song itself was written by

Cliff Burton just prior to dying in the horrendous coach accident in Sweden. But there's no evidence to back up that theory, and given their enormous respect and admiration for the late bassist, it's hard to believe that Hetfield and Lars Ulrich, who are noted as the song's authors, wouldn't have given due writing credit for any role Burton had had.

Finally, some have tried to insist that part of the lyrics were lifted from the David Lee Roth track 'Perfect Timing' (from his 1988 album 'Skyscraper'). While it's true that he uses the phrase: 'Cuz that light at the end of the tunnel/Is the front of an oncoming train', and there is a similar line in this song, since it's a well-known phrase in everyday use, it's hard to accept that Metallica have directly lifted anything from the one-time Van Halen frontman.

NO LIFE 'TIL LEATHER

The famous demo – probably the band's most renowned – that led to a deal with Megaforce Records and set them up for the glories to come.

Taking its title from a line in the song 'Hit The Lights', it features seven tracks, all of which were to make it onto the debut album 'Kill 'Em All'. The track listing is as follows:

'Hit The Lights', 'The Mechanix', 'Motorbreath', 'Seek & Destroy', 'Metal Militia', 'Jump In The Fire' and 'Phantom Lord'.

The only songs from the album that were not on the demo are 'No Remorse', 'Whiplash' and '(Anesthesia) Pulling Teeth', although it's a re-written version of 'The Mechanix' that appears on 'Kill 'Em All' as 'The Four Horsemen'.

Recorded at Chateau East Studio in Tuscin, California, the band's line-up at the time was; James Hetfield (vocals/rhythm guitar), Dave Mustaine (lead guitar), Ron McGovney (bass) and Lars Ulrich (drums).

The demo itself is perhaps a little closer to the band's original influences than when the revised line-up, without Mustaine and McGovney (replaced by Kirk Hammett and Cliff Burton, respectively) got around to cutting that debut album. Listening to the tracks here, it's clear that the Diamond Head/Motorhead/Iron Maiden inspirations were being worn very much on the sleeve. But the sheer power, enthusiasm and no little skill of the band shines through.

Interestingly, it can be heard that much of Mustaine's guitar work remained unaltered by Hammett, and it's probably his guitar parts, together with Hetfield's vocals, that really make the difference. When you listen to this tape, you can understand, to some extent, why Mustaine bore such a grudge against Metallica for so long. He

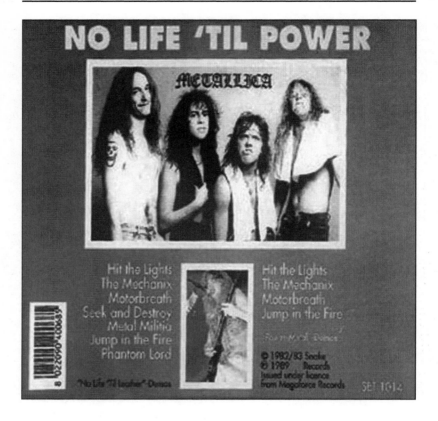

has always maintained that his contribution was crucial and that he was far from the temporary guitarist they claimed him to be at one point. In fact, he insists that he helped to shape the music. Says Mustaine:

"James didn't want to give me credit because he's jealous of me. His whole frontman persona he copped from me. In the beginning of the band he just sang, and I did all the guitar work. When he was done singing, he'd walk away from the microphone and I had to walk up to the mic and talk. I'm like, 'What's wrong with this picture?

I'm getting your beer tonight!' I think the most disappointing thing out of all of it is that when you look at all of the accomplishments they've made over the years, people are trying to make me invisible. My career's been successful, I've had a blast while I'm here but it would have been nice if Metallica fans really knew what my contribution was instead of them saying there wasn't any."

We shall never know what the 'No Life...' line-up would have gone on to achieve had it stayed intact, but the enduring quality of this tape is a testament to what might have been.

The demo has been put out un-officially twice in recent years and on both occasions it was claimed the releases had official status as live albums. The first time was under the title 'Metallica – Bay Area Thrashers' but analysis has shown that this was the 'No Life 'Til Leather' demo with added live noises, which are said to have been taken predominantly from the 'Cliff 'Em All' video. The second time it was titled 'Metallica – In The Beginning... Live', but again this proved to be the same tape, with the same crowd noises.

Metallica actually filed a lawsuit in November 1998 over these albums, citing copyright infringement. The lawsuit stated that amazon.com, Outlaw Records, Dutch East India Trading, Music Boulevard and others marketed and distributed the record without the band's knowledge or consent, and that they also fraudulently implied that the album featured live recordings released and approved by the band.

There have also been a number of bootleg versions available. A least 12 of these have all seven tracks. They include;

'Metal Militia', 'Metal Up Your Ass', 'No Life 'Til Power', 'The Real No Life 'Til Leather', 'Horsemen Of The Apokalypse', 'The Apokalypse', 'Fight Fire With Fire', and the oddly titled 'The Devil, Shaved Soap & Gasoline'.

So, how important was, and is, 'No Life 'Til Leather'? It was the tape that first convinced John and Marsha Zazula to start their own label, Megaforce, and give Metallica a deal. It was the tape that got the metal underground so excited about the band and proved they had something special to offer.

But more importantly, it seemed to focus everyone on a new dawn for metal. This was July 1982, and the New Wave Of British Heavy Metal was no longer as strong as it had once been. Everyone was waiting for something new and forceful to push through. If people had smirked at Metallica before this, now we all knew they were gonna be a handful. It put the group right in the box seat, and set them on a course that has led to them being the most successful metal band of all time.

NO REMORSE

From 'Kill 'Em All', this is one of the few tracks on that album not to have appeared on the 'No Life 'Til Leather' demo. It has proved very popular among those who love shoot 'em up style computer games, and, in fact, is said to have inspired one of the songs on the first 'Doom' game in 1993, among the first games of this style.

The origins of the song go right back to the era when the band's line-up was James Hetfield (vocals, rhythm guitar), Lloyd Grant (lead guitar), Ron McGovney (bass) and Lars Ulrich (drums). They wrote two songs back then called 'Hansom Ransom' and 'Lets Go Rock 'N' Roll'. In the end they combined the riffs from these two songs to make what we know today as 'No Remorse'.

It is an anti-war song in many respects. While the lyrics contain lines like 'No remorse/No repent' and 'Blood feeds the war machine/As it eats its way across the land', in truth this is far from a celebration of battle. What Metallica are doing is hammering those who actually enjoy war, as is obvious in the lines: 'Another day, another death/Another sorrow, another breath'.

The song was covered by Cannibal Corpse on their 2003 'Worm Infested EP' and Metallica used a snippet from this on the version of 'Battery' that appeared on the 'Live Shit: Binge & Purge' release in 1993.

NOTHING ELSE MATTERS

One of the main reasons that so many diehard Metallica fans railed against 'The Black Album', this track was seen as something of a lame love song, completely at odds with the more direct, driven and dynamic lyricism of their previous records.

Co-written by James Hetfield, Lars Ulrich and producer Bob Rock, the lyrics were penned by Hetfield to a former girlfriend, although now he can't actually work out why he wrote them! But he did actually start the writing process while on the phone to a girlfriend, using his free hand to put down ideas. Presumably it was a form of love letter proclaiming that, no matter how far he was away on tour, he was always thinking of her. Now, exactly which girlfriend inspired this even Hetfield can't now recall – he seemed to go through a lot at this point in his life.

Originally, Hetfield didn't want this song in the public domain because he felt it was just too personal. But Ulrich persuaded him that it was far too good just to languish at the back of a drawer somewhere.

One amazing fact about the track is that it doesn't feature Kirk Hammett at all – even the guitar solo is handled by Hetfield. There's only one other song in Metallica's album history that doesn't have Hammett on it in some fashion, and that's '(Anesthesia) Pulling Teeth'. As this is a bass solo, that is understandable.

The video for this track, while shown on MTV, is not aired during the day because of the nudity included. Well, there are nude posters up in the studio that are clearly in view. The song is also on the 1999 'S&M' orchestral album, and given its power ballad base, it would seem an ideal song for interpretation with a string section.

It's actually been released twice as a single, firstly in its original form, as the third one from 'The Black Album', and then as the first from 'S&M'. On both occasions it was a huge hit.

In addition, there have been a number of covers, ranging from German industrial band Die Krupps, Finnish cellists Apocalyptica and American nu metallers Staind, to Canadian singer Biff Naked, British popster Lucie Silvas... and the Vienna Boys Choir!

Today, Metallica view the song more as a tribute to the loyalty and devotion of their fans rather than as a love song per se.

Possibly the most unusual performance of the song was in 1991, when Metallica teamed up with Chris Isaak for a Bay Area radio station.

Chris Isaak

natural experience, what Hetfield was actually writing about was the transformation in his personality that happens when he gets drunk. Given this interpretation, one perhaps starts to view lines like 'I feel I change/Back to a better day' take on a different slant. It's probably the first time that Hetfield has admitted in a song that he might have an alcohol problem, something that was to consume him a decade later.

Undoubtedly it's a lot easier to admit to problems in the context of a song than it is in real life, so it is possible Hetfield was using his art and artistry to admit the guilt he felt due to his growing dependence.

There are also those who feel that the song is about re-connecting with the baser and more animal instincts, ones so often lost in the modern world. It might also be Hetfield re-affirming to the fans that, while 'The Black Album' took them a little further from

OF WOLF AND MAN

A track from 'The Black Album' written by James Hetfield, Lars Ulrich and Kirk Hammett. Hetfield has said that the lyrics and storyline were inspired by the movie 'Wolfen'. Made in 1981, this werewolf film starred Albert Finney as a New York cop trying to solve a series of unexplained murders, all of which seem to have been perpetrated by animals.

The film was released during a time when there was a real revival in the genre, and, inevitably, it turns out that werewolves are responsible.

There are those who believe that, far from being about a super-

their roots, nonetheless the band were still very much in touch with those feelings, beliefs and musical inspirations that had always driven them. The frontman might have seen a diehard backlash coming, and was anxious to avoid this if at all possible.

The band used this song on the 'S&M' album, although Hetfield re-titled it 'Of Wolfgang And Man' in acknowledgement of their classical surroundings and as a nod and tribute towards the great composer Wolfgang Amadeus Mozart.

ONE

One of the greatest moments in Metallica's career, and a landmark in that, not only did it win them the Grammy for 'Best Metal Performance' in 1990, but they also shot their first ever video for this song.

The track was written in 1987 by James Hetfield and Lars Ulrich, appears on the '...And Justice For All' album, and was released as the second single from the record.

'One' has a very ominous, doomy atmosphere. It starts with the sound of gunfire and an artillery barrage, before Hetfield comes in with a mournful guitar tone. It builds from there to a series of climaxes, each more devastating than its predecessor.

Hetfield himself has said that the opening was inspired by a Venom track called 'Buried Alive', which begins with the soundscape of a funeral service.

The lyrics were based around the Dalton Trumbo book 'Johnny Got His Gun', which tells the story of how a soldier during the First World War, Joe Bonham, loses almost everything during a mortar shell attack (in the song it's

said that a landmine caused the devastation), and is left without arms or legs and lies in a hospital bed deaf, blind, mute and almost immobile. After coming out of a coma and realising that he can't communicate with the rest of the world, Bonham reflects on his short life.

Eventually, in an act of desperation, he seemingly goes into spasms, but they are recognised as morse code – 'Kill me', he pleads.

The video for this song was directed by Bill Pope and Michael Salomon. It's shot virtually in black and white and features the band playing in a stark warehouse setting. Metallica also bought the rights to the 1971 movie of the book, which was adapted and directed for the big screen by Trumbow himself. It starred Timothy Bottoms as the ill-fated Bonham, and several scenes, together with pieces of dialogue, were cut into the final version of the video, which was premiered on January 20, 1989 on MTV.

Actually, there are three edits of this video: the full one with the film scenes, a shortened version of this and one that only has the band playing live. Two of the three versions are featured on the '2 Of One' video released in 1990 – the long edition with the movie scenes, plus what was called 'The Jammin' Version', with just the band playing the song. There's also an introduction from Ulrich.

'One' was covered by Korn for an 'MTV Icons' show in tribute to Metallica and was a hidden bonus track on the band's 2003 album, 'Take A Look In The Mirror'. Apocalyptica also tackled it for their 'Inquisition Symphony' album, and Tenacious D claim that they got the idea for their own song, 'Tribute' after band member Jack Black had played the track, claiming it to be 'the

best song in the world', to fellow member Kyle Gasser. Death metallers Crematory also covered 'One' on the album 'Tribute To The Four Horsemen: A Tribute To Metallica'.

Metallica themselves re-visited 'One' for the 1999 album 'S&M', when the orchestrations provided by the San Francisco Symphony Orchestra actually gave everything an even eerier feel.

The original version of 'One' charted at number 35 as a single in the US, and reached number 13 in Britain.

But we must end by pointing out something odd. The story is of a soldier in the First World War. And yet in the introduction to the song a helicopter can definitely be heard with its blades whirring. Helicopters were not in production at the time and certainly never used in that particular war. Presumably, Metallica felt that the familiar chopping sound of a helicopter's blades added to the effect, even if it was factually inaccurate. Artistic license.

ONE ON ONE STUDIOS

It was here that Metallica recorded their breakthrough record, 'The Black Album', in 1991. The band were actually holed up here from October 1990 to June 1991 working on it. This was the second time the band had used this studio. They'd booked in here for the '...And Justice For All' album,

originally intending to work with producer Mike Clink. But when that didn't work out, the band returned to Flemming Rasmussen, the man who'd been behind the 'Ride The Lightning' and 'Master Of Puppets' records. Although Rasmussen would have preferred to work at his own Sweet Silence Studios in Copenhagen, he had to come out to Los Angeles because Metallica had already booked studio time in One On One.

ORION

This is the instrumental track from the 'Master Of Puppets' album. Some of the solos used here were originally part of the demo version of another song from the same album, 'Welcome Home (Sanitarium)'.

It's really a Cliff Burton composition as he wrote most of it, with a little help from James Hetfield, Kirk Hammett and Lars Ulrich. The title itself was inspired by the near space rock nature of some of the sounds heard at key points in the song. It features multiple guitar/bass harmonies, definitely a sign that the band were becoming more adventurous, and it also includes one of the bass player's finest solos towards the climax.

The full version of the song was played at Cliff Burton's funeral, but it wasn't until June 3, 2006 that the band actually performed the song in its entirety onstage. This was at the Rock Am Ring Festival in Nuremberg as they started their 'Escape From The Studio '06' tour, during which they played the whole of the 'Master Of Puppets' album.

This was the third instrumental of the band's career to that date, following on from '(Anesthesia) Pulling Teeth' (on the 'Kill 'Em All' album) and 'The Call Of Ktulu' (from 'Ride The Lightning'). It was covered by Mastodon for the 'Master Of Puppets: Remastered' album, given away free with 'Kerrang!' magazine in April, 2006 and it was sampled by DJ Shadow for his track 'The Number Song'.

Cliff Burton regarded this as his favourite Metallica song – perhaps because it features two bass solos. People are often puzzled about this because Burton pulls off the trick of making his bass lines sound like a guitar. But there are indeed two trademark Burton solos here.

OSBOURNE, OZZY

The Prince Of Darkness. The Double O. Ozzy is an icon among metal fans, and you'd have thought the connections between him and Metallica would be long and loud. While there are not many direct ones, a few do exist.

In 1986 Metallica got the chance to open for Ozzy on his 'Ultimate Sin' tour of America. In all they played 60 dates together, starting in Wichita, Kansas, on March 27 and ending in Seattle on June 22. Says Ozzy:

"I remember Metallica opening a tour for me. I would walk past their bus before shows and hear them playing old Sabbath songs, and I thought they were making fun of me. And they wouldn't talk to me and always kept their distance, and I thought it was really weird. I asked their tour manager about it and said, 'Is this their idea of a joke?' And he said, 'No, they think you're... gods'."

The importance of this tour, not only to Metallica but also to the whole thrash movement, cannot be overestimated. For the first time a true giant of metal – one of the elite old guard, if you wish – agreed to tour with a young band spearheading the new guard of the genre.

In 1986 Ozzy was far from being the mainstream celebrity he is these days. But there's no doubt of his heroic status in metal circles, as a man of the people. He had fronted Black Sabbath throughout the 1970s, the band that virtually invented what we know now as 'heavy metal'. His fringed jacket, flashing peace signs, frog jumps, and a voice that sounded like a nasal burp had all endeared him to a huge global audience. But, when he was fired from Sabbath as the

'70s slipped sloppily into history, there were many who feared we'd never see or hear from him again. Wrong! Carefully nurtured by shrewd manager Sharon Arden (now Ozzy's wife/manager Sharon Osbourne), the man was re-born and emerged into the new decade with a fresh sound and a guitar hero in Randy Rhoads, who was the biggest breath of excitement guitar aficionados had know since the emergence of Eddie Van Halen a few years earlier.

Rhoads was electrifying and defied conventions, helping Ozzy to achieve new heights on his first two solo albums, 'Blizzard Of Ozz' and 'Diary Of A Madman'. It also helped that Ozzy was still very much a controversial figure. Biting the heads off doves let loose at a record company convention, snorting a line of ants while on tour with Motley Crue, pissing on The Alamo... all of these things helped to fuel the legend, and further endeared him to those who loved metal.

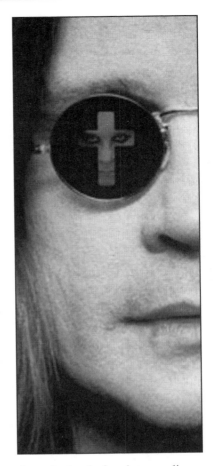

The tragic death of Rhoads in a freak plane accident seemed to knock him back quite a bit. But, with former Ratt/Rough Cutt guitarist Jake E. Lee in the fold, he was soon on the march again. By 1986 Ozzy had also eclipsed his old band. There was no doubt that he was the bigger attraction in any battle with Sabbath and his tours were guaranteed sell-outs.

So for Metallica to land the opening spot on a major American tour was a big deal. It worked for them because not only were they playing before huge audiences every night, but they were now in front of a different type of fan. These were the more old school devotees, and winning them over expanded the band's horizons. More than that, it was another cunning step in proving that this group were unquestionably way ahead of the thrash pack.

Metallica had been the first of the genre to sign a major label deal (with Elektra in America). The first to hook up with big management (Peter Mensch and Cliff Burnstein). Now they were also the first to get the opportunity to work with one of the metal greats.

It all opened doors, not only for them, but also for other bands of the genre. Metallica's success reflected back on everyone else, and gave them the chance to move forward. Ulrich said at the time:

"I guess we know that this band is starting to get genuine success because not only have we got two bottles of vodka per night on our dressing room rider, but this isn't the cheap stuff we've been used to – rather it's Absolut!"

However, Ulrich very nearly got the band kicked off the tour, by innocently asking Ozzy is he washed his hair after a gig. Totally drunk at the time, Ozzy was apparently insulted rather than amused by this query. So much so that the unfortunate drummer genuinely thought he'd wake up the next morning to find that Metallica were off the tour!

It was also a clever move by Ozzy to get Metallica on the bill. As with Motley Crue a few years earlier, it meant he was directly appealing to a younger crowd. There would be those persuaded to go and see Ozzy because Metallica were on the bill, so he was tapping into a new energy. Everybody won on that tour. Metallica themselves have learnt the lesson well. Now *they* are the venerable sages, drawing in younger fans by putting the heroes of the day on the bill.

Aside from this tour, there are also two other connections with Ozzy. Metallica covered 'Sabbra

Cadabra' for the 'Garage Inc.' album – well, it was a medley of that track and also 'A National Acrobat'. It's the only Black Sabbath cover the band have ever done – and it must be said, Sabbath's influence on them isn't as great as that of, say, Iron Maiden or Motorhead. Or Diamond Head, for that matter.

Finally, there's the matter of the bassists. In 2003 Metallica brought in Robert Trujillo to replace Jason Newsted. Trujillo had previously been part of Ozzy's band, a time he recalled with fondness:

"I must say, Ozzy, Sharon, Zakk, Mike Bordin, all the team and family members mean the world to me. Love and respect, my family 100 percent. I'm very stoked, excited and look forward to my new journey with my Metallica brothers."

Trujillo had played on Ozzy's 'Down To Earth' album and had also re-recorded the bass lines for the re-issues of the 'Blizzard Of Ozz' and 'Diary Of A Madman' albums. This was, perhaps, one of the most controversial moves of Ozzy's career. The decision was taken to wipe off the original rhythm section (bassist Bob Daisley and drummer Lee Kerslake), because of an ongoing legal battle, and to bring in Trujillo and drummer Mike Bordin to rework them.

Trujillo had also been on Ozzy's 'Live At Budokan' album, before accepting the offer to jump ship and join Metallica.

At the same time, in one of those quirks of fate, Ozzy elected to bring in Newsted to replace Trujillo for the 2003 US Ozzfest tour.

"He is a great bass player, has a good attitude in my band – and I have no hard feelings with Robert Trujillo," said Ozzy of Newsted.

The bassist at the time seemed delighted with the offer to join Ozzy, commenting:

"This is something I'm doing firstly out of respect, so it took zero seconds to decide. As for the physical part, I will push myself to make this happen... It's a huge blessing."

The relationship between Ozzy and Newsted only lasted that Summer, before the latter jumped ship and went on to work with Voivod. But it proved to be one of the more interesting, and surprising, swap deals in metal history. It also worked for all parties.

www.ozzy.com

OUTLAW TORN, THE

This is the last track on the 'Load' album – and its positioning is significant because it had to be cut by a full minute in order to fit everything on the record. There were 14 songs in all, and when it was realised that the band had overstepped the mark, they agreed that the jam which ends this particular one would have to be curtailed.

Weighing in at nine minutes and 49 seconds, this holds the distinction of being the longest original song on any Metallica studio album. The overall record is held by 'Mercyful Fate', which is 11 minutes and 11 seconds, but as this was a medley of songs from the Danish metal band of the same name, it doesn't count in this context.

So, what is this song all about? There are a couple of possible explanations. On the surface it is about losing a loved one, and longing to find a replacement, but one never comes. Some see this as an allegorical reference to the late Cliff Burton, even though he'd been dead for about a decade by the time this emerged. It's often been said that James Hetfield found it impossible to accept Jason Newsted as an adequate replacement for the lost bassist. Perhaps this song is another key to the puzzle, as Hetfield lays the blame, not on Newsted's inabilities, but on his own failure to overcome the grief.

Another possibility is that this is a dialogue between Christ and God, as the former awaits a re-union with the latter, knowing that his time is fleeting and running out fast. This may have something to do with Hetfield's own Christian Science upbringing, and an effort to understand the value – or otherwise – of Christ.

Certainly the imagery is powerful, but it is less likely to be about Christ and religion than about Burton. The demo version of this track was recorded at Lars Ulrich's home studio on March 6, 1995, and went under the title of 'Outlaw'.

The band restored the full version of the song for 'The Memory Remains' single. It was known then as 'The Outlaw Torn (Unencumbered By Manufacturing Restrictions Version)', and weighed in at a hefty ten minutes and 52 seconds. Most of what was restored is a Hetfield solo, Kirk Hammett having taken the first solo earlier in the song.

The track also turns up on the symphonic 'S&M' album from 1991, and it was one of the most successful adaptations made between the band and the San Francisco Symphony Orchestra. It was finally played live for the first time on April 12, 1999 at a show in Oahu, Hawaii.

One final point: many people have noted the similarity between 'The Outlaw Torn' and 'Fixxxer' from the subsequent 'ReLoad' album. This isn't just musical – both songs are about pain, and trying to deal with its consequences, something of a recurring theme at this juncture in Hetfield's increasingly unhappy life.

OVERKILL (MOTORHEAD)

One of the seminal Motorhead classics, this was the title track of their 1979 album, the one which really propelled them onto the path to greatness. It's arguably among the premier double kick bass drum tracks of all time, as Phil 'Philthy Animal' Taylor drives on the sound and style with real menace and venom. Few bands would have had the bravery to try and emulate what Motorhead did here.

But then, we all know that Metallica aren't like most bands – they go for the less obvious, and aren't scared by reputations. So it was that the band decided the best present they could give Motorhead leader Lemmy, as he celebrated his 50th birthday in 1995, was to do a special Motorhead EP.

They elected to cover four masterpieces from the Motor men, these being; 'Damage Case', 'Stone Dead Forever', 'Too Late Too Late', and 'Overkill'. Of all of these the last-named was the real challenge, and even though it was asking the near impossible for Lars Ulrich to match what Taylor had done nearly 20 years before, Metallica proved up to the task.

Watch out for a moment towards the end when James Hetfield

nearly stumbles and falls over the lyrics. But, as this was done virtually live, the band had no desire – nor chance – to go for a second take. So what you hear is how this was recorded in the first place – live and without a net. Well, almost. Is it up to the standard of the original? Actually, no, but then that would be expecting just too much, and Metallica come closer than most to doing the job on a par with the giants.

Aside from being used to celebrate Lemmy's half-century, the track appeared as a bonus song on the single 'Hero Of The Day' in 1996. There were actually two CD versions of this single release and 'Overkill' appeared on the other. Two years later, of course, the song turned up on 'Garage Inc.'.

Incidentally, Motorhead got to make their first appearance on the BBC TV show 'Top Of The Pops' with their single version of 'Overkill'. Sadly, Metallica weren't invited to do this.

PANIC

One of the most unusual names associated with Metallica, this was the band formed by Dave Mustaine prior to joining Metallica.

Mustaine had got into metal by trading pot for albums with a girl at a record store. That's allegedly how he first discovered the joys of Iron Maiden, Judas Priest and Motorhead, and also how he first learnt to play guitar – by strumming along to tracks by these masters.

In 1981 chance took a hand when Mustaine went to see a thrash-esque band called Metal Might at Slymuckers club. He got talking to a singer, one Charles Goodison, and eventually they decided to try their hands at putting together a band. The pair elected to name this fledgling metal crew, Panic. However, they were quickly hit by a tragedy – one that was to be mirrored five years later in an incident suffered by Metallica.

The band were involved in a road accident, as a result of which the drummer and driver were killed. Fortunately, Mustaine wasn't in the vehicle at the time, but one can only wonder whether his mind returned to this incident when he heard the news that Cliff Burton had been killed.

Panic never recovered from this blow, and Mustaine eventually decided that there was no future in sticking with the band, moving on to his next port of call – some band called Metallica.

As far as is known, there are no studio recordings in existence of Panic, although if you hunt hard enough you might be lucky and find a bootleg. Nor did Mustaine take anything from this short period over to Metallica, or Megadeth. Apart from one brief snippet in the song 'Rust In Peace... Polaris' by Megadeth, which is said to have been something he wrote while in Panic.

There have been a number of other bands called Panic over the years, although none have any connection to this lot.

PANSY DIVISION

A San Francisco band formed in 1992 and the self-styled found-

ers of queercore – the term says it all. Kirk Hammett guested on the song 'Headbanger', which appeared on their 1997 album 'More Lovin' From Our Oven'.

PANTERICA

Not so much a one-off band, as a one-song band. It happened in Mexico City on April 30, 1999, when Pantera frontman Phil Anselmo joined Metallica for the

song 'Creeping Death', in front of 50,000 fans.

PARADOX

The first band started by Jason Newsted when, in 1982, he re-located to California from Arizona. Apart from Newsted on bass/vocals, the rest of the line-up featured guitarist brothers Mello and Dave Golder, plus drummer Kelly Smith. It was very short-lived.

PARKER, BRAD

A rhythm guitarist who joined Metallica for only their fourth ever gig, but never made any further contribution. This was April 23, 1982 at the Concert Factory in Costa Mesa. At the time, James Hetfield was keen to concentrate on his singing, so the addition of Parker allowed him to shed the guitar. For this show the rest of the line-up was Dave Mustaine (lead guitar), Lars Ulrich (drums) and Ron McGovney (bass).

Parker was one of several rhythm guitarists the band brought in as they tried out different formations. In the end, of course, they decided that Hetfield should keep the guitar, and opted for the four-piece set-up that they use to this day.

Since his brief tenure with Metallica, Parker has made no impact on the rock scene. Like so many others he will forever be known as the man who had a moment with one of the biggest bands in history – that might be good enough for him, though. Better to be a footnote in a story like this than never be known at all.

PHANTOM LORD

A track from the band's debut album, 'Kill 'Em All', it first appeared on the 'No Life 'Til Leather' demo, which was effectively the same set of songs as would appear on the subsequent album. In fact, 'Phantom Lord' is the seventh track on both.

Written by James Hetfield and Lars Ulrich, it's got a storyline that is primal and typical of the genre, being about a battle between two heavy metal beasts. When performing the track live the band would often dedicate it to those people in the audience who were bumping heads, and, in turn, getting their heads bumped.

Phantom Lord was also the name of one of Hetfield's bands prior to joining Metallica. His first had been called Obsession, who started out in 1978. Two years later, he formed Phantom Lord with pals Jim Mulligan and High Tanner. Soon afterwards Hetfield met and jammed with Lars Ulrich, wasn't impressed and went back to Phantom Lord.

At this juncture he brought in Ron McGovney on bass – the pair had met at Downey High School. The band changed their name to Leather Charm, but fell apart, leaving Hetfield and McGovney high and dry. Fortunately, at this point Ulrich came back into the picture, contacting Hetfield after persuading Metal Blade boss Brian Slagel to put a Metallica track on the first 'Metal Massacre' compilation. Only trouble was that Ulrich had no band. The rest, as they say, became history.

There are also suggestions that at least part of the track was written during this period. There may also have been a Judas Priest influence at work here. On their 1978 album 'Stained Class', the Priest had a song called 'Exciter', which features the line: 'Fall to your knees and repent if you please'. A line from 'Phantom Lord' proclaims: 'Fall onto your knees for the Phantom Lord'.

Aside from this, the importance of the song is that it's regarded as the most mature on the album, and really an indication of where the band planned to go, musically. It even has a clean guitar sound, which was at odds with the way they recorded most of that first album.

Anthrax covered this for the compilation album 'ECW: Extreme Music', and, talking of the ECW (Extreme Championship Wrestling), one of its top stars during the 1980s, a certain Mike Awesome, used it as his entrance theme.

The same band also covered the track on the album 'Tribute To The Four Horsemen: A Tribute To Metallica'.

PHONOGRAM

Now known as Mercury Records, Phonogram is the UK record label that the band singed to when they left Music For Nations.

Metallica themselves had started in the UK and Europe with MFN, an independent label that nurtured them and guided their career through an extraordinary twist of success. But in the US, the band had already gone to a major in Elektra, and once the Peter Mensch-Cliff Burnstein axis came on board as Metallica's new management team, they made it clear that the future lay worldwide and in signing with a bigger record company.

Phonogram Records were regarded as one of the premier labels for hard rock and metal bands at the time. Their roster already included Rush, Black Sabbath, Dio and Bon Jovi. The label itself had started out in 1962 as a joint project between Philips Records and Deutsche Grammophon, before an alliance with Polydor led to the formation of PolyGram. A takeover by Universal again changed the structure, but despite a number of bands being dropped over the years, Metallica's sales base is so huge that there was never a danger that they'd be one of the victims of any cull.

It's probable that a deal was done with Phonogram, after the release of 'Master Of Puppets' though Music For Nations, because Mensch and Burnstein had a close relationship with the label through another of their clients at the time, Def Leppard.

The success of the Sheffield band would almost certainly have allowed them to negotiate a very favourable deal for the growing Metallica.

The first record to be put out by Phonogram for Metallica was 1987's 'The $5.98 EP: Garage Days Re-Revisited', a landmark release in itself and also in that it introduced new bassist Jason Newsted to the world. It was their most successful release to that date, reaching number 27 in the UK charts.

Both 1991's 'The Black Album' and 1996's 'Load' were chart toppers in Britain, while '…And Justice For All', 'ReLoad' and 'St. Anger' all made the top five. Even what one might call vanity albums, 1998's 'Garage Inc.' and 'S&M' a year later, made the Top 40, peaking at positions 29 and 33, respectively.

On the singles front, Phonogram/Mercury have also had a great deal of success with Metallica. Their first chart hit was 'Harvester Of Sorrow' in 1988, which made it to number 20. Their biggest impact came with 1991's 'Enter Sandman' and 'Until It Sleeps' five years later, both of which reached number five.

In all, Metallica have had 12 Top 20 singles, and five others have made it to the Top 40, with one – 'The Unnamed Feeling' – getting to number 42.

That's an impressive record for a band who are not known for being overtly commercial, and says much about their strong relationship with Phonogram/Mercury, for whom they continue to be a blue riband act. Now, 20 years on, it seems that the switch of labels did no harm at all to the group.

Carey, Huey Lewis & The News and Deftones.

PLANT STUDIOS, THE

Based in Sausalito, California, this is the studio where Metallica recorded both 'Load' and 'ReLoad'. The studio complex opened in 1972, and its first big album project was the huge selling 'Rumours' by Fleetwood Mac in 1976.

Since then the list of top names has included Carlos Santana, Prince, John Fogerty, Mariah

POOR TWISTED ME

A song from the 'Load' album, which was cunningly called 'Untitled' on the original demo, and deals with people who are constantly getting themselves into difficult situations in order to get sympathy from others.

Now, whether the band had anyone in particular in mind when they wrote this has never really been mentioned. However, in a sense, they might be talking about old bandmate Dave Mustaine, a man know for using his sacking from Metallica as a means of getting sympathy from others because of what he perceived as ill treatment. These lines do tend to suggest that Mustaine could easily have been the subject of this song: 'Oh poor twisted me/Oh poor twisted me/I feast on sympathy/I chew on suffer/I chew on agony'.

Beyond Mustaine, though, it might also refer to a lot of people who Metallica had met during their time in the music industry, where attention seekers dominate.

POWER METAL

This was the title given to a demo recorded by the band in April 1982. It was the band's second and featured the songs 'Hit The Lights', 'Jump In The Fire', 'The Mechanix' and 'Motorbreath'. The first two, of course, were also featured on the band's first tape, 'Ron McGovney's '82 Garage Demo', which had been recorded a month previously. 'The Mechanix' was the first song written for the band by guitarist Dave Mustaine, who joined James Hetfield (vocals/rhythm guitar), Ron McGovney (bass) and Lars Ulrich (drums) on these sessions.

This was never actually released, but seemed to acquire the title of 'Power Metal' from the term used on the band's business cards at the time – and it may well be the first time that the phrase itself was ever used. Today it's regarded as an important sub-genre of heavy metal.

A few years later, when Metallica had established themselves as a major force, a bootleg appeared called 'No Life 'Til Power' that had the whole of the 'No Life 'Til Leather' demo on one side of the vinyl and all four tracks from

'Power Metal' on the other. It used the same artwork as that for the original 'Power Metal' demo, which was a classic scene of a nude male and female (the male with a snake entwined around his body) in what might have been a temple setting.

All of these songs are featured on the band's debut album, 'Kill 'Em All'… well, 'The Mechanix' had been changed. The original song was about a randy garage mechanic trying to bed a female customer. But when Mustaine was fired, Metallica re-wrote the lyrics and changed the title to 'The Four Horsemen', but they still gave Mustaine a credit on it. 'The Mechanix' itself, as envisioned by Mustaine, turned up on the debut album from Megadeth, 'Killing Is My Business…And Business Is Good'.

Talking about the song, Mustaine himself says:

"'The Mechanix' is not 'The Four Horsemen', 'The Four Horsemen' is 'The Mechanix'. Get over it. Buy a calendar, learn to count, have a Coke and a smile.

"Listen, if I wasn't here, there'd be no Metallica, because James Hetfield sang, Lars played drums and there was Ron McGovney on bass. Did it ever dawn on anyone that I was the only guitar player? That I had a more integral part than you gave me credit for?

"James didn't want to give me credit because he's jealous of me. His whole frontman persona he copped from me. In the begin-

ning of the band, he just sang and I did all the guitar work. When he was done singing, he'd walk away from the microphone and I had to walk up to the mic and talk. I'm like, 'What's wrong with this picture? I'm getting your beer tonight!'."

Incidentally, 'Power Metal' was also the title of the first Pantera album with vocalist Phil Anselmo, released in 1988. Although whether this is in homage to a Metallica demo made six years earlier remains open to debate.

PRESIDIO SESSIONS, THE

This refers to recording sessions from 2001, prior to James Hetfield being admitted to rehab.

Says Hetfield himself:

"There are quite a few songs that didn't make it onto 'St. Anger'

from those sessions. Presidio was the name of the old barracks at the San Francisco army base, where we were recording in San Francisco before I went into rehab. And there was probably about 15 songs or something that didn't quite make it onto 'St. Anger' [from those sessions] - maybe more. And we've got 'em. They're cool – they're not finished, but they'll appear sometime somewhere, there will be a right time for those.

But for us, 'St. Anger' is doing really pretty darn good, and it's hard to not keep writing, so it would be tough to go back and redo some of that stuff, or get it in the shape to put it out. That would remind me of, like, 'Load' and 'ReLoad' – working backwards. But there's just so much good vibe going on now, there's no use in kind of turning around. So those things will appear in their form some way or another."

While it seems none of the recordings from these sessions made it onto the 'St. Anger' album – some of the songs, in different form, did, of course – nonetheless it's claimed they shaped the mentality and approach the band were to take further down the line.

Of course, these sessions are featured in the documentary film 'Some Kind Of Monster', and one can readily see the way this documentary was to shape up from these early sequences, and also appreciate, by watching the band working on the songs, that they really were in no state to focus properly.

Nonetheless, the Presidio Sessions have become something of a mythical time in the band's career. In some ways they represent the end of an era. In other ways they gave birth to the most controversial record Metallica have released, namely 'St. Anger'.

Thankfully enough material survives for us to look forward, one day, to their inevitable release.

PRIMUS

There are three connections between the wacky San Francisco trio and Metallica. Firstly, when Cliff Burton died, bassist Les Claypool was auditioned as a potential replacement. This wasn't long after Primus had actually started, and when he didn't land the job, Claypool threw himself

wholeheartedly into making his own band work.

Being based in the vicinity, Primus played a number of shows with Bay Area thrash bands, and Claypool was at one time almost recruited by Exodus.

Aided by guest appearances by the like of Tom Waits, albums such as 'Sailing The Sea Of Cheese' and 'Pork Soda' gave them considerable commercial clout. They also had a cameo role in the film 'Bill & Ted's Bogus Adventure', recorded music for 'Beavis & Butt-Head' and wrote/performed the theme for 'South Park'.

The second connection happened with their 1999 release 'Antipop' – their last studio album. James Hetfield plays guitar on the song 'Electric Electric'. Former Faith No More guitarist 'Big' Jim Martin also appears on the same track.

In addition, Kirk Hammett has recently recorded a song with Les Claypool (the pair were at school together) and former Faith No

More and current Ozzy Osbourne drummer Mike Bordin. There are no details yet on when or how this is to be released. And there's more. Hammett played onstage with Primus at Portland, Oregon on December 11, 1990, performing the Primus original 'Tommy The Cat' and also 'Master Of Puppets'.

Finally, Primus covered 'The Thing That Should Not Be' for the album 'Tribute To The Four Horsemen: A Tribute To Metallica'.

www.primusville.com

PRINCE, THE (DIAMOND HEAD)

Metallica's remarkable devotion to Diamond Head is seen on 'Ron McGovney's 1982 Garage Demo', recorded in 1982. This featured no less than four Diamond Head covers – half the track listing – included this song, which again turned up on the 'Garage Inc.' album, and is also included on the 'Harvester Of Sorrow' single. This is one of Diamond Head's most evocative songs, and was first recorded by them for the 1980 album known both as 'Lightning To The Nations' and 'The White Album' (so-called, because original pressings came in a plain white sleeve, with the band's autographs as the only sign of any artwork).

Written by vocalist Sean Harris and guitarist Brian Tatler, this song is said to be about Niccolo Machiavelli, the 15th Century Italian political master, whose most famous writings were contained in a book called 'The Prince', wherein he describes the methods that someone can use to retain control of his kingdom. Most people have always thought this book backs the principle that the end justifies the means. This isn't the case, however, as Machiavelli stops short of claiming that any action, however ruthless, is justified in order to reach the desired goal.

The difference between Metallica's version and the Diamond Head original isn't too great. In fact, in their early days, the Americans were, if anything, guilty of paying too much respect to one of their prime influences. But there's little doubt that Metallica's patronage has been a major reason for Diamond Head's name being kept alive for so long, despite the fact of their own star being on the wane.

Amusingly, Lars Ulrich is sometimes referred to as The Prince Of Denmark, a title partly inspired by this song, but probably more to do with his alleged 'control freak' attitude than anything else.

PRINCE CHARMING

A track from the 'ReLoad' album, this has nothing to do with the Adam & The Ants hit song of the same title. One can't help but feel there might be a certain sense of anger from James Hetfield here, as the story is one of being rejected by your parents, and taking it out on everyone around you.

Hetfield comes from a Christian Science background, and that coloured not only the early part of his life, but also many of the songs that he's written. What he may well be saying here is that the religious beliefs held by his mother and father were allowed to override any feelings of affection for their son, and he's now giving vent to his frustrations in his lyrics – a more productive way of doing so than is the case of the 'hero' of the song, who attacks all those around him.

However, there may also be an element of Hetfield trying to explain himself here, perhaps attempting to get those around him to understand some of his behaviour, to understand his latent anger.

Incidentally, the song was originally to be titled 'Drivin''.

PURIFY

This is the penultimate song on the 'St. Anger' album. Some see it as the band publicly shedding the excess baggage of the past and both lyrically and musically determined to go for a more strippeddown and angry sound. Others believe it's something much more personal from James Hetfield, as he exposes his own demons and holds them up for public ridicule and debate. Whatever, it's a cathartic song, even if a lot of its

inherent power is lost due to misguided production.

PUSHEAD

An artist who has provided some of Metallica's most vibrant illustrations and sleeves whose real name is the rather more prosaic Brian Schroeder. His list of artworks for Metallica include the covers for 'St. Anger' and for both the 'One' and 'Eye Of The Beholder' seven inch singles, as well as working on the 'Cliff 'Em All' and 'A Year And A Half In The Life Of Metallica' video sleeves and the '…And Justice For All' inner sleeve.

He's also designed T-shirts for the band and is probably the artist most closely associated with them. Rather like Derek Riggs and Iron Maiden (he created 'Eddie'), the relationship between Pushead and Metallica has been mutually beneficial.

Away from Metallica, Pushead has worked with Misfits, Soundgarden, Prong, Tad and Hirax. He's also worked with 'Thrasher' magazine (a skateboard publication), and for Zorlac Skateboards, for whom he has designed both adverts and also graphics for skateboards.

His artwork is characterised by a judicious use of skulls and is extraordinary in the way it draws from horror, anatomy and also surrealism. Like few others, his designs are instantly recognisable and are both gore-infested yet clean. While not known for holding back or pulling his punches, he never seems to simply go for pure shock value. His art is definitely of a style that appeals to both metal fans and punks alike and his work is hugely popularity among fans of both genres.

Away from the drawing board (as it were) Pushead has also found time to develop a career as a musician, fronting Septic Death, active from 1981-86 and said to have had a major impact on bands like Infest and Citizen's Arrest as pioneers in the thrashcore area. The group also featured Jon Taylor (guitar), Mike Matlock (bass) and Paul Birnbaum (drums).

They did few shows during their five years together, but did release records on Pushead's own label, Pusmort. If you want to check them out, then pick up a copy of the compilation 'Zorlac Anthology'. It has every studio recording, plus a lot of live stuff as well.

Aside from Septic Death's own records, Pusmort also released titles from Onslaught, Exit Condition and Attitude Adjustment.

In more recent times, Pushead has started a new label, Bacteria Sour and remains very much in demand as an underground artist.

Q. PRIME

The management company who've been with the band for some 23 years, Q. Prime Inc. was started by Peter Mensch and Cliff Burnstein, who had first met when they were involved with the mighty CCC Management company, responsible for acts like AC/DC, Aerosmith and the Scorpions.

Mensch had majored in Human Studies at Brandeis University, before getting a masters degree in Marketing from the University of Chicago. He'd began his 'musical' career as Aerosmith's tour accountant.

Burnstein had started out in as an A&R man; one of his first signings were cult hard rockers Legs Diamond. But it was at CCC, originally known as Leber-Krebs, that he found his niche.

In 1982, Mensch and Burnstein decided to split from CCC and head out on their own. At first, the business was run from two flats, in Hoboken, New Jersey (where Bunstein was based) and Earl's Court, London (home for Mensch). Their clients included Def Leppard, whom Mensch had persuaded to join CCC, and AC/DC, again a band whom Mensch and Bunstein took from CCC.

The first contact with Metallica came in late 1984. Looking to expand their roster, and always on the hunt for young talent, Mensch contacted 'Kerrang!' writer Xavier Russell, who had become a close friend of Metallica. He passed on the message of interest to Lars Ulrich, who famously phoned Mensch from a phone box

Peter Mensch

– the result being an agreement that's lasted to this day.

Today, Q. Prime (as the company is now known) manage a raft of top names, including Jimmy Page, Shania Twain, Muse, Garbage and Snow Patrol. And, over the years, some of the biggest names in the world have passed through their offices. These include the Red Hot Chili Peppers, Madonna and the Rolling Stones. Madonna worked with them on her 1998 album 'Ray Of Light', and the Mensch-Burnstein axis is credited with helping to make this such a huge success. The Stones hired them as consultants for their 1989 album 'Steel Wheels' and the subsequent tour.

Over the years, Mensch and Bunstein have had to deal with some significant problems within bands. The death of Bon Scott in February 1980 threw AC/DC into a state of potential turmoil. Def Leppard drummer Rick Savage lost an arm in a road accident at the end of 1983. And, from Metallica's viewpoint, the death of Cliff Burton in 1986 was a landmark tragedy that could have torn the band apart. But their policy has always been the same: allow the band to make their own decisions. In fact, this has always been the hallmark of the Mensch-Bunstein ethos – they never smother their artists in cotton wool.

When Def Leppard decided to fire founder-guitarist Pete Willis in 1982, Mensch told them they would have to face him and do it themselves – there was to be no hiding place. And the business duo quickly made it plain to their bands that, while everything would be looked after on tour, once they came off the road, the musicians themselves would be responsible for personal lives.

However, while the pair have a strong and impressive reputation, and a consistently successful record, they're not without critics. One of Def Leppard's original managers, Frank Stuart-Brown, has always believed that Mensch and Bunstein used unfair tactics to entice their charges away to join CCC. And when courting Queensryche a few years later, the duo tried to overwhelm the Seattle band by impressing them with the vast amounts of cash Leppard were making on tour. At first that failed, as Queensryche decided to stay with co-managers Kim and Diana Harris – but Q. prime did eventually get their men.

On the Metallica front, many thought it was a mistake for Mensch and Bunstein to look for ways to get the band out of their contract with independent label Music For Nations in 1986. Mensch once proclaimed that he didn't believe in any of his clients being on a small label.

In the end, Metallica signed a UK/European deal with major company Phonogram (now Mercury). But there are some who maintain this wasn't a sensible move, and that their new home did little more than go with the flow, rather than aggressively marketing the band to new heights. However, whether MFN could have made 'The Black Album' as big as it turned out to be all over the world is a moot point.

Today, with the departure of Def Leppard, Metallica are Q. Prime's longest-serving clients, which probably says a lot about both parties.

QUEEN

In Metallica terms, there are two strong connections between the celebrated British band and Metallica. The first was a cover of 'Stone Cold Crazy', which appeared on Queen's third album, 1974's 'Sheer Heart Attack', and was recorded by Metallica for a compilation put together by their US label, Elektra, to celebrate their 40th anniversary. Called 'Rubaiyat', it was released in 1990. Amazingly, it won the band a Grammy for 'Best Metal Performance'.

The band are still convinced that this happened, because when that category was introduced into the Grammy system, Metallica had been sensationally beaten by Jethro Tull of all bands – hardly metal, right? Now, the Grammy committee seemed determined to make it up to Metallica. Well, that's what the band thought.

Subsequently, this version turned up on 'Garage Inc.'. There are differences between Queen's original and Metallica's rendering in both the music and the lyrics. Inevitably, Metallica were harder, faster and more brutal. But they also altered some of the words, so that whereas Queen were humorous and tongue-in-cheek, Metallica went for a more full-frontal assault. For instance, Queen used the line, 'Walking down the street/ shooting people that I meet/with my rubber tommy water gun'. But Metallica shifted it to, 'Walking down the street/shooting people that I meet/with my fully loaded tommy gun'.

The second important relationship beween the two bands happened on April 20, 1992, when the Freddie Mercury Tribute Concert For AIDS Awareness was staged at Wembley Stadium in London and Metallica were among the many major names on the bill.

The origins of this show go back to Mercury's death from the dreadful AIDS virus on November 24 the previous year. The three remaining members of Queen – guitarist Brian May, bassist John Deacon and drummer Roger Taylor – started to formulate a plan, together with band manager Jim Beach, as how best to celebrate the life, talent and legacy of their late singer. In February 1992, at the annual BRIT Awards, Taylor and May announced the gig for April. Amazingly, all 72,000 tickets were sold out within two hours of going on sale, despite the only confirmed act being the Queen trio.

The gig itself was divided into two parts. During the first half, bands influenced by Queen performed. These included Metallica, plus Guns n' Roses, Extreme and Def Leppard. In between bands, clips of Freddie Mercury in his prime were shown on giant video screens. Metallica played three songs: 'Enter Sandman', 'Sad But True' and 'Nothing Else Matters'.

The second half featured the trio of May, Taylor and Deacon, joined by a host of top names, to perform mostly Queen songs. James Hetfield was the sole Metallica representative for this part, doing 'Stone Cold Crazy', with Black Sabbath guitarist Tony Iommi also on stage.

Elsewhere, Def Leppard's Joe Elliott and Slash from Guns n'

Roses did 'Tie Your Mother Down'. Robert Plant was on hand for 'Innuendo' (interspersed with snippets from 'Kashmir') and Led Zeppelin's 'Thank You' before concluding with 'Crazy Little Thing Called Love'. David Bowie and Annie Lennox did 'Under Pressure'. George Michael sang ''39' and 'Somebody To Love'. Elton John and Axl Rose lent their talents to 'Bohemian Rhapsody', while Axl himself did 'We Will Rock You', and Elton John teamed up with Iommi for 'The Show Must Go On'. At the end, everyone got together for the grand finale, 'We Are The Champions'.

Many remember the day for the extraordinary moment when Bowie got down on his knees for a recitation of 'The Lord's Prayer', and Metallica weren't even mentioned in a lengthy review of the show published by 'The Times'.

However, footage from the event – especially backstage – was used by Metallica in their video 'A Year And A Half In The Life Of Metallica'. The concert itself got an official release in 1993 in both the US and Japan, in video and laserdisc format, although there was no British release until 1997. And, in this format, Spinal Tap's performance of 'The Majesty Of Rock' was cut out, as were two songs each by Extreme and Def Leppard, plus Plant's rendering of 'Innuendo' – all due to space restrictions. Talking about the gig, Hetfield said:

"That gig was really cool, but actually the rehearsal was even cooler. I thought it was going to be a little rehearsal room, but it was a little bigger. There was a few more people there than I expected. And I was already nervous as shit. But as soon as I talked with the guys, they were really cool, really mellow, they made me relaxed right away."

The gig was put out in DVD format in 2002, but only the second half of the event was there, something for which this release received a lot of understandable criticism.

On a wider level, just what is the influence of Queen on Metallica? It's probably two-fold. Like almost every major rock band of the past 25 years, Metallica have inevitably been inspired to some extent by the British giant's musicality. And their extraordinary range has clearly had its effect. While Metallica have never written anything close to 'Bohemian Rhapsody', nontheless the fact that a song as complex and diverse as this could become a cultural icon does have its echo in the fact that Metallica themseves could confidently come up with similar length songs, all of which are individual and go through a number of changes throughout.

If this is one aspect of Queen's importance to Metallica, then the other is perhaps even more profound. The former's philosophy was always to transcend the trappings of any genre. They drew vociferously from such a wide range of inputs that all one can say about Queen is that they were…Queen. Rock? Yes. Metal? Occasionally? Rockabilly? Just a tad. Electronica? Even this. But it was all combined in a manner that suited the whole. Queen created their own environment, and that is definitely the same for Metallica. Even though they're still revered as the masters of thrash, in reality they quickly got past this sort of restriction.

The fact that the thrash movement almost grew up around them shouldn't hide the fact that, even on their debut album, 'Kill 'Em All', Metallica were far from being a composite thrash band. They always had a musical belief and aspiration that went beyond the mere desire to 'bang that head that will not bang'. Throughout their career, Metallica have striven to be different. Like Queen, they've made some bad errors of judgement. Yet, also like Queen these were their own errors – and it's never diminished the fans' dedication to their heroes.

While musically, bands such as Black Sabbath, Iron Maiden and Slayer are closer to Metallica, spiritually it might be suggested that Queen are among their closest allies. Who knows, perhaps one day Metallica will do their own version of the 'Hot Space' album... then again, perhaps not.

www.queenonline.com

QUINTANA, RON

The man credited with giving the band their name. The story goes that, in late 1981, with the fledgling metalheads still struggling to come up with a suitably impressive moniker, Lars Ulrich

had a conversation with his friend Quintata, who was trying to come up with a title for his planned fanzine. There were two that Quintana had in mind: one was Metal Mania, the other was said to be Metallica.

Impressed with the idea of Metallica as a name, Ulrich convinced Quintana to go for Metal Mania as the title of the fanzine, so that he could take Metallica for the band!

Says Quintana of his relationship with the young drummer:

"Lars would visit San Francisco, and crash on my floor. He broke my cassette deck by constantly playing, and rewinding, my best live Diamond Head tapes, but always brought enough cool tapes and 'zines to make me forget about any problems."

However, there is another story about where the name came from. In late 1980, a book was published in the UK called 'Encyclopaedia Metallica'. Co-written by 'Record Mirror' journalists Brian Harrigan and Malcolm Dome, it was a history of the genre, with a foreward from Saxon singer Biff Byford. This came out a year before the landmark conversation between Quintana and Ulrich. Given the latter's obsession with anything to do with British metal, and the fact that he spent quite considerable time in the UK, it is inconceivable that the drummer didn't at least know about the books' existence. In which case, one can only assume

that, by the time Quintana came up with that precise name, he may have forgotten about the book. Or perhaps it jogged his memory.

Ulrich has always denied that the book had anything to do with the choice of band name, except for one occasion, when the drummer did admit that it may have had an influence. Whether Quintana knew of the book remains open to speculation.

Incidentally, the actual term 'Encyclopaedia Metallica' was coined by Harrigan, basing it on the 'Encyclopaedia Britannica'. But whatever the truth about the origins of the name, Quintana himself did go on to publish the 'Metal Mania' fanzine, and was to be one of the most important figures in promoting the bay Area thrash scene. Not only through the fanzine itself, but also thanks to

his DJ stint on a show called Rampage Radio, on station KUSF.

Trivia fiends might be interested to know that Quintana, an avid tape trader at the time, put a classified advert in the fourth issue of 'Kerrang!' magazine, trying to find liked-minded people with whom he could correspond and trade. Among those who answer the ad were photographer Harold Oimen, who took some of the earliest pictures of the band, and a lighting engineer called Pat Scott, who would go on to work for Metallica in their club days.

Today, Quintata still does shows on KUSF, under the Rampage Radio banner (check out www. rampageradio.com). And you'll find copies of 'Metal Mania' on eBay. And they're not too over-priced, either.

RADIO CITY

The venue in Anaheim where Metallica played their first ever show, on March 14, 1982.

RAMONES

One of the great punk bands, New Yorkers Ramones got major Metallica treatment on the various formats for the 'St. Anger' single. Altogether, five Ramones covers were featured: 'Commando', 'Today Your Love, Tomorrow The

World' (on CD1), 'Cretin Hop', 'Now I Wanna Sniff Some Glue' (CD2) and 'We're A Happy Family' (12 inch vinyl).

The Ramones started out in 1974, and kept going until 1996, when they split up.

Although they never achieved significant commercial success, their influence is both enormous and enduring. Their biggest album, 1980's 'End Of The Century', only made it to number 44 in America and number 14 in the UK.

Altogether, eight members were involved, all taking the surname 'Ramone': Joey, Johnny, Marky, Dee Dee, C.J., Richie, Tommy and Elvis.

Sadly, three members of the band have died in recent years, these being Joey, Dee Dee and Johnny.

www.officialramones.com

RASMUSSEN, FLEMMING

Its worth getting something straight – although Flemming Rasmussen is often cited as having produced the albums 'Ride The Lightning', 'Master Of Puppets', plus '…And Justice For All', in fact, he didn't. At least not by himself. Rasmussen was more the engineer on the projects, with the band producing themselves.

However, with this in mind he still played a major role in the development of their sound and style.

"What Flemming does with Metallica is that he records the band. To me, the word 'produce' means to create something, and most of that comes from the band in the songwriting stages,"

said Lars Ulrich at the time of '...And Justice For All'.

Rasmussen came into Metallica's world thanks to Rainbow. He'd worked on their 1983 album 'Difficult To Cure', and the band liked the sounds he got. They'd already decided to record in Europe, so after a brief European tour in June 1984, supporting Twisted Sister, they headed for Copenhagen and Sweet Silence Studios.

Says Rasmussen of the first time he came across Metallica:

"Everybody else was running round doing disco and shit, and I hated that. Most of the other people in the studio thought that Metallica was the worst piece of shit they'd ever heard in their lives, but I loved that."

Over the next two years, the combination of Rasmussen and Metallica gave us the remarkable pair of albums 'Ride The Lightning' and 'Master Of Puppets'. But, the death of Cliff Burton threw everything into turmoil. And it seemed that the band might end their association with Rasmussen and Sweet Silence.

For 'The $5.98 EP: Garage Days Re-Revisited', Metallica, with new bassist Jason Newsted, headed for Los Angeles, and the same was true for the next album, '...And Justice For All'. They began to record the latter with Guns n' Roses producer Mike Clink, but it just didn't work out. So,

locked into a studio booking at One On One in LA, the band contacted Rasmussen and persuaded him to fly out in order, "To save our asses," as Hetfield succinctly put it.

Despite controversies over the raw sound and the way that the bass lines seemed to be buried so low in the mix, the album was mostly well received. It was nominated for a Grammy in the 'Best Hard Rock/Metal Performance' category, but amazingly lost out to Jethro Tull.

This, though, marked the end of the working relationship, although Rasmussen remains on good terms with the band.

READING FESTIVAL

Metallica have headlined the event on two occasions. On August 24, 1997, they played the following set:

'Ecstacy Of Gold', 'No Remorse' (jam), 'So What', 'Master Of Puppets', 'King Nothing', 'Sad But True', 'Fuel', 'Hero Of The Day', 'Ain't My Bitch', 'One', 'Until It Sleeps', 'For Whom The Bell Tolls', 'Wherever I May Roam', 'Nothing Else Matters', 'Enter Sandman', 'Stone Cold Crazy', 'Creeping Death', 'Battery', 'Last Caress', 'Motorbreath'.

That same year, Suede, the Manic Street Preachers, Embrace

and The Verve were the other main attractions at the festival.

Six years later the band were back, headlining on August 24, 2003, when their set was:

'Ecstacy Of Gold', 'Battery', 'Master Of Puppets', 'Harvester Of Sorrow', 'Welcome Home (Sanitarium)', 'For Whom The Bell Tolls', 'Frantic', 'Sad But True', 'St. Anger', 'No Remorse', 'Seek And Destroy', 'Blackened', 'Fuel', 'Nothing Else Matters', 'Creeping Death', 'One', 'Enter Sandman'.

Also on the bill in 2003 were Linkin Park, Blur, Blink-182, System Of A Down and the Black Rebel Motorcycle Club.

RECYCLER, THE

This is the Southern Californian newspaper that first introduced Lars Ulrich and James Hetfield. It was here that Ulrich advertised in 1980 trying to find like-minded metalheads with whom to jam, and start a band. The advert read: 'Drummer looking for other metal musicians to jam with, Tygers of Pan Tang, Diamond Head and Iron Maiden'.

Hetfield answered the ad. and met up with Ulrich. But he wasn't impressed at all with the young Dane, part of the reason being that his cymbals kept on falling over.

Recalls Hetfield:

"Lars had a pretty crappy drum kit, with one cymbal. It kept falling over, and we'd have to stop, and he'd pick the fucking thing up. He really was not a good drummer."

So, the pair parted. Ulrich headed for the UK to follow Diamond Head around on tour for three months, before going back to LA and taking up the cudgels for his own musical ambitions.

Ulrich persuaded Brian Slagel to put his (non-existent) band onto the 'Metal Massacre' compilation, showcasing young American metal talent, and then contacted Hetfield again. With the carrot of a track on a record being dangled, Hetfield this time agreed to team up with Ulrich.

But, without that fateful ad in the first place, who knows where metal history might have gone?

RED VETTE

One of three names shortlisted by Lars Ulrich and James Hetfield for their band, prior to choosing Metallica.

RELOAD

Some people have decried this album as being no more than a dumping ground for the songs that didn't make the 'Load' record. That is unfair, and also slightly inaccurate.

In fact, the band had wanted to release 'Load' as a double album, but this was scuppered by unavoidable circumstances. So Metallica had to settle for putting out two single albums. In reality, they could probably have been issued in reverse order, because there's little to choose between them.

"We wrote 27 songs for 'Load' and were developing it as a double album," said Lars Ulrich in 1996. *"We then got the offer to play Lollapalooza in 1996, so we put one record out now with most of the songs that are done, and then we'll come back after a year and finish the rest of them.*

As far as I'm concerned, you can take any of these songs and interchange them on the two albums. The only fear we had was getting to it quick. We didn't want to leave it lying around for three years and worry about what it would sound like when we came back to it."

Starting with the revved-up 'Fuel', a driving entry into the record, things go a little mysterious with the haunting 'The Memory Remains', which features an unforgettable guest appearance from Marianne Faithfull. Hetfield had wanted to introduce a female voice into the mix, someone who had a

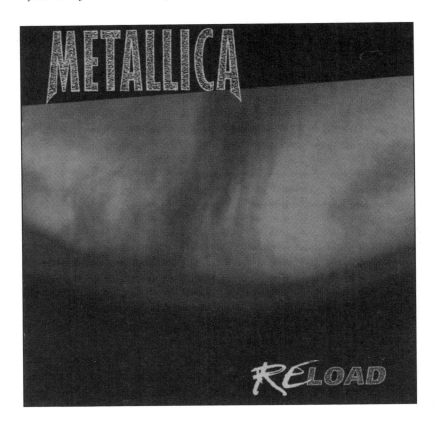

certain lived-in charm, but also the charisma to carry it off. A number of candidates were discussed, but after thinking about Patti Smith and Carly Simon, they went for Mick Jagger's former muse.

Hetfield amusingly said that it was the first time that a woman had been on a Metallica album, apart from Hammett!

Elsewhere, people were intrigued by 'The Unforgiven II', a sequel no less to 'The Unforgiven' from 'The Black Album'. In many respects, it is a different song completely, starting off from the same base, but then building an altogether more individual atmosphere.

'Low Man's Lyrics' took the band even further away from their roots, incorporating a hurdy gurdy, played by David Miles, while 'Fixxxer' is a dark, deep song dealing with the consequences of abuse: mental, physical and drug induced. It was the final track on 'ReLoad', and one wonders whether Hetfield was preparing the ground for what was to come a few years later, when he had go into rehab and start dealing with his issues.

It is tempting, in fact, to look back on the record now as being somewhat confused, angry and revealing more of Hetfield's tortured soul than had been the case before. But then that's the beauty of hindsight. At the time, this was seen as a collection of songs left over from the 'Load' sessions and thrown out just to maintain momentum, while the band decided on their next move. But Ulrich disagreed at the time, insisting that all songs on both albums were treated equally.

"I think a lot of people think it's just the scraps, but it's not. I have to sit there and convince myself that I've written 27 songs that are all equally good. If No. 17 wasn't good enough, I'd throw it away. I believed from minute one. That's why we kept writing these fucking songs. We normally stop at 12 when we write albums, but we knew that we wanted to develop all 27 of these songs, that they were all good enough."

Released on November 18, 1997, there were elaborate marketing plans put into place to maximise the attention. Firstly, they organised a free show. For the 'Load' release, Metallica had played on the back of a flatbed truck, driving around San Francisco, something that got huge attention from MTV. Now, taking an idea from country star Garth Brooks, who'd done it in New York's Central Park, the band and their business advisors looked for a suitable location for a fully free gig. They tried to get locations in Cleveland, Boston and Detroit, but were turned down.

Eventually, they came to an agreement to do a free gig on November 11, 1997 in a parking lot in Philadelphia. Dubbed 'The Million Decibel March', it proved to be a huge publicity success. Local paper 'The Philadelphia Inquirer' said: 'It was part burlesque show, part rugby match, and hearing-loss loud. The band was profane on stage, and charming before. Police pronounced the fans better behaved than a Philadelphia Eagles crowd (the Eagles are the city's NFL team). And neighbours who feared the worst from the self-styled Loudest Band in the World complained more about the sound from the news choppers circling overhead.'

Elektra also pushed the boat out in the retail outlets, with countdown calendars, 'coming soon' banners and any sort of paraphernalia that could generate excitement and anticipation. Amusingly, the US release date for the album was the same as that for Celine Dion's 'Let's Talk About Love' – one can just envision two very different fan bases flocking to the stores!

The record label also used 'South Park' to push up sales, taking out ads during the animated hit series, which was seen as locking straight into the band's core audience.

However, there was one caveat to all of this: would the title make people think this was a re-mix record? In the end, no-one need have worried. It topped the American albums chart, going on to sell three million copies there. It went gold in the UK, shifting over 100,000 units and making number four in the charts. It was a huge seller across the globe and 'Better Than You' got the band yet another Grammy for 'Best Metal Performance'.

Tracklisting

'Fuel', 'The Memory Remains', 'Devil's Dance', 'The Unforgiven II', 'Better Than You', 'Slither', 'Carpe Diem Baby', 'Bad Seed', 'Where The Wild Things Are', 'Prince Charming', 'Low Man's Lyric', 'Attitude', 'Fixxxer'.

RIDE THE LIGHTNING

If 'Kill 'Em All' kickstarted the thrash genre, then it was with 'Ride The Lightning', the band's second record (which was released in August, 1984), that they really showed this was to be more than a passing phase. In fact, whenever diehard fans discuss just what is the greatest Metallica album of them all, the choice usually rests between this one and 'Master Of Puppets'.

'Ride The Lightning' is probably the record that bridged the gap between the ultra-fast approach of the debut and the more symphonic, epic qualities that would stand them in good stead for the next decade, thus establishing the style for which Metallica have become most respected.

After working in Rochester, New York on 'Kill 'Em All', this time the band headed for Denmark, and specifically Sweet Silence Studios in Copenhagen.

Prior to beginning work on the new record, Metallica had been in Europe, supporting Venom on their 'Seven Dates Of Hell' tour, so they didn't have far to travel.

They took their time, painstakingly getting the sounds that would make the album so different from anything else in the metal world at the time. Everyone knew that, if Metallica were to survive and prosper as a credible force, they had to break the mould, and in so doing, set fresh challenges for everyone else.

Mind you, there were problems almost immediately. The band had had equipment stolen in Boston a few months earlier, including a Marshall Amp that James Hetfield particularly loved.

Before starting in the studio, Hetfield spent ages trying to track down an amp with a similar sound. Eventually, he found one

that suited him – in a Danish music shop.

So, what's the record like? Opening with the ferocious 'Fight Fire With Fire', it was immediately clear that on this album Metallica had developed, mutated and were now ready to try something a little different. They'd even the confidence to lead listeners in this full-on attack via an acoustic start.

The title track is one of two numbers here that were co-written by the departed Dave Mustaine, although Cliff Burton's input helped to re-fashion these somewhat.

'For Whom The Bells' begins with a Burton solo – one that he'd actually composed before joining Metallica. It then opens up into a formidable anthem that complements the heavy nature of 'Ride The Lightning' itself.

'Fade To Black' might be something of a slow-pacer, almost a ballad, but spiritually it is very dark, and oppressive. If Metallica were able to vary the tempos on this album, then they never strayed too far from imagery and lyrics that were strictly downbeat. But as the first truly mournfully paced number the band had committed to tape, it immediately pushed them away from the thrash pit. However, fans had no problem embracing this as a classic, which says a lot about the dedication the band elicited at the time.

'Trapped Under Ice' is a claustrophobic nightmare, both musically and lyrically. It offers little respite, and is perhaps the song here that most closely follows the blueprint of the debut. Interestingly part of the riff was brought over to Metallica by Kirk Hammett from Exodus, his previous band.

'Escape' slows down the pace again, ending in a wail of prison sirens dealing, as it does, with an escaped prisoner. While 'Creeping Death', the song with which the band opened their set on their 'Sick Of The Studio '07' tour remains a huge fan favourite, with its biblical connotations, and the vast chorus of 'Die by my hand'. But this isn't strictly a Metallica song. It was another idea re-located by Hammett when he quit Exodus.

"The riff was Kirk's – although it did date back to his time with us – but he also took one lyrical idea," says Exodus guitarist Gary Holt. *"You know the part where it goes, 'Die by my hand'? That was an adaptation of a song I wrote called 'Dying By His Hand' – it even sounds the same. You can imagine how I feel listening to 60,000 people singing what is effectively my line! I did tackle Kirk about it once and he said, 'Man, I'm sure I asked you if that was OK'. Kirk, you didn't, and what's more, you know you didn't.*

But, it doesn't actually bother me now. Good luck to him. Of course, if I had even half-a-cent for every copy of 'Ride The Lightning' sold it would make a big difference, but I've long since forgiven him!"

The album finishes with the phenomenal instrumental 'The Call Of Ktulu', which again gives Dave Mustaine a writing credit. In fact, this is the last song on any Metallica record to acknowledge an input from the Megadeth mainman.

This song was originally called 'When Hell Freezes Over', but it's believed that Burton changed the title to one inspired by fantasy author H. P. Lovecraft, who's works he avidly read.

The whole was simply a tremendous piece of work, one that proved Metallica were world beaters in the making. The reviews were positive and there was a belief in the air that this was a pivotal moment in metal history. The band themselves knew they'd taken things up a notch or two.

"We don't want to repeat what's gone before," Ulrich said at the time. *"We've done 'Kill 'Em All'. If that's what people want, then they've got it. No, we're ready to move on. I think this will appeal to a wider audience."*

There was also an intriguing development on the business front, as Bronze Records tried to sign up the album for release in America. In fact, they were so confident of succeeding that they hired a special bus to go to all the major European festivals where Metallica were playing during the Summer of 1984, to promote the record and their involvement. But the deal never happened. In the end, Metallica signed to Elektra in the States (they were still on Music For Nations in Europe and Britain).

Looking back now, it's hard to comprehend quite what this album meant at the time. It wasn't just a crucial period for Metallica. It was also perhaps the moment when everyone stopped smirking at this silly nonsense called thrash and realised it was the future for metal.

To date, the album has sold over five million copies in the US alone, where it peaked at number 100 on the 'Billboard' chart. In the UK, it's sold over 10,000 copies, reaching number 87 in the charts at the time.

Incidentally, on the first pressing a bad mistake was made, and 400 copies were printed with a green sleeve instead of the blue one we know and love today. If you've got one of these, then you're holding onto a real collector's item.

Summing up the album at the time, Ulrich said:

"This time we've learnt that it is possible to slow down the pace, without losing any power. We have got intensity still, but there's also subtlety. It's moving in a new direction."

Tracklisting

'Fight Fire With Fire', 'Ride The Lightning', 'For Whom The Bell Tolls', 'Fade To Black', 'Trapped Under Ice', 'Escape', 'Creeping Death', 'The Call Of Ktulu'.

ROCHESTER, NEW YORK

This is where Music America Studios was based, where Metallica recorded their debut album, 'Metal Up Your Ass'. Well, that was the intended title for the record. But, under duress, the band agreed to alter it to the less contentious 'Kill 'Em All'.

ROCK AND ROLL HALL OF FAME

On March 13, 2006 Metallica were given the honour of inducting Black Sabbath into the Rock And Roll Hall Of Fame, during a ceremony at the Waldorf Astoria Hotel in New York City. Lars Ul-

rich noted that every heavy band owed a debt to the Sabs: "I wonder how many times on this very night in the last 20 years that the words 'If it weren't for you, we wouldn't be here' have been uttered. Well, here we go once more. Bill, Geezer, Ozzy, and Tony - if it weren't for you, we wouldn't be here."

James Hetfield added that the band were crucial and central to all of metal and hard rock:

"Never have I known a more timeless and influential band. They have spread their wonderful disease through generations of musicians. They are always listed as an influence by heavy bands to this day, (and) they are loved and highly respected as the fathers of heavy music. It truly is a dream come true to induct into the Rock And Roll Hall Of Fame such a significant group of musicians – and in the words of our fearless leader Ozzy Osbourne,

'Let's go f**king CRAZY!' Here is Black Sabbath!"

Metallica paid a further tribute to Sabbath on this occasion by performing the songs 'Hole In The Sky' and 'Iron Man'.

Incidentally, the main criterion for being eligible for induction into the Hall Of Fame is that you must have had at least a 25-year career – Metallica now qualify.

ROCK, BOB

The producer who's most associated with Metallica, Bob Rock worked with them from the landmark 'Black Album', through to the controversial 'St. Anger'. But who is Bob Rock?

Born in Winnipeg, Canada, he first got noticed as guitarist with 1980s band The Payolas, who had a huge hit with 'Eyes Of A Stranger'. Subsequently, he also worked with Payolas singer Paul Hyde in a project called Rock & Hyde who had a hit with the song 'Dirty Water'. In the late '80s he fronted his own heavy rock act, Rockhead, but with little success.

However, he really made his name as a producer. Starting out as an assistant at Little Mountain Studio in Vancouver, he has worked with a string of artists over the years, including Bon Jovi, Aerosmith, Motley Crue, Quireboys, Cher, Skid Row, David Lee Roth and the Lostprophets.

But he is perhaps most famously connected with Metallica, although if the band had carried through their original plan, Rock would only have been brought in to mix 'The Black Album', which the group intended to produce themselves. And what brought him to their attention? The sound quality on Motley Crue's 'Dr. Feelgood'.

"There was something about the way that record sounded that was . . . fuck! Major hard-on,'"

Lars Ulrich said at the time.

However, Rock turned down the whole idea of being simply a mixing engineer, and insisted that he either produce the project from the start, or he wasn't interested. Ulrich:

"He'd seen us live on the '... Justice tour'. He loved our shit, and loved the fact of a band that was on the edge. But he felt we'd never captured in the studio what we could get across live. We told him how we recorded in the studio, and he fell off his chair laughing. 'Is it actually possible for all four of you to be in the studio at the same time?'"

But if Rock's high point was 'The Black Album', then he was also responsible for the perceived disaster of 'St. Anger', a time he recalled as follows: "Metallica had all these problems personally, and they never wanted to be with each other in the same room, or speak to each other again. They broke up. There was a couple of weeks to a month where it was over.

"I was there as a friend and not as a producer, and if I made a mistake – that was it. I didn't do what other guys would do which is say, 'Just phone me when you got the songs'. There are producers that do that. They don't

really do anything; they go, 'Just write the songs and when they're good, I'll record them'. I didn't do that – these guys are my friends. I love these guys. They're falling apart, and I've got to be with them, so be it.

"I stuck with them for two-and-a-half years of my life, because they needed someone. We stuck together, and basically what Metallica fans have got to realize is that 'St. Anger' is the reason why they're still a band, and if I was the sacrificial lamb then so be it. I'd rather have those guys now, as human beings, and me not work with them than anything. They're just a huge band and amazing musicians. I've nothing, but great things to say about them."

'St. Anger' marked the end of the alliance between Rock and Metallica. But there's no doubt that, commercially, he was at the helm for the band's most productive period.

ROCK STAR SUPERNOVA

A misfiring 'supergroup' featuring Jason Newsted, Motley Crue drummer Tommy Lee and former Guns n' Roses guitarist Gilby Clarke, this trio were put together for the second series by US reality TV show 'Rock Star', the idea being that they would then audition hopefuls for the singing slot, and one lucky person would get to record an album and tour with the band.

After 11 episodes, Canadian Lukas Rossi was the man who emerged as the winner. But neither the subsequent, self-titled album, nor the tour were a success.

Newsted, in fact, missed the tour through a shoulder injury, and was replaced by ex-Black Crowes man Johnny Colt.

RODS

From the East Coast of America, The Rods were a trio who seemed destined for great things at the start of the 1980s. But they never happened. In Metallica terms, their claim to fame is that they were due to tour the UK in March 1984 with James Hetfield, Lars Ulrich, Cliff Burton and Kirk Hammett, a series of dates that was also due to feature Canadians, Exciter. Dubbed 'Hell On Earth', sponsored by 'Kerrang!' magazine and organised by record company Music For Nations, anticipation was high – but the tour was scrapped, due to poor ticket sales.

Said Gem Howard, Metallica's tour manager at the time:

"About two weeks before the start of the tour we noticed to our dismay that our best-selling show was the Newcastle Mayfair where we'd sold a massive 14 tickets. It was at that moment that we thought the tour might not be

the success we wanted it to be, so we cancelled it immediately."

It may be difficult to believe now, but that was the reality back then. In the end, Metallica did two sold-out shows of their own at the Marquee Club in London, on March 14 and 27. The problem was that the band had taken time out of Sweet Silence Studios to do the tour – they were working on the 'Ride The Lightning album – and couldn't get back in for a while. Exciter ended up playing one show at a club called the Royal Standard in Walthamstow, North London.

The Rods were led by pint-sized guitarist/vocalist David 'Rock' Feinstein, a cousin of Ronnie James Dio. The pair played together in Elf, which ended when Ritchie Blackmore recruited almost the whole band for the first incarnation of Rainbow – Feinstein wasn't included, and retired to consider his next step.

The Rods actually started out as David Feinstein's Thunder, with bassist Joey De Maio and drummer Carl Candey. Musically, though, De Maio's ethos was at odds with that of Feinstein. So the bassist went on to form Manowar, while Candey stuck with the guitarist.

Settling on the name The Rods, the new bassist Steve Starmer lasted long enough to work on the band's debut album 'Rock Hard', before being replaced by ex-Rainbow man Craig Gruber, and then Gary Bordonaro. Originally on their own Primal label, the record was picked by Arista, and revamped with two new songs featuring Bordonaro. It was also re-titled 'The Rods'. Such was the buzz on the band that they got the chance to support Iron Maiden in Europe during 1982, before recording their second album 'Wild Dogs'.

But all the expectation and potential was never fully realised. Despite a decent run of albums, they split in 1990, with Feinstein effectively retiring to run two restaurants. However, as the 21st century dawned, he returned with a solo album and then new band Feinstein, before teaming up again with Candey and Bordonaro for a Rods re-union at the Wacken Festival in Germany during 2004.

Maybe it's time to re-visit 'Hell On Earth' – except that this time it's doubtful whether The Rods would headline over Metallica!

www.rockfeinstein.com

RONNIE

This is a song from the 'Load' album, originally to be titled 'Dusty', with lyrics inspired – if that's the right term – by a shooting at a Washington school in 1995. The villain of the piece was one Ronnie Brown, also known as Ronnie Frown. It wasn't until the Colombine tragedy in 1999 that people really started to notice the subject matter referred to in this song.

However, in a bizarre twist, killer Ronnie Pituch, sentenced to 50 years in jail during 2005 for murdering his mother and an 11-year-old boy, claimed that Metallica were, in fact, talking about him – despite the fact he'd committed his crimes several years after the song was written. Pituch, who said he was possessed by the devil, seemed to empathise with 'Ronnie's' theme, about a loner who committed murder.

On a lighter note, there are those who've tried to suggest that, as there is a musical similarity to classic era Rainbow on this track,

the 'Ronnie' is in fact also a reference to Ronnie James Dio, vocalist with Rainbow in the 1970s.

RON MCGOVNEY'S GARAGE DEMO

The name given to a demo that was recorded in bassist Ron Mc-Govney's garage on March 14, 1982. This was the band's first attempt at making a demo tape, and, while it didn't get much circulation, it certainly was the start of something major.

The band's line-up at the time was McGovney, James Hetfield on vocals and rhythm guitar, Dave

Mustaine on lead guitar and Lars Ulrich on drums.

Altogether the fledgling band cut eight tracks, only two of which were originals. These were 'Hit The Lights' and 'Jump In The Fire'. Amazingly, not only did they make it on to the 'Power Metal', 'No Life 'Til Leather' and 'Metal Up Your Ass' demos, but also survived to take their place on the debut album, 'Kill 'Em All'.

In addition, the band did six covers. These were 'Killing Time' from Irish band Sweet Savage, 'Let It Loose' by Savage (an English band who were not related at all to Sweet Savage) and Diamond Head's 'Sucking My Love', 'The Prince', 'Am I Evil?' and 'Helpless.

Of the covers, only 'Sucking My Love' and 'Let It Loose' failed to make the 'Garage Inc.' record.

The whole process was a little primitive. They recorded onto a ghetto blaster (worth all of $49), which was suspended in the air, while Hetfield sang through a guitar amp.

But, as McGovney explains, this demo helped them to get the gig with Saxon at the Whiskey A-Go-Go in Los Angeles that was to give them a major boost.

"We'd heard that Saxon was gonna be playing the Whiskey in Hollywood. So I went over to the club with our demo, and as I was walking up, I ran into (drummer) Tommy Lee and (singer) Vince Neil from Motley Crue. I told them that Saxon was doing

a gig at the Whiskey and I wanted to try to get my band to open up for them. They said, 'Yeah, we were gonna open up for them, but we're getting too big to open. Come on in, and we'll introduce you to the chick that does the booking. So I dropped off the tape, and she called me back the very next day."

Ratt were booked to open on the first night, but Metallica got the second one – all thanks to the chance meeting with Motley Crue. And it was only the young metal band's third ever show.

Interestingly, McGovney recalls that the tape he took up to the Whiskey featured only three of the songs recorded in his garage, these being 'Hit The Lights', 'Let It Loose' and 'Killing Time'.

ROSSINGTON, GARY

The Lynyrd Skynyrd guitarist had the distinction of playing on a Metallica track. He guested on the song 'Tuesday's Gone', one he knew well, as it was no less than a cover of a Lynyrd Skynyrd classic, one that he'd co-written. Rossington played guitar on this and the track features on 'Garage Inc.'.

Rossington himself is one of the elite of southern rock. He actually co-founded Lynyrd Skynyrd in 1964, with pals Ronnie Van Zant, Allen Collins, Larry Junstrom and Bob Burns. And Rossington was an ever-present as the band became a major force in the rock world.

In 1976, the guitarist crashed his car into an oak tree, while under the influence of alcohol and drugs. The rest of the band were not amused, as his injuries meant the postponement of a planned tour. They actually fined him $5,000 and Van Zant and Collins wrote the song 'That Smell' about him; this appears on the 'Street Survivors' album.

Rossington learnt his lesson, though, give up his addictions, and declared future Skynyrd tours would be free of drugs and booze. Of course, in October 1977 the band were torn apart by a fateful plan crash that killed Van Zant, guitarist Steve Gaines and backing singer Cassie Gaines, Steve's sister. Skynyrd split up for ten years during which time Rossington and Collins started the Rossington-Collins Band with the former's wife Dale Krantz on vo-

cals. But, after two albums, they split up, following the death of Collins' wife, Katie.

Today, he tours with the reformed Skynyrd, although in recent times he has also been battling against illness. Rossington remains one of only two members of the 1970s-vintage Skynyrd in the current line-up, the other being keyboard player Billy Powell. Bassist Leon Wilkeson and Allen Collins have also since passed away.

RUBIN, RICK

The man seemingly now charged with revitalising Metallica's career, Rick Rubin has proven in the past to have the magic touch. He was the producer behind Slayer's most celebrated album, 'Reign In Blood'. He worked miracles with both Neil Diamond and Johnny Cash, was the pioneering spirit that drove the Beastie Boys and also re-vamped The Cult's sound on 'Electric'.

Born Frederick Jay Rubin in 1963, the young Rick showed his entrepreneurial instincts by starting up Def Jam Records while still at school. The label's first release was a band called Hose, punks influenced by the likes of Flipper, featuring Rubin himself on guitar.

Rubin's dabble out front was short-lived, and he quickly discovered the joys of hip-hop, through an association with DJ Jazzy Jay of Zulu Nation. Through Jazzy Jay,

Rubin met promoter Russell Simmons, and the pair really set about putting Def Jam on the map. The first serious release was LL Cool J's 'I Need A Beat'. Over the next few years, things really took off, as Public Enemy, Run-DMC and the Beastie Boys all signed up for a dose of the Rubin magic. It was his idea for Run-DMC to cover Aerosmith's 'Walk This Way', and to get the latter's Steven Tyler and Joe Perry to guest – that, of itself, revived Aerosmith's flagging career.

By 1988, Simmons and Rubin had parted. Now, Rubin created the Def American imprint, in the process working with significant rock and metal acts such as Slayer, Dazing and Masters Of Reality. He also produced the breakthrough album for the Red Hot Chilli Peppers, namely 'Blood Sugar Sex Magic'.

In 1994, he coaxed the legendary Johnny Cash into the studio for 'American Recordings', the album that gave his career a timely boost. It won Cash a Grammy and proved – along with his work with Mick Jigger, Tom Petty and Donovan – that Rubin could get something extra out of established artists. AC/DC even turned to him for the 'Ballbreaker' album.

Very much in demand, he's already contracted to work with both Slipknot and U2 in the near future. So it was to Rubin that Metallica turned in their determination to re-discover their essence. In many ways, Rubin has always been at his best when working with stressed artists who seem to have hit the buffers. From Johnny Cash to the Red Hot Chilli Peppers, and Neil Diamond to The Cult, he has succeeded in putting them back on track. However, there is a down side to Rubin, in that the trick only seems to work once with any artist. As Slayer discovered after 'Reign In Blood', it's as if he removes himself from the battlefield after one foray, almost

bored. Having worked the spell once, he's no desire to repeat.

But, this will surely be to Metallica's advantage. We await the results.

RUTHIE'S INN

This was the venue in Berkeley, California, where Metallica, among many young metal luminaries, played during the early part of their career. Other thrash bands to appear included Megadeth, Exodus, Possessed and Death Angel. This all happened between 1983-87. In actuality, the venue was more renowned for being a punk-friendly club than for its metal affiliations.

The club was converted into a restaurant called Roundtree's in 2002.

S&M

This is the title of the orchestral album recorded by Metallica with the San Francisco Symphony Orchestra at two shows, on April 21 and 22 1999, in SF. The orchestra was conducted by Michael Kamen, who in terms of rock music, already had a catalogue of top names on his CV, including Pink Floyd, Queen, Eric Clapton, Aerosmith, Rush, David Bowie and Queensryche.

The band's set spanned their career to that date, from 'Ride The Lightning' to 'ReLoad', and also featured two new songs, 'No Leaf Clover' and '- Human'.

"Michael Kamen came to us with the idea almost two years ago," said James Hetfield in 1999. *"He'd done projects with other rock people, like David Bowie, Eric Clapton and Pink Floyd. He wanted to get a little more extreme, so he chose us. I'm sure there's something more extreme – he could have picked, like, Graveworm – but I think we were a pretty good choice. We said, 'Hell, yeah'. You don't pass these things up. It took two years to pull together – from the initial idea to deciding which orchestra, to picking the songs. "We really had a big problem choosing songs. Nobody really could imagine what would work and what would not. We were tossing ideas and songs around and around. For example, we wanted to leave out 'Enter Sandman' because we thought our fans wouldn't like it in a classical arrangement, but Michael had such a great arrangement that we had to give in, we just didn't have any other choice. Then we thought we'd give 'The Unforgiven' a try, but it just didn't work. Even Michael couldn't do anything with it."*
"I say let Metallica be Metallica, and let the Symphony be the Symphony," said Kamen. *"The two have more in common than not. But Metallica will need to go full-tilt to be heard over a 100-piece orchestra!"*

The shows happened at the Berkeley Community Theatre in California. But not all of the audience were impressed. Some of the season ticket holders (those who had seats for the more traditional classical recitals at the venue) didn't come back after the interval. Hetfield described such people as, "Musical elitists... but at least we got in their faces for half-an-hour." One of these was famed director Francis Ford Coppolla.

Apart from recording the shows, Metallica also filmed them. Directed by Wayne Isham, this was released on video (the concert only) and also on DVD (featuring a bonus 41-minute documentary, two different clips for 'No Leaf Clover' and various other sections unique to this format; the sound was also 5.1).

Released on November 23, 1999, the album reached number two on the prestigious 'Billboard' chart in the US, while 'The Call Of Ktulu' got the band a Grammy in 2001, as 'Best Rock Instrumental Performance'. In the UK, however, it only made it to number 33 on the album charts.

Metallica repeated the S&M shows in November, 1999, firstly in Berlin on the 19th, and then four days later at Madison Square Garden in New York.

Tracklisting

CD1 – 'The Ecstacy Of Gold', 'The Call Of Ktulu', 'Master Of Puppets', 'Of Wolf And Man', 'The Thing That Should Not Be', 'Fuel', 'The Memory Remains', 'No Leaf Clover', 'Hero Of The Day', 'Devil's Dance', 'Bleeding Me'.

CD2 – 'Nothing Else Matters', 'Until It Sleeps', 'For Whom The Bell Tolls', '- Human', 'Wherever I May Roam', 'The Outlaw Torn', 'Sad But true', 'One', 'Enter Sandman', 'Battery'.

ST. ANGER

No question. The most controversial album of the band's career. One that stutters and stumbles, and strips away all the pretence within Metallica. This was stark, staring horror – telling of four musicians who didn't seem to have any connection at all.

Although it topped the charts in no less than 30 countries on its release in June, 2003, sales of 'St. Anger' quickly tailed off. It seemed that the diehards – the ones that have to have everything bearing the band's name – were out in force very early on, but when word got out about how the album sounded, many others stayed away from the temptation.

The process had actually begun in April 2001. Metallica hired a location called The Presidio in San Francisco – a converted army barracks – for the purpose of recording, building their own makeshift studio. By this time Newsted had departed and, as there was no immediate replacement, producer Bob Rock was asked to temporarily step in. Now, even though Rock had been part of the Metallica team since 'The Black Album', there was a sense that this was a band who were incomplete – and seemingly content to remain so. The tight-knit infrastructure that had boosted and bolstered Metallica in the past now had a gap – and a large one.

Just three months after starting on the album the band had to call a halt. In July, 2001, James Hetfield went into rehab, needing treatment for alcoholism and other addictions. Yet another sign that the family might have turned dysfunctional.

Eventually, the band managed to get the fraught process finished. But, as was documented on the 'Some Kind Of Monster' film, in many ways 'St. Anger' couldn't have been anything other than it was. Relationships within the band were strained to the point of snapping, and the music is sufficiently insane to reflect that dark period.

Remembering those times, James Hetfield has said: "We went from one extreme to the other; from hating each other to not talking to hugging and crying over every note… It was crazy – one to the other. They're both unrealistic. Somewhere in the middle is where we need to live, and balance is difficult at times, especially for myself, who likes the extremes, or thinks I like them.

"All the work that we went through on 'St. Anger', it was said that it was not for that album, it was for the next record, and that makes total sense. 'St.

Anger' was pretty much a statement – it felt like a purging of a feeling. And this record is more us working together – in harmony, in friction, in happiness, in sadness… all of that put together. And we're able to get through it – we've walked though fire; we know how hot it can get, and we don't need to go through there again."

The record might also have been inspired somewhat by Icelandic band Sigur Ros. After seeing them in San Francisco, Ulrich wrote them the following note:

"Thank you, thank you, thank you! We are in the studio right now struggling to make some sort of album. I'm going to go back after this completely inspired."

The album got mixed notices, but for the most part, as time has worn on, its impact has tailed off. In fact most Metallica devotees would rather forget it even exists. Prior to its release, Jason Newsted predicted that it would be a flop:

"They don't know what to do. They've not one riff idea between them. And, trust me on this, there won't be any guitar solos."

Newsted was spot on. One of the biggest criticisms was the absence of any Hammett solos. Bob Rock pitches the 'blame' squarely on the guitarist's shoulders:

"The truth is that Kirk had a chance to do a solo on every one of the songs. The only thing we said is, 'If the solo doesn't add something – then we're not going to add it'. That's the truth. It was like, 'Kirk, you've got as much time as you want. Come up with something original and great... That doesn't date it'. They were just trying to reach for something new and basically every time he did a solo, we all said, 'No, it's better without'. And it came down to nothing is really sounding great so let's not have solos."

The other massive downer was the truly appalling drum sound. Ulrich tried to defend himself by claiming that if this had been used on 'Master Of Puppets', then everyone would have copied it. Wrong! If that had been the case, then Metallica might well have buried themselves then and there. Here's what Bob Rock had to say:

"It was the fact that there were NO real songs. That was because the guy who writes the songs couldn't do it, because of where he was personally. So, what 'St. Anger' became was

what the band could do at that point, and it is exactly that. It was riffs strung together. The way I look at it was like raw power or a garage band. It was just riffs. It was garage band and that was supposed to sound like that, and what I learned out of it is that people in metal just don't want it to change."

Typical of the sort of reception the band were getting at the time was the album review in 'Rolling Stone' magazine. It pointed out that Metallica had lost their way, and spent the previous decade trying to re-discover their roots. The reviewer, Barry Walters, praises the band for being more brutal and ferocious here than had been the case for many years, but concludes that this is more of a masterful retreat than a breakthrough to a new era.

Inevitably, the band went out on tour determined to break in the new songs. But slowly Hetfield in particular began to back away from the album, with only Ulrich steadfastly defending its worth and value. And when, during 2007, the band took time off from recording their new album to do a brief tour ('Sick Of The Studio '07'), it was significant that not one song from 'St. Anger' was included – and no-one complained.

Released on June 5, 2003, 'St. Anger' topped the 'Billboard' charts in America, and made it to number three in the UK.

Tracklisting

'Frantic', 'St. Anger', 'Some Kind Of Monster', 'Dirty Window', 'Invisible Kid', 'My World', 'Shoot Me Again', 'Sweet Amber', 'The Unnamed Feeling', 'Purify', 'All Within My Hands'.

ST. ANGER (SINGLE)

This was released in 2003, and made number 76 in America, but hit number nine in the UK. It came in three formats, as follows:

CD Single 1 – 'St. Anger', 'Commando' (Ramones cover), 'Today You Love, Tomorrow The World' (Ramones cover), 'St. Anger' (radio edit).

CD Single 2 – 'St. Anger', 'Now I Wanna Sniff Some Glue' (Ramones cover), 'Cretin Hop' (Ramones cover), 'St. Anger' (music video).

12 inch vinyl – 'St. Anger', 'We're A Happy Family' (Ramones cover).*

SABBRA CADABRA (BLACK SABBATH)

This is a track from the Black Sabbath album 'Sabbath Bloody Sabbath', released in 1973. At Lars Ulrich's suggestion it was covered by Metallica for the 'Garage Inc.' album. However, what Metallica did wasn't just 'Sabbra Cadabra'. They also added in part of another Sabbath song of the same vintage, 'A National Acrobat'. The band wanted to record a Sabbath number, but not something wholly obvious.

Says Ulrich of the choice:

"I remember on the 'Load' tour, talking with Kirk about this project one night in Frankfurt, staying up and watching the sun rise, and saying, 'If we do any Sabbath, it's got to be 'Sabbra Cadabra''. Black Sabbath were not a direct influence on our music – they had been going for too long. But they were a big influence on the four of us as we were growing up."

It has been claimed by some that the Sabbath original actually contains backwards messages – but, like most of these accusations, there seems to be very little evidence to support this.

Metallica's version does feature one of those moments when lyrics are misheard. The actual words you're listening to are: 'You have to let your body sleep, to let your soul live on'. However, this can been heard as: 'You have to let your body sleep, to let your soul evolve'.

SAD BUT TRUE

A song from 'The Black Album', this was also released a single – the fifth one to be taken from the record.

Lyrically, it was inspired by the 1978 movie 'Magic', a psychological thriller written by the celebrated William Goldman and starring Anthony Hopkins and Ann-Margaret. Hopkins plays ventriloquist Corky, who suffers from multiple personality disorder, and believes his dummy, Fats, talks to him. Murder and intrigue follow – but is it really the dummy who's behind all the twists, or is it Corky?

Well, that's the premise on which Metallica based the song, which musically is very melodic, and pitches an insistent bass riff against some heavy yet tuneful guitars.

Kid Rock actually sampled this track for his own 'American Badass', and Snoop Dogg performed a snippet when he appeared on the 'MTV Icons' programme in 2003, a show which paid tribute to Metallica.

There's also an Internet-based Metallica tribute band called Sad But True. The band features musicians from across America, united in cyberspace by a love of Metallica. You'll find their website at www.sadbuttrue-band.com – and they offer free downloads of Metallica covers.

The single version of the song, released in 1992, reached number 98 on the Top 100 in America, and number 20 in Britain.

SAN FRANCISCO

This is the city most associated with Metallica, even though they actually formed in Los Angeles. It was Cliff Burton who persuaded Lars Ulrich and James Hetfield to re-locate to the SF – in fact he made this a condition of leaving Trauma for Metallica.

San Francisco is always regarded as being more like a European city than Los Angeles, and a lot more laidback. But in the 1980s SF's Bay Area was unquestionably the Mecca for the growing metal scene in the States.

It was here that so many of the genre's most revered names started out. From Testament to Exodus, Possessed to Death Angel.

There were also a number of venues that would become legendary through their connection to the scene. The Stone is where Cliff Burton made his live debut with Metallica, on March 5, 1982. Two weeks later, the band were back at the venue, and parts of their performance that night were filmed and used in the 'Cliff 'Em All' video.

Ruthie's Inn in Berkeley gave early opportunities to bands like Metallica, Megadeth, Exodus and Death Angel, and was a hub for thrash until about 1987. These days it's a restaurant called Roundtree's.

Elsewhere in the city, Metallica played two shows at the Kabuki Theatre in 1985, and The Warfield also embraced thrash in the 1980s.

So, why did the Bay Area become such a hotbed for this sort of music? Rick Ernst, producer of the 'Get Thrashed' documentary says:

"I grew up in New York so I would read stories about it in magazines such as 'Metal Forces'. It seemed like such an incredible place for thrash, and being a New Yorker, I would buy any album from a bay area thrash band and 99 per cent of them were awesome; there was just something in the air out there that made these bands so good. Having filmed in the bay area and having hung out with fans, bands etc. I can tell you I'm blown away by how tight knit the thrash community is out there. It's indescribably cool, amazing actually."

SAN FRANCISCO SYMPHONY ORCHESTRA

The orchestra used by Metallica on the 'S&M' album, in this case conducted by Michael Kamen. The orchestra was started at the beginning of the 20th century and was then conducted by Henry Hadley, who also founded the Seattle Symphony Orchestra.

During the mid-1930s, as The Great Depression took hold in America, the orchestra's very existence came under threat, and a public fund was set up to raise the necessary money to keep it functioning.

It was the association with Metallica – as well as other rock giants – that introduced the orchestra to a wider audience than ever. But the 'S&M' album was far from their first. In fact, they released a record as far back as 1925, some 14 years after its founding. This was an acoustic piece by French composer Daniel Francois Esprit Auber called 'Fra Diavolo'.

SATENSTEIN, SKYLAR

Lars Ulrich's second wife, Satenstein was born on June 23, 1971. The pair got married in Las Vegas on January 26, 1997.

Said Ulrich:

"When I proposed, we'd known each other for 254 days, so I had it set up that they would bring

out 255 roses – one for each day we had knows each other, and one for the future."

The couple got divorced in July 2004, after four months' separation. They have two sons: Myles (born in 1998), and Layne (born three years later).

SATRIANI, JOE

One of the most respected and acclaimed guitarists in rock, Satriani taught guitar for a time at a music store in San Francisco – and Kirk Hammett was amongst his most celebrated pupils.

SCARY GUY

The skull-based logo which adorned both the 'Live At Wembley' three-track CD and also the 'Live Shit: Binge & Purge' box set. It was created by James Hetfield and was also used on other merchandise at the time. A stencil for the logo was included with the 'Live Shit...' release.

SCRAP METAL

A one-off band featuring members of Metallica's road crew, they appeared at the Aardshock Festival in Zwolle, Holland in 1987 where they played a covers set. Metallica headlined the event.

SEEK AND DESTROY

A real fan favourite, this appears on the debut album 'Kill 'Em All'. Heavily influenced by the Diamond Head track 'Dead Reckoning', it deals with the desire to kill someone out of a thirst for revenge – but someone who does deserve to die.

In the early 1990s, the band took to stretching the song to more than 15 minutes in length, as they jammed along at the end, while the crowd were urged to shout out 'Seek & Destroy!' as a constant mantra.

It has also been used as the intro music for two wrestlers, namely WCW star Sting and AAA man Cibernetico.

Virtually an ever present in the Metallica live show for the past 25 years, you can hear stage versions on the DVD 'Cliff 'Em All' and also as part of the 'Live Shit: Binge & Purge' box set, where Jason Newsted does lead vocals.

One interesting fact is that Kirk Hammett's studio guitar solo seems to feature a 'bum' note. Listen about three minutes and 46 seconds in, and you'll hear this odd moment. Hammett has since apologised, admitting it was a mistake that wasn't corrected.

Amusingly, this song was also referred to under the title 'She Can Destroy' in the band's early days. This was due to 'Kerrang!' journalist Xavier Russell, seeing the track performed live and mishearing what it was called.

SEGER, BOB

Born in Detroit, Seger spent years slogging away on the local circuit, before finding huge suc-

cess in the 1970s with The Silver Bullet Band. Seger formed the band in 1974 and had a minor hit with 'Get Out Of Denver' that same year. In 1975 the song 'Katmandu', from the album 'Beautiful Loser', took him to number 43 in the US singles charts. It was the 'Live Bullet' album in 1976 that really broke Seger and the Silver Bullet boys. It was a major commercial success, thanks in no small measure to 'Turn The Page'. Originally on the 'Back In '72' record, this is the track that Metallica chose to cover for the 'Garage Inc.' project. But back to Seger.

In 1977, both the album and single entitled 'Night Moves' were huge successes. The former went into the Top Ten, while the latter made it to number four. A year later the 'Stranger In Town' album had no less than three big hits: 'Still The Same', 'Hollywood Nights' and 'We've Got Tonight'. And he made it to the top of the album charts in 1980 with 'Against The Wind'.

However, the prevailing winds of musical change, together with the onset of the MTV generation, hit Seger hard. He went into a steep and rapid decline, and all but disappeared with albums and tours happening only sporadically. But he's since enjoyed an upswing in fortunes with the album 'Face The Promise' selling remarkably well, and the accompanying US tour a sell-out. He also guested on the song 'Land-

ing In London', which was on the 3 Doors Down album 'Seventeen Days', released in 2005.

Metallica's cover of 'Turn The Page' also helped introduce Bob Seger to a new audience, one that had perhaps never appreciated his depth and talent – until, that is, 'Garage Inc.' gave him a certain cachet.

www.bobseger.com

SENATE JUDICIARY COMMITTEE

On July 11, 2000, Lars Ulrich provided a statement for the Senate Judiciary Committee looking into the future of the Internet and how it might affect copyright. The following is the statement in full. There is no better way of indicating where Metallica stood on the issue.

"Mr. Chairman, Senator Leahy, Members of the Committee, my name is Lars Ulrich. I was born in Denmark. In 1980, as a teenager, my parents and I came to America. I started a band named Metallica in 1981 with my best friend James Hetfield. By 1983 we had released our first record, and by 1985 we were no longer living below the poverty line. Since then, we've been very fortunate to achieve a great level of success in the music business throughout the world. It's the classic American dream

come true. I'm very honoured to be here in this country, and to appear in front of the Senate Judiciary Committee today.

"Earlier this year, while completing work on a song for the movie 'Mission: Impossible II', we were startled to hear reports that a work-in-progress version was already being played on some US radio stations. We traced the source of this leak to a corporation called Napster. Additionally, we learned that all of our previously recorded copyrighted songs were, via Napster, available for anyone around the world to download from the Internet in a digital format known as MP3. As you are probably aware, we became the first artists to sue Napster, and have been quite vocal about it as well. That's undoubtedly why you invited me to this hearing.

"We have many issues with Napster. First and foremost: Napster hijacked our music without asking. They never sought our permission – our catalogue of music simply became available as free downloads on the Napster system.

"I don't have a problem with any artist voluntarily distributing his or her songs through any means the artist elects, at no cost to the consumer, if that's what the artist wants. But just like a carpenter who crafts a table gets to decide whether to keep it, sell it or give it away, shouldn't we have the same options? My band authored the

music which is Napster's life-blood. We should decide what happens to it, not Napster – a company with no rights in our recordings, which never invested a penny in Metallica's music or had anything to do with its creation. The choice has been taken away from us.

"What about the users of Napster, the music consumers? It's like each of them won one of those contests where you get turned loose in a store for five minutes and get to keep everything you can load into your shopping cart. With Napster, though, there's no time limit and everyone's a winner – except the artist. Every song by every artist is available for download at no cost and, of course, with no payment to the artist, the songwriter or the copyright holder.

"If you're not fortunate enough to own a computer, there's only one way to assemble a music collection the equivalent of a Napster user's: theft. Walk into a record store, grab what you want and walk out. The difference is that the familiar phrase a computer user hears, 'File's done' is replaced by another familiar phrase: 'You're under arrest'.

"Since what I do is make music, let's talk about the recording artist for a moment. When Metallica makes an album we spend many months and many hundreds of thousands of our own dollars writing and recording. We also contribute our in-spiration and perspiration. It's what we do for a living. Even though we're passionate about it, it's our job.

"We typically employ a record producer, recording engineers, programmers, assistants and, occasionally, other musicians. We rent time for months at recording studios which are owned by small businessmen who have risked their own capital to buy, maintain and constantly upgrade very expensive equipment and facilities. Our record releases are supported by hundreds of record company employees and provide programming for numerous radio and television stations. Add it all up and you have an industry with many jobs – a very few glamorous ones like ours, and a greater number of demanding ones covering all levels of the pay scale for wages which support families and contribute to our economy.

"Remember too, that my band, Metallica, is fortunate enough to make a great living from what it does. Most artists are barely earning a decent wage and need every source of revenue available to scrape by. Also keep in mind that the primary source of income for most songwriters is from the sale of records. Every time a Napster enthusiast downloads a song, it takes money from the pockets of all these members of the creative community.

"It's clear, then, that if music is free for downloading, the music industry is not viable; all the jobs I just talked about will be lost and the diverse voices of the artists will disappear. The argument I hear a lot, that 'Music should be free', must then mean that musicians should work for free. Nobody else works for free. Why should musicians?

"In economic terms, music is referred to as intellectual property, as are films, television programmes, books, computer software, video games, and the like. As a nation, the US has excelled in the creation of intellectual property, and collectively, it is this country's most valuable export.

"The backbone for the success of our intellectual property business is the protection that Congress has provided with the copyright statutes. No information-based industry can thrive without this protection. Our current political dialogue about trade with China is focused on how we must get that country to respect and enforce copyrights. How can we continue to take that position if we let our own copyright laws wither in the face of technology?

"Make no mistake, Metallica is not anti-technology. When we made our first album, the majority of sales were in the vinyl record format. By the late 1980s, cassette sales accounted for over 50% of the market. Now, the compact disc dominates. If the next format is a form of digital downloading from the Internet with distribution and manufacturing savings passed on to the American consumer, then, of course, we will embrace that format too.

"But how can we embrace a new format and sell our music for a fair price when someone, with a few lines of code, and no investment costs, creative input or marketing expenses, simply gives it away? How does this square with the level playing field of the capitalist system? In Napster's brave new world, what free market economy models support our ability to compete? The touted 'new paradigm' that the Internet gurus tell us we Luddites must adopt sounds to me like old-fashioned trafficking in stolen goods.

"We have to find a way to welcome the technological advances and cost savings of the Internet, while not destroying the artistic diversity and the international success that has made our intellectual property industries the greatest in the world. Allowing our copyright protections to deteriorate is, in my view, bad policy, both economically and artistically.

"To underscore what I've spoken about today, I'd like to read from the 'Terms of Use' section of the Napster Internet web site. When you use Napster you are basically agreeing to a contract that includes the following terms:

'This website or any portion of this web site may not be reproduced, duplicated, copied, sold, resold, or otherwise exploited for any commercial purpose that is not expressly permitted by Napster.'

'All Napster website design, text, graphics, the selection and arrangement thereof, and all Napster software are Copyright 1999-00 Napster Inc. All rights reserved Napster Inc.'

'Napster, the logo and all other trademarks, service marks and trade names of Napster appearing on this web site are owned by Napster. Napster's trademarks, logos, service marks, and trade names may not be used in connection with any product or service that is not Napster's.'

"Napster itself wants – and surely deserves – copyright and trademark protection. Metallica and other creators of music and intellectual property want, deserve and have a right to that same protection.

"In closing, I'd like to read to you from the last paragraph of a 'New York Times' column by Edward Rothstein: 'Information doesn't want to be free; only the transmission of information wants to be free. Information, like culture, is the result of a labour and devotion, investment and risk; it has a value. And nothing will lead to a more deafening cultural silence than ignoring that value and celebrating... [companies like] Napster running amok'.

"Mr. Chairman, Senator Leahy and Members of the Committee, the title of today's hearing asks the question, 'The Future of the Internet: Is there an Upside to Downloading?' My answer is, yes. However, as I hope my remarks have made clear, this can only occur when artists' choices are respected and their creative efforts protected."

SEPULTURA

The Brazilian thrashers' connection with Metallica comes through the song 'Hatred Aside', from their album 'Against'.

It was co-written by Jason Newsted, who also supplied guitar and backing vocals.

www.sepultura.uol.com.br

SERRANO, ANDRES

The image on the cover of 'Load' is called 'Blood And Semen III'. It's a photograph taken by Serrano, with an effect achieved by mixing bovine blood together with the photographer's semen, between two pieces of Plexiglas.

Born in 1950, Serrano has become infamous in his home country of America, thanks to his photos of corpses and also the 'Piss Christ', a photo of a crucifix submerged in a glass container of the artist's own urine. His talents have led him to snap members of the Ku Klux Klan, morgues and burn victims. It would seem that, for Serrano, nothing is out of bounds. He once went into the New York subway system armed with lights and photographic paper, determined to portray the homeless living there as art objects.

Serrano is especially obsessed with bodily fluids. In his time, he's used not only blood, urine and semen, but also mother's milk.

Inevitably, Serrano has been roundly condemned by some. In 1989 he was denounced by the Rev. Donald E. Wildman, who saw himself as a protector of family values and launched a major campaign against the artist's 'Piss Christ' image.

Even within Metallica there wasn't unanimity over using 'Blood And Semen III' for the 'Load' cover.

Said Hetfield at the time:

"To Kirk and Lars, it's art, and it's so deep. To me, it's just a picture some guy took. I remember when I first saw it, it was, 'So what?' Then they told me what it was, it was: 'Oh, it's definitely more interesting to me now'. But that's about it.

"I was worried about not being able to get the music into the K-marts of the world because of a cover they don't like. I think it's bullshit. I want to get music to people who want it. I want it readily available for everybody. Controversy? I don't give two shits about that."

It was Kirk Hammett and Lars Ulrich who drove the idea of

using this image for the cover. Hammett:

"We had no concept for the album; no title, no artwork. When I first saw the picture, I thought it looked like hot-rod flames, because I have a hot-rod flame tattoo."

Hammett saw the photo in a book called 'Body And Soul', and it was he who first mooted the idea. With Ulrich's enthusiastic backing, the pair got their way, with Newsted so strongly against it that, at the time, he refused to talk about it.

"I'm always trying to expand my audience, and it's great when a band like Metallica comes to me," Serrano himself said a decade ago. *"The thing about 'Semen And Blood III' is that it can function on a very abstract level. People will appreciate it for that, and not think twice about it. Maybe other people will know what it is and have a slightly different reaction."*

Metallica – or rather Hammett and Ulrich – were clearly delighted with the results, as another Serrano image – 'Piss And Blood' – was used on the cover of 'ReLoad'.

SHOOT ME AGAIN

A song that appears on the 'St. Anger' album. If you watch the footage shot of the band re-hearsing this (www.youtube.com/watch?v=eOxMu4zAOJc), it's clear that there is a hellish ferocity about the song. The performance is more fired-up than Slipknot, and stands comparison with any of the younger de-tuned demi-gods. Hetfield's vocal style is almost resigned, mirroring the lyrics which are, at times, world weary – perhaps an inevitable reflection of the fact that Hetfield was battling his personal demons at the time.

SHORTEST STRAW, THE

Metallica go political? Definitely. This song, from the '...And Justice For All' album, refers to the bigotry that was taken as normal in America during the 1950s and 1960s, when the country was still gripped by McCarthyism. It was started by Senator Joe McCarthy who denounced Communism and anyone sympathetic to that cause. He stirred up feelings of fear, loathing and pernicious hatred of anything that was different. Neighbour turned on neighbour, and black lists became the norm.

More importantly, Metallica wonder in this song whether much has changed. Can we really accept a contra viewpoint as having a right to exist?

There are those who believe the song was inspired by the spies Ethel and Julius Rosenberg, convicted of selling American nuclear secrets to the Russians. They were executed, but afterwards new evidence came to light which cast doubts on the verdict.

SLAGEL, BRIAN

This is the man who gave Metallica one of the biggest breaks in their career. In 1982 he agreed to put a track, 'Hit The Lights', on the first 'Metal Massacre' compilation album – it was the birth of a legend, but who knew at the time?

Brian Slagel grew up in Woodland Hills, California, and had an early love for heavy music. So much so that, as a teenager, he worked in a local record store called Oz.

"I was at a cousin's house when I was 11. I wasn't really all that into music back then. My cousin put on 'Machine Head' by Deep Purple, and hearing it changed my life. I was like, 'What is that?' I immediately went out and bought the record the next day, and have

pretty much been hooked on hard stuff ever since."

It was at this point that the New Wave Of British Heavy Metal was starting to take hold, giving metal a fresh, exciting focus. Not slow to see what was happening, Slagel imported some of these records and noticed that there was a growing audience for this sort of sound in America. Enthused, he started one of the first metal fanzines in the States, 'The New Heavy Metal Review'.

"Actually, I started out bootlegging. I would tape live concerts and trade. I was into the whole tape-trading thing. I would trade demos and live concerts with people around the world. That's kinda how I got turned onto the whole New Wave of British Heavy Metal. A kid that I knew in Sweden turned me onto Iron Maiden when the first Iron Maiden record came out."

In 1982 he took another step towards getting talented young bands across to the masses. He decided to release a compilation called 'The New Heavy Metal Review Presents Metal Massacre'. It was here that Metallica got that opportunity, as Lars Ulrich persuaded Slagel to give them a chance. Trivia hounds might wish to note that early pressings of the album contained the band's named misspelt as 'Mettallica'.

Alongside Metallica were the likes of Ratt, Cirith Ungol, Steeler, Bitch and Malice – all of whom

would achieve some status in the future. Slagel goes on:

"I also started writing for 'Kerrang!' and 'Sounds' magazines in England. Doing some LA correspondence stuff. I was helping out with the local heavy metal radio show, and doing all sorts of things while working at the record store. I kinda got the idea that since no one was really paying any attention to what was going on in L.A. at the time, it would be fun to do a compilation album – kinda in the spirit of the NWOBHM. I just came up with the name and I went to all of the bands and asked whether

they'd want to be on a record if I did one. They all said sure.
"Lars was a friend of mine, and he was always saying he was going to put together a band. I was like, 'Yeah, sure you are Lars'. So it is pretty amazing what happened with them. The first track was great. The only disappointment for me was that they wanted me to do the first album when they had just their demo, but I didn't have the money."

The 'Metal Massacre' album quickly sold out its initial pressing of 5000 copies. Emboldened, in 1983 Slagel became a label mogul of sorts, by founding Metal Blade.

His first batch of releases included Slayer's 'Show No Mercy', which caused an underground sensation, selling over 40,000 copies worldwide, an astonishing quantity for such an extreme band.

"We were just a bunch of fans starting out," recalls Slagel.

"I was just trying to get some coverage for metal. I never thought metal would get as big as it did. Nor did I ever think I would be doing this for this long!"

As it grew ever bigger, Slagel kept a determined hand on the reins, running Metal Blade solo

until 1988 – quite a feat. Since then it has continued to expand and adapt to modern demands, in the process earning a reputation as one of the premier metal labels on the planet. Says Slagel:

"I am still a big metal fan, so just being able to work with music that I love, that still makes it exciting. Plus, it is still a thrill to find new bands and help them get their music out. Also, I am lucky enough to work with so many great people and bands."

But, back to 'Hit The Lights', according to ex-bassist Ron McGovney, there might actually be two versions on 'Metal Massacre'…

"I believe on the very first pressing of 'Metal Massacre' they kept Lloyd Grant's lead tracks (he was the guitarist prior to Dave Mustaine). Lloyd actually only came over twice, and then they ended up recruiting Dave Mustaine on guitar. As I remember, Dave played the two leads on 'Hit The Lights', but they kept the second lead which Lloyd played because they liked it better. Now, on the second pressing of the album, it was all Dave's leads."

SLITHER

This song features on the 'Re-Load' album, released in 1997. A straightforward track, it seems to be a warning that if you go looking for trouble, then the chances are you'll find it.

SMALL HOURS, THE (HOLOCAUST)

There's little doubt that the lengthy list of bands who owe their reputation almost solely to Metallica would have to include Scotland's Holocaust close to the top. In 1987, Metallica covered their song 'The Small Hours', which was the first time many people had even heard the name Holocaust. It appeared on 'The $5.98 EP: Garage Days Re-Revisited', the record that introduced bassist Jason Newsted to the world as the new man in Metallica.

Subsequently, it appeared on the 'Garage Inc.' album.

Holocaust themselves never got beyond the stage of being a club/pub band, and owe any reputation they have to this day to Metallica.

SMITH, TONY

Metallica's tour manager for many years, and the man who also founded both their official fan club and fanzine (the latter being titled 'So What!'), which he edited for a while. He retired from working with the band in 1999 and now runs BANDitems (www.banditems.com), a site through which he sells rare memorabilia.

SNAKE

The 'Snake' logo which adorns the cover of 'The Black Album' was inspired by the Culpepper Minutemen flag, from which the legend 'Don't Tread On Me' was also taken. The flag dates back to the late 18th Century, and the snake in question is actually a rattlesnake. There were various versions of this flag but the one used by Metallica was based on the yellow one.

SNAKE PIT

The small section right at the front of the stage, created by Metallica during their 'Wherever We May Roam' arena/stadium tour in 1991-92. This allowed a select few fans to stand right under the band, thereby creating a club atmosphere within a far bigger venue.

The authors have experienced the opening of a Metallica show at both Wembley Arena and Milton Keynes Bowl in the Snake Pit, and can attest to the deafening power of the band's pyrotechnics, not to mention the heat they give off.

SOUTH PARK

The contentious animated series has two connections with Metallica. Firstly, in an episode called 'Christian Rock Hard', main characters Stan, Kyle and Kenny are arrested for illegally downloading music. Having an epiphany, they then decide to start a movement aimed at stopping the practice, and Metallica join in the protest.

The second connection involves the movie 'South Park: Bigger, Longer & Uncut' in which James Hetfield sings the number 'Hell Isn't Good' during a sequence where Kenny goes to hell.

SO WHAT (ANTI NOWHERE LEAGUE)

This was originally released in 1981 by the British punks Anti Nowhere League, as the B-side to their hard-hitting version of Ralph McTell's 'Streets Of London'. As you might have expected, the League didn't exactly spare the boot.

Apparently, it was written in a pub one night, when the band overheard two men trying to outdo each other with remarkable stories. It's a real put-down of people who try to puff up their own importance by exaggerating a story to the point of incredulity.

Inevitably, the swearing factor in the song was inordinately high, so much so that police seized all copies of the first pressing, using the Obscene Publications Act as an excuse.

Subsequently, the track has turned up on re-issues of the Anti Nowhere League album 'We Are… The League'. Metallica covered this as an extra track on the Japanese version of 'The Black Album' and for the B-side of 'The Unforgiven' single. It also appears on the 'Garage Inc.' album. On October 25, 1992, Metallica played this live for the first time at Wembley Arena. And they got Anti Nowhere League vocalist Animal to guest with them. He recalls the moment just before walking onstage:

"As I waited on the edge of the stage waiting to go on, it suddenly dawned on me I was just about to stand in front of 10,000 punters who didn't know me from Adam, and sing a song that I couldn't fucking remember… all that kept running through my head was, 'Run, you silly old fucker!'"

In addition to being a song covered by Metallica, 'So What' is also the name of their official fan club. This was started in 1993 by the band themselves, who have a very hands-on approach to it.

SOME KIND OF MONSTER

There are two distinct aspects to this entry. On the one hand, this is a song from the 'St. Anger' album. The title came from James Hetfield attempting to describe the thinking behind the lyric to producer Bob Rock, and coming out with the idea that it deals with a Frankenstein creature. Fans of the American TV series 'Supernatural' might recall that in the episode 'Phantom Traveller', one of the central characters, Dean Winchester, hums this tune to calm himself while on a flight.

The track was released as a single, and reached number 40 in the UK and number 19 on the US mainstream rock chart. It was the last single to be put out from the album.

"EPIC STORYTELLING! *Some Kind of Monster* is one of the MOST REVELATORY ROCK PORTRAITS EVER MADE."
-Owen Gleiberman, ENTERTAINMENT WEEKLY

METALLICA
SOME KIND OF MONSTER

FROM THE AWARD-WINNING FILMMAKERS OF **PARADISE LOST** AND **BROTHER'S KEEPER**

"Chronicles the intimate emotions of the most successful heavy metal band of all time.
ENTERTAINING, MOVING AND HISTORICALLY SIGNIFICANT."
-THE NEW YORK TIMES

On the other hand, 'Some Kind Of Monster' is also the title given to the documentary made around the recording of 'St. Anger', which has taken on a life of its own and really caught everyone's attention.

Producer/directors Joe Berlinger and Bruce Sinofsky were given unprecedented and unfettered access to the band, and what they found made for both fascinating footage, and also for some embarrassing moments.

"We thought we would be spending about two weeks doing behind-the-scenes stuff around the new album. But as soon as we arrived, the shit hit the fan," says Berlinger. "The band started disintegrating. But because we were friends with

Berlinger and Sinofsky

them, we convinced them to let us film it and they had the courage to let us.

"I look back at this film and I'm amazed it came to be. I'm amazed at the access they gave us, amazed the label didn't shut us down. Promotional films are intended to promote – filming people in the best of situations, not the worst of situations."

Berlinger and Sinofsky had gotten to know Metallica thanks to one of their previous projects, 'Paradise Lost'. Now the pair were brought in to make a promo style film around the new album. At first it was simply seen as a marketing tool.

"The film was originally being paid for by the record label as a promotional vehicle," recalls Berlinger. "But, as time unfolded and it became clear we had something special, the record label started forcing its will and wanting to turn this into a real-ity television show, timed to the release of the album. And we all felt like, 'Well, the beauty of this film is that it was completely unplanned', and if we turn it into a reality TV show like 'The Osbournes', it would trivialise and cheapen the material, and it would make it seem like this was the plan from the start. 'Oh, let's go into therapy and turn it into a reality show', which would have destroyed the integrity and the credibility of the material."

So, after a meeting between all parties concerned, Metallica decided to foot the bill themselves, and keep the cameras rolling everywhere. It cost them $2 million just to buy the rights to what had been done up until that point. What the directorial pair ended up with was literally hours of footage documenting a band falling apart. They had arguments between all of the members, Lars discussing tracks with his father and former tennis professional Torben Ulrich advising his son on what songs to put on the record. And most damning of all, it chronicled the way that 'performance enhancing coach' Phil Towle makes himself indispensable to the whole process of making the album.

Brought in by the band's management, Q.Prime Inc., to play a role in getting the band to work better as a unit, he slowly turns the situation to his advantage. Towle is sometimes referred to as a 'therapist'. Not true. He had voluntarily rescinded his licence from the Kansas Behavioral Sciences Regulatory Board a decade earlier for allegedly attempting to persuade clients to continue treatment beyond the point where it was useful. He used a similar tactic to keep himself inside the Metallica camp.

When the band decide it's time to dispense with his services, Towle responds: "We've still got some trust issues that I think we need to sort out."

The film was released in 2004, to a mixed response. One man very angry was former Metallica member Dave Mustaine. He had been filmed here confronting Lars Ulrich about issues still haunting him over his sacking two decades earlier.

"I feel that I've been used," Mustaine insists. *"The filming was very lengthy, and I asked for them to send me a copy of what was going to be used, because I was concerned how I'd come out of it. In the end, they* *didn't do that, despite giving me their word. And they've used such a brief clip in the final edit that I come across really badly. Yet again, I've been betrayed by Metallica."*

SQUINDO, TONY

An artist working with Metallica, Squindo designs T-shirts for them, having begun by doing cartoons for the 'So What!' fanzine. He has also worked with Ramones, Misfits, Korn and The Offspring and says of himself:

"In the Pennsylvania Mountains, a small cabin is a rockin'. Fuelled by pizza and supercharged by Red Bull – Tony and Wendy Groholski-Squindo are cranking out amazing artwork and photos that you need. With a turnaround time that will have your head spinning and an attention to detail that'll please the micromanager from hell, Squindo Studios."

SPASTIK CHILDREN

A real conglomerate of like-minded musicians who got together to drink heavily, wear daft clothing, make fools of themselves and generally have fun while playing a style of music that was more punk than metal. The three founding members – Fred Cotton, James McDaniel and Rich Sielert – might not be household names, but a number of those who have appeared with the Spastik Children over the years are renowned in the world of metal.

Firstly, there's James Hetfield who, under the pseudonym of Bobby Brady, played the drums and sang. Then there's Kirk Hammett, who, as Goddamn It, struck up on the bass. Jason Newsted also played bass occasionally. The original four-stringer was Cliff Burton, with both Hammett and Newsted taking the man's place when he died. And then there's

'Big' Jim Martin of Faith No More who struck up on guitar. Cotton, as Johnny Problem, was the lead vocalist, while McDaniel (alias Slucky McDonald) also played guitar. Among the songs these nutters would play in bars and clubs around North California were:

'Let Me Flush' - this is supposedly about someone whom Hetfield knew, who got drunk and just shat in his pants. The poor bloke thought that he'd only farted and not 'followed through', as it were. He had to flush his offending underwear down the bar's toilet.

'What's That Smell' - a delightfully sensitive song about farts.

'Thermos' - this is a cover of a song Steve Martin sang in the movie 'The Jerk'.

'Bra Section' - about tossing-off while browsing through the bra section of a mail order catalogue – and having your mum walk into the bathroom while you're mid-stroke.

'Benefit Baby' - about a guy who sponges food from girls.

'Cunt' - about an ex-girlfriend.

As you can readily imagine, these weren't sensitive singer-songwriters, but a bunch of muso pals out to let rip.

The band's philosophy was summed up thus:

"The concept behind Spastik Children was to have fun in as unprofessional a context as possible. Songs were written on-the-spot during practices, musicians

preferred playing instruments they had no past experience with, and the band hosted a revolving door policy of members that would come and go as desired. If the band had any kind of mission, it was merely to get as drunk as possible and see if we could still play, and abuse the crowd. That was the whole object."

SPUN

The name Metallica used when they played a secret gig at Club Kim's in San Francisco on June 4, 2002 – their first gig for over 18 months. Bob Rock stood in on bass, as the band did Ramones covers, oldies like 'Hit The Lights' and a new song called 'Dead Kennedys Roll'.

STONE COLD CRAZY (QUEEN)

One of Queen's more obviously metal-oriented numbers, this appears on their third album 'Sheer Heart Attack', released in 1974.

Although all four members of Queen are credited with writing it, in fact Freddie Mercury probably had more to do with this than the other three, having performed the track with his previous band, Wreckage. This is the first song Queen ever played live – making it a landmark indeed. However, it did undergo considerable change

before finally being ready to commit to vinyl (as it was back then).

The lyrics are all about someone daydreaming of becoming a gangster, hence the name-checks for people like Al Capone. And stylistically, it is definitely a proto-thrash song, which is presumably why it appealed to Metallica. They covered it for an album titled 'Rubaiyat', released to celebrate the 40th anniversary of their US label, Elektra and which features acts of the time covering songs by famous names who had been on the label. The track was the B-side for the single 'Enter Sandman', and features on the 'Garage Inc.' album. It also won Metallica a second Grammy in 1991 for 'Best Metal Performance'.

STONE DEAD FOREVER (MOTORHEAD)

A track originally from the Motorhead classic, 'Bomber', which was released in 1979. The album was a huge success despite being recorded under difficult circumstances – producer Jimmy Miller was increasingly under the influence of heroin, at one point disappearing from the studio, to be found asleep at the wheel of his car.

Metallica performed the song live in December 1995, as part of their set at the 'Motorheadache '95' concert, held to celebrate Lemmy's 50th birthday. It was released on the single 'Hero Of The Day' in September 1996.

STRUGGLE WITHIN, THE

The song that ends 'The Black Album', this has never been played live by Metallica. It's said to be about someone suffering from a self-defeating personality.

Some believe it to be a sequel to 'The Frayed Ends Of Sanity' from the previous album, '…And Justice For All'.

SUICIDAL TENDENCIES

The band with whom Rob Trujillo first made his name. Although born as more of a hardcore/punk band in 1981, their influence on the thrash scene has been profound.

The California band didn't have an auspicious start to their career, being voted 'Worst Band/Biggest Assholes' in 1982 by 'Flipside' magazine. But by the time the 1987 album 'Join The Army' came out, not only had their sound become more metallic (thanks, in part, to guitarist Rocky George), but they had also left behind many of the problems caused by alleged gang associations.

By 1989 Trujillo had been drafted in, and his slight funk/hip hop inspirations helped to propel the classic 1990 record 'Lights… Camera… Revolution!' which is

not only regarded as, arguably, the band's finest, but also the moment when they reached their commercial peak.

'Still Cyco After All These Years' followed in 1993 (effectively a re-recording of their rare, self-titled debut), with 'Suicidal For Life' the next year. But the group then fell apart, with Trujillo opting to join Ozzy's band.

Since then, there have been various attempted comebacks, led by perennial, yet troubled frontman Mike Muir, but nothing that's captured the imagination like the Trujillo years.

www.suicidaltendencies.com

SWEET AMBER

A track from the 'St. Anger' album. 'Amber' is street slang for heroin, and the song is said to be based on James Hetfield's time in rehab. It contains the warning that it's 'never as sweet as it seems', which is a reference to how addiction takes over your life. There are also those who believe that amber is more likely to refer to alcohol than heroin.

The fact that Amber is also a girl's name has led to speculation that, far from being a personalised letter from Hetfield about his addiction problems, it's actually more about a relationship.

Interestingly, the line 'Wash your back so you don't stab mine' was originally said by Hetfield in response to a major radio corporation in America threatening to ban Metallica from airplay because the band had refused to do a promo for them.

SWEET SAVAGE

An Irish band who briefly flirted with fame during the New Wave Of British Heavy Metal era, but have become no more than a footnote in music history. They started in Belfast during 1979, and got the opportunity over the next couple of years to support Wishbone Ash and Motorhead when they toured Ireland. In 1981, they made it to the mainland, opening for Thin Lizzy.

There are now two reasons why people recall Sweet Savage. Firstly because of guitarist Vivian Campbell. His departure in 1983 to join former Rainbow and Black Sabbath singer Ronnie James Dio in his new band, Dio, was a major blow from which the young Irish hopefuls never fully recovered. This happened just after Sweet Savage had recorded three tracks for a Radio One 'Friday Rock Show' session. These were 'Killing Time', 'Into The Night' and 'Queen's Vengeance'. It's often claimed that the debut Dio album, 'Holy Diver', features a number of songs that were, in effect, reworkings of Sweet Savage material – perhaps, given Campbell's presence, that's not a surprise.

The second reason why the band are remembered is because

Metallica covered 'Killing Time'. This appeared on the B-side of the single 'The Unforgiven' and it also features on the 'Garage Inc.' album. The huge upsurge of interest in the band following Metallica's patronage led to them re-forming in 1996, to have another stab at fame. Campbell's place was taken by 15-year-old prodigy Simon McBride. But this didn't lead to any lasting success, and Sweet Savage have remained overshadowed by their former guitarist's profile – after a stint with Whitesnake, he's now with Def Leppard – and Metallica's cover.

SWEET SILENCE STUDIOS

The famous Copenhagen studio where Metallica recorded all of their albums from 'Ride The Lightning' to '...And Justice For All'. It was built in 1976 by Freddy Hansson and Flemming Rasmussen, the latter, of course, being closely involved with Metallica as a producer/engineer. Aside from our heroes, other luminaries such as Rainbow, Cat Stevens and Ringo Starr have recorded there. According to their official website: 'The Studio has a big recording room with enough space to record string and horn sections etc., a medium sized room and a small 'dry' room. All rooms are with windows that allow you too see/communicate between the rooms. Sweet Silence soon became famous for its good sound, and a staff of qualified engineers and producers'.

In 1999, the studio was actually moved, because the building in which it was housed was due to be demolished. Rasmussen built a new complex over a period from September 1999 to March 2000. So the current studio is not the one where Metallica did some of their finest work.

TANK

A trio from Croydon, who started out in 1980, Tank features one-time Damned member Algy Ward on bass/vocals, Pete Brabbs on guitar and his brother Mark on drums. Often regarded as being close to Motorhead in attitude and approach, their 1982 debut album, 'Filth Hounds From Hades', was produced by none other than 'Fast'

Eddie Clarke. The highlight of the album is a storming rendition of The Osmonds' 'Crazy Horses'.

Constant touring with the likes of Motorhead and Girlschool helped the band to build a strong following, something that was reinforced and underlined by their second album, 'Power Of The Hunter'. The third effort, 'This Means War', was released in 1983 on new label Music For Nations (the band's original record company, Kamaflage, having gone out of business) and saw Tank become a four-piece, with the addition of second guitarist Mick Tucker.

However, the Brabbs brothers left the band soon afterwards, replaced by Cliff Evans (formerly with blues-rockers Chicken Shack) and Graeme Crallan (ex-White Spirit, along with Janick Gers, now with Iron Maiden) on bass and drums, respectively. It was this incarnation that toured Europe in 1984 with Metallica.

This was to prove a high point on which the band could never quite capitalise. More line-up changes followed throughout the 1980s, especially on drums, with Gary Taylor (ex-Streetfighter) and Steve Clarke (previously with Fastway) each getting their chance.

Tank's cult status remains high, and a number of bands have covered their songs over the years – although Metallica have yet to join that list.

www.tankfilthhounds.net

THIN LIZZY

The great Irish band, whose version of the traditional song 'Whiskey In The Jar' was the one that inspired Metallica to cover it themselves. Lizzy started in Dublin during 1969, having a hit with the aforementioned 'Whiskey…' in 1973. But Lizzy's purple period really started after this hit, with the 'Fighting' album in 1975. From this point, until their split in 1984, the band were hugely influential and successful, their ability to improvise and innovate leaving an indelible mark.

Despite having some of the greatest guitarists of their era – Gary Moore, Brian Robertson, Scott Gorham, John Sykes – Lizzy is always seen as the domain of bassist Phil Lynott, who also had a distinctive buzz as vocalist. His clever and emotive lyrics helped to lift the band beyond cult status, and his death in January 1986 robbed the rock world of a visionary. Lizzy have re-grouped subsequently, and tour regularly, but only to play the classics. They've recorded nothing new since Lynott's death.

One of the highlights of the group's career was getting the chance to be the first band to headline a show at Slane Castle in County Meath in 1981; this is now a regular stop on the gig circuit for

major acts. The support bill that day included U2, and Lizzy finished the show with… 'Whiskey In The Jar'.

www.thin-lizzy.com

THING THAT SHOULD NOT BE, THE

A track from the 'Master Of Puppets' album and inspired by the short story 'Shadow Over Innsmouth', written in 1936 by celebrated fantasy author H.P. Lovecraft. It is actually unique among Lovercraft's short stories because this was the only one to appear in a book while he was alive; others published during his lifetime were in magazines. It was covered by Primus in 1998 on the 'Rhinoplasty' album, by Dream Theater for their official bootleg of the 'Master Of Puppets' record and again by Scottish metalheads, Mendeed in 2006, for the 'Kerrang!' magazine CD 'Master Of Puppets: Remastered', given away free with the magazine in April of that year.

Guitar fiends might be interested to know that this was the first song written by Metallica to use alternative guitar tuning. It has every guitar string tuned down a full tone, from E standard to D standard.

Primus also recorded the track for the album 'Tribute To The Four Horsemen: A Tribute To Metallica'.

THORN WITHIN

A track from the 'Load' album, which is Jason Newsted's favourite song on the record. Some interpret this as a girl having to confess to her father that she is pregnant. The embryo being the thorn within. Others see it as a guilty person seeking the salvation that he is constantly being denied.

THROUGH THE NEVER

This track from 'The Black Album' is thrashier than most on the record, but was quickly dropped from the band's live set. There's been constant speculation that this is due to James Hetfield's dislike of it. Some people have attempted to tie the song in with fantasy author H.P. Lovecraft's famous Cthulu Mythos writings, which of course gave rise to the Metallica song 'The Call Of Ktulu'. But that might be fanciful.

TOO LATE TOO LATE (MOTORHEAD)

The B-side to the Motorhead single 'Overkill'. In 1995, during the recording sessions for the 'Load' album, Metallica decided to cut versions of the Motorhead classics 'Overkill', 'Damage Case', 'Stone Dead Forever' and 'Too Late Too Late' as a birthday present to Lemmy, who was 50 on December 24 that year. Twelve months later it was included on the second CD of the 'Hero Of The Day' single, and is also on 'Garage Inc.'.

TRAUMA

The band with whom Cliff Burton started his career. Contemporaries of Metallica's, by August 1982 they were starting to get attention thanks to a one-track demo featuring the song 'Such A Shame'. It was after seeing a Trauma show at The Whiskey A-Go-Go (or The Troubadour – there is disagreement as to the actual location) in Los Angeles that Lars Ulrich and James Hetfield decided Burton was the man to replace Ron McGovney. 'Such A Shame' appeared on the 1982 compilation album 'Metal Massacre II', alongside names like Overkill, Armored Saint and Warlord. But the band never recovered from the loss of Burton.

Of major interest to Metallica fans, and students of the early days of the thrash era, is very rare footage of Trauma, which you

can access at www.simulstream. com/cliff. This was shot just three months before Burton joined Metallica. It was directed by Don Wrege, who says of Trauma:

"In the summer of 1982 I was working in Los Angeles and was contacted by a British fellow calling himself Tony. He asked me if I would be interested in directing a long-form music video for a heavy metal band he was managing out of San Francisco, called Trauma. We met and I was impressed with his enthusiasm for the band and heavy metal in general. I went to a rehearsal to check them out. What I encountered was loud, and I was immediately struck with how good the bass player (Cliff Burton) was. Their show included such interesting attractions as a scantily-clad woman in a leather S&M outfit chained to a huge cross; another girl in virginal white who was sacrificed on an altar during the song 'I Am The Warlock', and the drummer's solo during which he set his kit on fire, nearly blinding himself in the process. On the day of the shoot, as preparations were made to the studio stage, I stepped outside to have a smoke and Cliff joined me in my car. He mentioned that he didn't think he was long for the group, that they weren't motivated enough and he intended to be famous fast. That was fairly prophetic."

TRUJILLO, ROB

The bassist who replaced Jason Newsted, and whose recruitment by Metallica was regarded as something of a coup at the time. Born on October 23, 1964, in Culver City, California, Trujillo played in a number of local acts before joining Suicidal Tendencies in 1989. His more funk oriented style took Suicidal in a different direction for both 1990's 'Lights… Camera… Revolution!' album, and 'The Art Of Rebellion' two years later. Subsequently, he and Suicidal frontman Mike Muir formed the more funk-friendly offshoot, Infectious Grooves. At the end of the last decade, Trujillo joined Ozzy's band, appearing on 2001's 'Down To Earth', as well as controversially re-recording the bass lines for new versions of the 'Blizzard Of Ozz' and 'Diary Of A Madman' records, replacing Bob Daisley's efforts. He has also worked with Black Label Society, Jerry Cantrell and Glenn Tipton.

On February 24, 2003, Trujillo was to become Metallica's third bassist to record an album, following the late Cliff Burton and Jason Newsted. He made his studio debut with 'St. Anger' that same year. It's said that he was offered $1 million as an upfront fee to tempt him into the fold, money

that would be set against future earnings. His audition and recruitment feature in the documentary 'Some Kind Of Monster'.

Those who've seen Trujillo play live with Metallica over the last few years believe that he's brought a fresh dimension to their performances. This may be due to the fact that, like Burton, he prefers to play with his fingers, rather than a pick, whereas Newsted was more into the latter approach. But he has fitted seamlessly into the line-up and is more lively onstage than Newsted. Moreover, it's been suggested that the attitude of both Ulrich and Hetfield towards the new man is more inviting than was ever the case with Newsted. Trujillo has been immediately welcomed as an equal member, something Newsted himself feels that he was always denied. Perhaps Trujillo has benefitted in this respect, from Metallica learning from the mistakes made with Jason? Who can tell.

TRUMBO, DALTON

A controversial figure, Trumbo was a 20th century novelist and screenwriter, whose book 'Johnny Got His Gun' directly inspired the Metallica song 'One'. Famous in the 1940s for working on the scripts for movies like 'Kitty Foyle', 'Thirty Seconds Over Tokyo' and 'Our Vines Have Tender Grapes', he hit the headlines in 1947, when he refused to tes-

tify about Communist activities in Hollywood before the House UnAmerican Activities Committee, part of the Communist purge of the time; though Trumbo was actually not a member of the Communist Party. As a result, the writer was held in contempt of Congress, blacklisted and spent 11 months in jail. The blacklisting was removed in 1960. He wrote the anti-war story 'Johnny Got His Gun' in 1939, inspired by the true tale of a British officer badly disfigured in the First World War – it won a National Book Award in the States at the time. Trumbo died in 1976 from a heart attack.

TUESDAY'S GONE (LYNYRD SKYNYRD)

A Lynyrd Skynyrd song, originally featured on their 1973 debut album 'Pronounced Leh-Nerd Skin-Nerd', this is about the ending of a relationship due to the demands of being on the road, and has become a Skynyrd classic. Metallica covered the song for the 'Garage Inc.' album, and their version has a guest appearance from Skynyrd guitarist Gary Rossington, as well as John Popper, frontman with Blues Traveler. The original Skynyrd version was featured in the movies 'Dazed And Confused' and 'Happy Gilmore', which did much to raise its profile.

Metallica performed the song live at the Bridge School Benefit Concert, organised by Neil Young in October, 1997, in Mountain View, California. The band were joined onstage by Alice In Chains frontman Jerry Cantrell and Popper. The latter also guested with them on 'Last Caress' during the same show.

TURN THE PAGE (BOB SEGER)

A Bob Seger song, written and recorded for the veteran Michigan man's 1973 album 'Back In '72'. Dealing with life on the road, the live version – on the 1975 album 'Live Bullet' – has become a mainstay of classic rock radio in America. Lars Ulrich apparently heard this song while driving across the Golden Gate Bridge, and Metallica covered it on their 'Garage Inc.' album. While the two versions are very similar, a saxophone solo on the original is replaced by Kirk Hammett on slide guitar. Others to cover this song include Anglo-Dutch rockers Golden Earring and country legend Waylon Jennings.

Metallica's version was released as a single in 1998, but failed to chart.

Kid Rock guested with Metallica onstage for this song on January 9 and 10, 2000.

2 X 4

A song from the 'Load' album and about the futility of violence. First played live by the band before the album was released, James Hetfield would introduce it as being about "A piece of lumber" – the term '2x4' generally being used in reference to a piece of wood. The guitar solo was, according to Kirk Hammett, inspired by jazz trumpeter Chet Baker.

ULRICH, LARS

While Lars Ulrich has never been regarded as one of the all-time great drummers, nonetheless, much of Metallica's success has been due to his vision, business acumen and sheer drive. It was Ulrich who first got the band's current management team of Peter Mensch and Cliff Burnstein onboard in 1984. When hearing that the duo, renowned then for their collaborations with AC/DC and Def Leppard among others, were interested in the young Metallica, Ulrich called Mensch from a phone box in order to set things in motion. That's the essence of Lars – committed and passionate about Metallica.

Born on December 26, 1993, in Gentofte, Denmark, the young Ulrich was at first thought to be destined for a career in tennis, follow-

ing in the footsteps of his father, Torben, who'd been a successful player from the 1940s all the way through into the 1970s. In fact, he had been ranked the top senior player in the world in 1976. Away from the court, Torben was also a well-known jazz musician, working with the likes of Miles Davis and Stan Getz; saxophonist Dexter Gordon was Lars' godfather.

The moment that was to change Lars' life forever came in February 1973, when Deep Purple played in Copenhagen. Torben Ulrich had got five passes for himself and his mates to see the gig. But when one of them dropped out, nine-year-old Lars got the spare ticket – later he recalled how mesmerized he'd been by the occasion. The next day he bought Deep Purple's 'Fireball' album – and his journey to the dark side had begun. By 13, he

had his first drum kit – a Ludwig – and at the age of 17 re-located to Los Angeles. Now, on the face of it, this was to help his still budding tennis career. But Lars had other ideas.

By then he was immersed in the growing New Wave Of British Heavy Metal movement, spending every spare coin he had on import records and also copies of the weekly UK music paper 'Sounds', regarded as the ultimate resource for anyone into this genre. He was especially fond of Diamond Head, following them on tour in the UK, and sleeping on floors when necessary. But Lars wanted to take things further. Hence the advert in 'The Recycler' newspaper that led to the meeting with James Hetfield, and the birth of Metallica.

Since then, the band have gone through some incredible highs and lows. Lars himself has been married and divorced twice. The first time was to a Birmingham girl named Debbie Jones, but this ended in 1990, while the band were recording 'The Black Album'. His second marriage was to Skylar Satenstein, who was a doctor. They divorced in 2004 after seven years, during which time the couple had two sons: Myles (born in 1998), and Layne (born three years later). More recently he's been dating Danish actress Connie Nielsen, the pair having a song in 2007 they named Bryce Thadeus Ulrich-Nielsen.

Ulrich has never been a stranger to controversy, one of the most intense being his fight against Napster. Ulrich testified against the online file-sharing resource when he discovered that the band's entire back-catalogue was available for free download via their system. His stance provoked a massive backlash against both him and Metallica from fans outraged that they were using their position to try and intimidate Napster and force them

to close down. He was even parodied for his attitude in an episode of 'South Park', when the animated Lars Ulrich is seen to be blubbing because he is struggling to pay for an inflatable gold bar fridge.

Perhaps his most emabarrassing moment came in 2004 when the drummer was rushed to hospital

after being taken ill on a flight from Germany to appear with Metallica as one of the headliners at the Donington Download Festival. Not only did he miss a band performance for the first time in his career (an ensemble of drummers, including Slayer's Dave Lombardo and Slipknot's Joey Jordison, successfully stood in for him), but rumours persisted at the time alleging that Lars' absence was due to drugs. It was officially passed off as an 'anxiety attack', but that other story simply refuses to go away.

On the other hand, when Beatallica, a band who mix Metallica and the Beatles, faced a major lawsuit from Sony, acting on behalf of the latter, Ulrich actually backed the band, even offering the services of Metallica's own lawyer, Peter Paterno, to help them out. And in 2001 he appeared on the quiz show 'Who Wants To Be A Millionaire?', raising $64,000 for charity. He's also had his own label, simply called The Music Company, which was more than a mere vanity project. He started it in 1998, and released records from Canadian punks DDT, metalheads Systematic (who briefly featured one-time Slayer drummer Paul Bostaph) and the Brand New

Immortals (with ex-Black Crowes bassist Johnny Colt). Sadly, the company doesn't exist now, being dissolved in 2004.

Away from music, Ulrich did the voice for a drag on the Disney cartoon 'Dave The Barbarian', has 'appeared' in 'The Simpsons' and is know for his love of both art and scuba diving.

But it is as a drummer that he's found most fame. And, while it is fair to say that he's often been derided in public by critics, fellow musicians and even members of his own band, his approach to the kit has become an integral part of the Metallica sound. He's also played a major role in guiding Metallica towards fresh musical challenges; it was said to be his love of Oasis that was behind the shift on 'Load' and 'ReLoad', and he is the one member of Metallica who, to this day, stands by 'St. Anger'.

Moreover, unlike most drummers, Lars Ulrich is articulate and never afraid to express an opinion. Over the years he may well have done more interviews on behalf of the band than anyone else.

To some, he'll always be the overgrown spoilt brat, used to getting his way, and a poor excuse for a drummer. To others, he's the engine room of Metallica, powering their sound. To yet others, he's a shrewd, intelligent even ruthless businessman. The reality is that Lars Ulrich is a combiantion of all of these, with a sprinkling of sentimentality and a fierce loyalty to those he regards as friends.

Perhaps Noel Gallagher of Oasis best summed him up:

"He's a strange character. A strange, strange man".

ULRICH, TORBEN

Lars' father, and as far as Metallica fans are concerned, the man who came to prominence on the 'Some Kid Of Monster' documentary, when he's seen giving advice to his son and the band as to the songs they should – or shouldn't – include on the 'St. Anger' album. But to dismiss him as some beardie-wierdie with too much to say for himself lacks

the respect due him for a distinguished life and career.

Born in 1928, he made his name as a top tennis professional from the late 1940s into the early 1970s. In that time he won numerous tournaments, before helping to found the Association Of Tennis Professionals in 1972. He also won the Wimbledon Seniors Doubles title in 1976 (aged 48), with Australian Owen Davidson.

He also has an impressive musical background, having helped to open the famous Blue Note club in Copenhagen in 1952, and recording and touring with numerous jazz bands and musicians – he's regarded as a fine clarinet, flute and tenor saxophone player.

He's also written extensively on music for various publications, exhibits his paintings (principally made with ball, racquet, rope and rice paper), and has acted as well.

These days he lives in Seattle, and is still active in the arts.

UNFORGIVEN, THE

This track from 'The Black Album' marked something a departure for Metallica in its style and structure. The rhythm guitar riff has similarities to 'Fade To Black' and 'To Live Is To Die', and there has been speculation that the long note which introduces the song might well have been sampled from the soundtrack to the film 'For A Few Dollars More', composed by Ennio Morricone. This has always been denied by Ulrich.

When put out as a single it peaked at number 35 in America, and number 15 in the UK.

UNFORGIVEN II, THE

From the 'ReLoad' album, this track is the sequel to 'The Unforgiven' from 'The Black Album'. People have debated as to what this song is all about. Hetfield once proclaimed it's meaning to be: "Forgiving no-one, and ending up alone". This song has only ever been performed once live, at the Billboard Awards in 1997.

The single only made number 59 in the US, but reached number 15 in the UK.

UNIVERSITY OF CALIFORNIA (NAPSTER)

One of three universities in America cited by Metallica in their law suit against Napster in 2000. The others were Yale and Indiana Universities. The schools were included because they refused to ban the software that allowed file-sharing through Napster.

UNNAMED FEELING, THE

A track from the 'St. Anger' album and one that deals with someone close to losing their san-

ity. The video for the song got a lot of attention as it featured the band playing in an empty room, the walls of which were slowly closing in on them. The cover artwork for the single was chosen after a fan contest. It was released in 2004, and while it failed to chart in America, it did make number 42 in the UK. It was also released as a single in Australia.

The full tracklisting for this EP is

'The Unnamed Feeling', 'The Four Horsemen' (live), 'Damage, Inc.' (live), 'Leper Messiah' (live), 'Motorbreath' (live) , 'Ride The Lightning' (live), 'Hit the Lights' (live), 'The Unnamed Feeling' (video).

UNTIL IT SLEEPS

This track from the 'Load' album, in demo form, was jokingly called 'Fell On Black Days', because of its strong resemblance to the Soundgarden song of the same title. The theme of the track is cancer – which claimed both of James Hetfield's parents. They were Christian Scientists, and therefore refused all medical help. The video for this won the 'Best Rock Video' category at the 1996 MTV Video Music Awards. Directed by Samuel Bayer, it was partially inspired by the work of 15th Century Dutch painter Hieronymus Bosch.

VENOM

The trio from the North-East of England who literally invented the concept of 'black metal' when they released their album of that title in 1982. Venom are among the most important underground metal bands of all time.

Formed at the end of the 1970s, they were closely associated with the New Wave Of British Heavy Metal, even though their sound had more to do with a dirty punk influence than the flamboyant metallic approach which drove many of their peers.

Never prepared to compromise, the band always maintained that they'd refuse to tour unless or until the finances were in place to deliver a breathtaking stage set. Thus, it wasn't until February, 1984 that they announced a proper European tour. Dubbed 'The Seven Dates Of Hell', Venom

took out Metallica as their support band, and this is where things got a little heated. Venom drummer Abaddon became very bitter years later about the young Americans' success, one that eclipsed Venom's own impact.

"You know James Hetfield, of Metallica, right? Well, I would swear that he's suddenly started to walk like Cronos," Abaddon claimed at the time. *"All of a sudden, he did."*

It was one of a number of comments made by the drummer over the years, as he claimed that Metallica had copied Venom and used the British threesome as a springboard to achieve their own status.

"They ripped us off!" he was to claim in the early 1990s. *"You look at what they did, and the way they did it. It's obvious. Metallica took everything they could from Venom, and then brushed us aside. Those fuckers owe us a huge debt – and it would be nice if, one day, they re-paid it. Fat chance!"*

However, band mainstay Cronos (bass/vocals) has been a lot more sanguine. In the booklet that accompanied the band's 2005 box set 'XXV' he commented:

"Sure, Metallica took the chance we offered them, and used it to their advantage. But, so what? Did they stop us from doing anything? No. The fact that we never became

as big as we all thought this band deserved was all our own fault. We never took our opportunities. They did, simple as that. For us to hold any sort of grudge against Metallica is just crazy. We gave them a helping hand, but they had what we didn't – the focus and the guts to take it further."

Metallica themselves have always had the utmost respect for Venom's importance:

"Black metal, speed metal, death metal – Venom started it all!" says Lars Ulrich.

Venom never did achieve the status their early potential promised. They've undergone a success of line-up changes and released some sub-standard albums, as well as the occasional gem. But today, their importance and impact is once again being acknowledged. And, after all, they did earn the distinction of having their single, 'Warfare' played on the 'Breakfast Show' on Radio One nearly 25 years ago!

Cronos recalls: *"We didn't do the single with that in mind at all. But the late Tommy Vance picked up on the song and loved it so much he started to give us a lot of airplay."*

The upshot was that Mike Reid, at the time doing the aforementioned Breakfast Show, decided to play a snippet from the song each day for a week, building up to airing the whole track, much to the shock of many listeners more used to smoother fare with their bacon and eggs.

"It wasn't a gimmick, because that was never something we wanted, or expected," Cronos adds, *"All we did was record what we felt was a true metal song, something that fizzed, had energy and growled in the usual manner of a metal song. The fact that others picked up on it was a bonus.*

"You know, a lot of supposed metal or hard rock bands record singles that are designed for radio airplay. That's an abomination to us. So, we went in completely the opposite way, and seemed to hit the right note with someone."

www.venomslegions.com

VERTIGO

The name under which Metallica played their only support slot in Britain, outside of festivals. It happened in May 1990, when the band supported Metal Church at the Marquee Club in Central London. They did it for a spot of fun, and were introduced onstage by Metal Church frontman Mike Howe, who said,

"This is a new band we like, who've only done a couple of shows before. Please give them a chance".

Amazingly, word hadn't got out on the streets, and fans turned up at the venue without any prior knowledge of who would be opening for Metal Church. They got the shock of their lives on seeing who 'Vertigo' were!

Metallica chose the name for the show as Vertigo was a subsidiary label of Phonogram, to whom they were signed in the UK and Europe, and one closely associated with heavy metal.

VIDEOS 1989-2004, THE

This DVD was released in December, 2006, and features all of Metallica's promo videos shot during the 15 years from 1989. In all, there are 21 clips, ranging from 'One' to 'Some Kind Of Monster'. 'One' was the first promo video that the band both shot and allowed to be seen, having aborted one previous effort. Metallica always insist on total control of their videos – if they don't like them, then they're scrapped. 'One' combines live footage with scenes from the 1971 movie 'Johnny Got His Gun'; the book on which the film was based had inspired the lyrics to the song. It also gave Metallica their first Grammy Award.

Other clips of interest include: 'Hero Of The Day', which incorporates computer effects – the first Metallica video to do so; 'The Memory Remains', with a guest appearance from Marianne

Faithfull; 'Turn The Page', the first promo shot by Metallica for a cover, and featuring porn star Ginger Lynn; 'Whiskey In The Jar' has two clips, one censored, the other in full, and 'I Disappear', which is the most expensive Metallica video to date. The clip for 'St. Anger' was shot in St. Quentin State Prison, after which the band gave a free show for the inmates; this was bassist Robert Trujillo's first gig with Metallica. And for 'The Unnamed Feeling', there were two guest appearances: from actor Edward Furlong and top surfer Rob Machado.

The DVD reached number three in the US charts.

Tracklisting

'One', 'Enter Sandman', 'The Unforgiven', 'Nothing Else Matters', 'Wherever I May Roam', 'Sad But True', 'Until It Sleeps', 'Hero Of The Day', 'Mama Said', 'King Nothing', 'The Memory Remains', 'The Unforgiven II', 'Fuel', 'Turn The Page', 'Whiskey In The Jar', 'No Leaf Clover', 'I Disappear', 'St. Anger', 'Frantic', 'The Unnamed Feeling', 'Some Kind Of Monster'.

VOIVOD

One of the most important extreme metal bands of all time, their combination of thrash, industrial and psychedelia have not only made them unique, but proven crucial to bands like Neurosis, Isis, Pelican and Mastodon, who've clearly taken influences from these French-Canadians.

They started in 1982, with each member of the band having a particularly silly stage name: Snake (vocals), Away (drums), Piggy (guitar) and Blacky (bass). But their impressive nature, and the rapid development displayed on early records like 'War And Pain', 'Rrroooaaarrr', 'Killing Technology' and 'Dimension Hatross' quickly dispelled the chortles.

With 'Nothingface', 'Angel Rat' and 'The Outer Limits', they switched from independent label Noise to MCA, and explored increasingly complex musical and lyrical issues.

Line-up changes dogged the band throughout the 1990s, but the arrival of Jason Newsted in 2001 (under the pseudonym of 'Jasonic') helped to put them back

on track for the 'Voivod' and 'Katorz' albums.

The tragic death of innovative guitarist Denis 'Piggy' D'Amour in 2005, from cancer, devastated the band. But, using guitar parts never previously heard, the remaining trio – including Newsted – put together a new studio album for release in 2008. It should have been out a lot earlier, but a shoulder injury sustained by the bassist delayed things.

www.voivod.com

VOODOO CHILDREN

A band who played just one show, in 1993, and featured Kirk Hammett on guitar and Jason Newsted on bass. Along with them in the group were Tony Prinzivalli on guitar (he'd also played with Newsted in another project the previous year called Kipper Biskits), drummer Tim Lau and keyboard player Whitey Chrobak (who'd featured in Fatso with Jason Newsted in 1994).

As mentioned above, Voodoo Children only did one gig, in tribute to blues guitarist John Campbell, who died on June 13, 1993 from heart failure. The benefit show, to raise funds for his six-month-old daughter Paris Campbell, took place in August of that year at The Lone Star in Dallas. Apart from the Voodoo Children, others to appear on the bill included Dr. John, Jimmie Dale

X – AS IN EX-MEMBERS OF THE BAND

Here's a full list of the most significant ones:

Lloyd Grant (guitar)

Damian Phillips (vocals, also known as Jeff Warner; he played one show with the band on May 28, 1982. This was the only time the Metallica played with a 'proper' singer)

Brad Parker (guitar)

Ron McGovney (bass)

Dave Mustaine (guitar)

Cliff Burton (bass)

Jason Newsted (bass)

YALE UNIVERSITY (NAPSTER)

The famous American university was named in a lawsuit taken out by Metallica in 2000. Determined to stamp out illegal file-sharing, the band's lawyers named three schools in its legal action against Napster. Yale, they claim, had been guilty of turning a blind eye to the use of Napster software by students. Until that point, the school had monitored the situation, but had taken no action. Faced with a potentially damaging lawsuit, Yale banned its use on college networks, and averted further legal proceedings. In response, the band issued the following statement:

"We appreciate the prompt and responsible reaction by Yale University in dealing with the gross violations of copyright laws and the protection of intellectual property."

ZEROPTION

An early 1980s hardcore band who were among Metallica's main influences when they started out. Formed in 1980, the Toronto band had stopped playing live by 1983. Their releases include 'What Price Glory?' and 'Herd Not Scene'.

ZAZULA, JOHN & MARSHA

The couple who signed Metallica to their Megaforce label and subsequently released the 'Kill 'Em All' album. John and Marsha Zazula (aka. Johnny and Marsha Z) actually started the label in 1982, because nobody else would sign the band. Based in Old Bridge, New Jersey, Megaforce grew out of a stall run by the Zazulas which specialised in metal records and tapes. It was getting a copy of the 'No Life 'Til Leather' demo that first convinced them that this young band had definite potential. This was cemented by the arrival of the next two-track tape, most commonly known as 'The Megaforce Demo'.

Recalling those early days with Metallica, John Zazula says:

"We sent them $1,500 to come across America. They got a one-way rental: a U-Haul van and a truck. Literally, they had two drivers and they slept in the back with all their gear, and they delivered themselves to my front door. It was basically, 'Well, we're here – what do we do next?'"

At first the band actually lived with the Zazulas. But one night, the intrepid foursome got a little too rock 'n' roll. They raided their hosts' drinks cabinet, found some unopened champagne, popped the corks, and off they went. But these were bottles saved from the Zazulas' wedding day – and the couple weren't at all amused. From then on, the band were banished to sleeping in their rehearsal area, which was located in the Music Building. Anthrax rehearsed in the same space and brought in a fridge, toaster and oven, so that Metallica could, at least, eat and drink. The Anthrax crew also allowed their new friends from the West Coast to shower in their homes.

But conditions weren't exactly ideal. The band were sleeping on the ground with little protection from the cold floor below – in a part of the building where all the rubbish was stored! But they coped, and waited for Zazula, who was managing them at this juncture, to turn them into superstars!

When Zazula realised that no label was going to sign up his new charges, he decided to start up his own – and Megaforce Records was born.

Although Metallica's relationship with the Zazulas was, professionally, short-lived, nonetheless, Megaforce grew as a result. Over the years the Zazulas have been associated with Anthrax, Testament, S.O.D., King's X, Manowar, Ministry and Bad Brains. John Zazula himself even tried the artistic route, as the mysterious Lone Rager. Loud and brash, John was a key character in powering the East Coast thrash movement in America during the mid-1980s, and his wife was the perfect complement. They're still active on the music scene to this day.